THE *Seasonal* PALETTE

Compiled and Edited by
ELIZABETH K. NORFLEET

Featuring paintings by
BOB TIMBERLAKE

You cannot fill your belly by painting pictures of bread.
– Old Chinese Proverb

Lillian's Blueberry Bread

TASTE·FULL.
PUBLICATIONS

PUBLISHER
EDITOR-IN-CHIEF
Elizabeth K. Norfleet

EDITORIAL ASSISTANTS
Gale Duque
Constance Nelson

EDITORIAL SUPPORT
Kelly Anderson

RECIPE COORDINATOR
Trent Colbert

RECIPE CONSULTANT
Donna Spears

DESIGN AND ART DIRECTION

ART DIRECTOR
Elizabeth K. Norfleet

PHOTOGRAPHER
Van Miller

FOOD STYLIST
Janet Grennes

PROP STYLIST
Susann Hodges

GRAPHIC DESIGN
Alice Heitchue
William R. Perkins, Jr.
Joanne Raulerson Thomas

PRINTER
Transcontinental Printing
Printed in Canada

ISBN: 0-9704345-3-7

Taste Full Toll-free Phone Number:
888-499-6283
Taste Full Web Address:
www.taste-full.com
Bob Timberlake Web Address:
www.bobtimberlake.com

The former loft of the Shoaf's 200-year old renovated barn has replaced Bob Timberlake's basement furnace room as his studio.

All the photographs in ***The Seasonal Palette*** were shot on location atop a wooded knoll near Lexington, North Carolina. The knoll, part of a 70-acre tract, is where Bob Timberlake moved a barn built in 1809 from the nearby Shoaf farm and, in a three-year project, carefully molded it into his studio with the help of area craftsmen. To marry ***Taste Full***'s recipe development with a Timberlake feel, the artist generously allowed us access to his vast collections — including agateware, pottery, antique toys, hand-carved and hand-forged tableware and hand-tied fishing flies. When Elizabeth thanked him for providing such an inspiring place for the photo shoot, he responded that he built it "as a place for people to be creative." What a gift!

Table of Contents

Seasonal chapters featuring appetizers, soups, salads, entrées and desserts

Notes from Oxford

Have food, will travel is my motto, although that *modus operandi* is my birthright. Whether scouting a farmer's market for the most tender butter beans or driving some distance to eat at someplace authentic, both my parents instilled in me a love of good, honest cooking – yes, occasionally at a place quite grand, but most often, just real. Through these early experiences I developed an appreciation for food and travel, which I shared through a regional lifestyle magazine, ***Taste Full***, from 1990-2000.

Through years of publishing ***Taste Full*** I shared a lot with our readers about the reasons I felt compelled to start the magazine. Bottom line: I love where I'm from, and the best way I knew how to celebrate my blessed home state of North Carolina was through the very thing I enjoy most – good food. Raw oysters, a backyard burger, Brunswick Stew, shad roe, you name it. My eclectic palate delights as much in simply prepared down-home dishes as it does in ones that have been flambéed, and ***The Seasonal Palette***, ***Taste Full***'s "best of" cookbook celebrates the flavor that diverse spirit offers.

By design ***Taste Full*** was established as a quarterly publication, flowing with the seasons. Seasonal living is as natural as breathing when you live in a region that stretches from the mountains to the coast, and where spring, summer, fall and winter all touch down during the year with a bounty of wild game, fresh fish and produce. From its inception, the magazine featured foods and flavors of each anticipated season, so, it seemed only fitting that my first cookbook should follow suit.

Naturally I've spent a lot of time pondering cookbooks, and more specifically, what it is that draws me back to my favorites. I've discovered that I look for a source of inspiration, something that immerses me in a point of view or helps me learn about a place or a person. Bob Timberlake's paintings and perspectives, which so lovingly illustrate the South, give ***The Seasonal Palette*** that inspiration and that vantage. While planning the cookbook's food photography, I worked to keep the feel of Mr. Timberlake's paintings and his attention to detail. Our crew even journeyed to the artist's countryside studio to photograph all the food on location so that we could capture the common images that stud his Southern landscapes: a potted geranium resting on an agateware plate, a wood pile, watermelon…old rustic chairs.

LONGTIME SUBSCRIBERS TO ***Taste Full*** may recall the few times I made reference to the magazine's inauguration coinciding with my wedding. The very first copy – a labor of love – arrived via FedEx just before I said my vows. The conception of ***The Seasonal Palette*** coincided with another very special time of my life: new motherhood. On the eve of publication, with a two-year-old son in one arm and an eight-month-old daughter in the other, I saw that it was an appropriate time to look back, reflect, and compile this collection of recipes that my family of staff had faithfully tested.

Accordingly, the magazine evolved with my life. When newly married, the early issues played up foods that were fancy, more special occasion. What I considered a weeknight meal then versus now makes me laugh. ***The Seasonal Palette*** celebrates a casual lifestyle that most of us have adopted alongside a renewed interest in home and family.

WHEN WE FIRST BEGAN pouring over ***Taste Full***'s recipe archives, Trent Colbert and I *oohed* and *aahed* over the specialty dishes. Time passed with our retesting of favorite recipes, and we kept coming back to tried-and-true dishes that through the years had become our family's new comfort foods. The variety in ***The Seasonal Palette*** will certainly add panache to your entertaining style, but more than anything you will sample foods that will nurture your family and friends, and, boy, they will be asking for more.

Once I make a dish from a cookbook that excites me, it becomes a part of my life. Think about it. One braves new recipes for the people who are special in your life as home-cooked meals spawn warm memories. Long after the table is cleared and the dishes are put away, the scents and textures of a dinner shared with good friends remain.

With ***The Seasonal Palette*** I have tried to capture a glimpse of where current Southern cooking thrives with a collection of recipes that incorporates the tastes and fusion of cooking styles that have become a part of my life and its seasonal joys. Whether preparing the Black-eyed Pea Salsa, considering our Asian Sweet and Sour Slaw, or dishing out plates of the zesty Black and White Pasta with Creole Scallops, I think we've canvassed the contemporary, versatile Southern palate.

I FEEL HONORED Mr. Timberlake shared his paintings with this volume of recipes. He has captured images of my homeland that my heartstrings never want to release.

Some of ***Taste Full***'s earliest recipe development is included in this cookbook, and I dare to say it's because my staff has always worked to make sure our food would, indeed, stand the test of time. Rest assured that ***The Seasonal Palette*** will still find a place on your table in 10 to 20 years. And the memories will last even longer.

– Elizabeth K. Norfleet

Seasonal Musings from Bob Timberlake

I LOOK FORWARD to each of North Carolina's four distinct seasons with childlike anticipation. Each season promises exciting changes at every turn. Of course, I have my favorites, but the transition is welcome and exhilarating all at the same time. Like most folks, I love to eat good food. And somehow, over the years, I have come to associate each time of year with particular activities and the wonderful foods that seem to go right along with them.

SUMMER TAKES US outdoors – into the smell of summer flowers and freshly cut grass. All these things bring back memories of summers past – snacking on hand-churned homemade ice cream, blackberries picked on the 4th of July, and sweet, juicy watermelon. Ah, watermelon. Mark Twain once claimed that, 'Once you have eaten watermelon, you know what the angels eat.' And who can forget fried chicken and church suppers on the grounds? This brings to mind one of nature's most savory gifts: the season's first, much-anticipated red-ripe homegrown tomato. Truly cause for celebration and benediction! My only negative thought – besides dreading the impending hot weather – is that I must temporarily give up my beloved raw oysters until cold weather returns. However, I am quickly cheered by visions of soft shell and great blue crabs, crab cakes, fresh tuna and other delights from the sea. Now you know why I love summer!

FALL USHERS IN football and tailgating, hunting and fishing, and "critter dinners" with friends and family. My long-absent favorite, fresh oysters, are finally back in season – mouth-watering oysters-on-the-half-shell and oyster stew. Let's not forget chicken stews simmering in big old black iron pots. Nary an autumn passes that my friend Jesse Capel in Troy, North Carolina, doesn't make sausage and put up hams to the delight of friends and neighbors. There's an excitement

during this time of year that is absent during others. Folks are awash in a flurry of activity – unlike the sluggish warm days of summer – with school back in session, preparation for the holidays, get-togethers with friends and family, and lots of good wholesome food. It's as if we're akin to the squirrels, storing up for cold days ahead and preparing ourselves for some exciting event that's just around the corner. We savor fall greens and the last country tomato to the very last slice – the absence of home-grown tomatoes being fall's only negative, in my opinion. So we ration them for country ham sandwiches at breakfast until the very last quarter-size tomato is gone.

WINTER IS MY very favorite time of year, and worthy of elaboration. Bring on the cold crispness despite the sun's shimmering brightness, and the fireside times, and holidays spent with family and friends! Best of all are the festive and glorious aromas that arise from the kitchen. The sense of smell is believed to be our keenest, and familiar smells coming from the kitchen are very powerful, indeed.

A recent jonquil study by the artist

Food in the winter is more robust with sharper flavors that bolster us against the colder temperatures. Lexington's local barbecue restaurants add to their menus hot, tangy soups and stews that always bring tears to my eyes. There are so many great soups to savor, and Preacher Moore's unbelievable oyster stew is the best of all. Then there's steamed clams á la Carol Lewark at Swan Island Hunting Club – fantastic! And, of course, my son Dan's three-bean soup that is never made the same way twice, proving that some foods are best prepared by instinct, using smell and taste instead of a recipe. Turkey and dressing is a perennial favorite around the holidays, but I believe it should be eaten year-round. Then there are the oyster roasts. Did I mention that I really like oysters?

Winter also brings hunts and the tried-and-true recipes for duck and other game that have been passed down through many generations along the coast and down to the Low Country. Mealtime takes on a new meaning at Swan Island Hunt Club when the food is prepared by Carol, and at Backwoods Quail Club by "Tiny" and "Lease".

Winter is a time for family gatherings. My children, like their mother, are fantastic cooks. My daughter Kelly unquestionably makes the finest chocolate chip cookies in the world – bar none! Growing up, she had to hide them from her brothers and me. What was it Charlie Brown said? 'I've never met a chocolate chip cookie that I didn't like.' He must have tasted Kelly's cookies! My eldest son Ed is also a terrific cook. Like their father, all my children enjoy good food.

SPRING COMES WITH its promise of renewal and birth just when we've grown tired of winter's cold dreariness. Blueberries and strawberries beckon from the fields of pick-your-own farms. Cherries in May beg to be picked, pitted and eaten. Cold mountain streams near Blowing Rock and Boone brim with delicious mountain trout. And of course, there's the race to plant the first tomatoes, fast-forwarding our thoughts to fresh and flavorful summertime foods. Then again, there's the last raw oyster of the season before summer's heat returns once more. But, as a consolation, there is always raw broccoli – my second favorite food. So I guess you could say that no matter what the season, the palette is beautiful and delicious – just the way the Creator intended.

I hope you enjoy the recipes we've brought together here. Elizabeth and I think it represents some of the best eating from our home state of North Carolina. Let us know what you think — we'd love to hear from you!

– Bob Timberlake

Spring

True Blue Pimento Cheese with Homemade Crackers

Taste Full's pimento cheese is spiced with sharp cheddar and Tabasco. Serve with easily made Homemade Crackers.

Easy • Makes 2 cups

- 8 ounces sharp Cheddar cheese
- 2 teaspoons minced garlic
- 1/2 teaspoon salt
- 1 teaspoon black pepper
- 1 4-ounce jar chopped pimentos
- 2 heaping tablespoons mayonnaise (Hellmann's)
- • dash of Tabasco
- 1 teaspoon lemon juice

Cut the Cheddar cheese in chunks and crumble with the metal blade of the food processor. Combine the cheese in a bowl with all the other ingredients. Mix well, chill and serve.

Homemade Crackers:

Average • Yields 48 crackers

- 1/2 cup milk
- 1/2 cup heavy cream
- 2 tablespoons warm water
- 1 teaspoon dry yeast
- 2 1/2-3 cups flour
- 1 teaspoon salt
- 1 tablespoon butter, room temperature

In a saucepan scald milk and cream. Set aside and cool to lukewarm. In a small bowl combine warm water and yeast; let sit for 5-10 minutes. Sift flour and salt into a large bowl. Add lukewarm milk and yeast mixture to flour. Blend well with a fork until you have a smooth dough, adding more flour if needed. Knead in soft butter; continue kneading 3 minutes. Let the dough rest in a covered bowl for 10 minutes.

Preheat oven to 350°. Divide dough into four parts. On a lightly floured board, roll each piece out to a very thin rectangle. Cut the dough into strips about 1" wide. Next, cut strips into 2" rectangles. Bake crackers on an ungreased baking sheet 15-20 minutes until light and crispy. Cool and store in an airtight container until ready to serve.

Previous page *Volunteers*, 1994

CROSTINI WITH SHRIMP GUACAMOLE

An easy and attractive hors d'oeuvre for parties. To make ahead, save the avocado pit, then place back in the prepared guacamole and seal airtight to prevent avocado from turning brown. A great way to use a little bit of leftover boiled shrimp.

AVERAGE • MAKES 25-30 CROSTINIS

1/2	pound cooked shrimp
1	ripe avocado, pit removed
2	tablespoons mayonnaise
1	tablespoon lemon juice
1	tablespoon minced red onion
1	clove garlic, minced
1/2	teaspoon cumin
•	salt and pepper to taste
•	French baguette
•	olive oil
•	cilantro leaves or paprika, optional

Peel, devein and finely chop shrimp. Peel and seed the avocado; save pit. Combine both in a small bowl breaking up avocado with a fork. Stir in mayonnaise, lemon juice, onion, garlic and seasonings.

To make crostini: Preheat oven to 350°. Slice baguette thinly in rounds and brush one side with olive oil. Toast for 10 minutes or until lightly browned. Spoon guacamole onto crostini and garnish with paprika or a cilantro leaf.

ASPARAGUS WRAPPED IN SMOKED SALMON

Smoked salmon, a perennial favorite, is even better when wrapped around fresh asparagus. A creamy Horseradish Sauce adds an interesting flavor bite.

EASY • 24 SERVINGS

24	asparagus spears
24	thin slices smoked salmon
24	sprigs fresh dill
•	Horseradish Sauce

Blanch asparagus in a large pot of boiling salted water until crisp-tender, 3-4 minutes. Drain and refresh under cold running water to stop cooking. Dry on paper towels.

Wrap a thin slice of smoked salmon around each asparagus spear. Tuck in a sprig of dill. Serve sauce on the side for dipping.

Horseradish Sauce

1/4	cup prepared horseradish
1	cup sour cream
1	hard-boiled egg yolk, mashed
1/4	cup whipping cream
1/4	teaspoon paprika
•	salt and pepper to taste

Squeeze horseradish in a paper towel or cheesecloth to remove liquid. In small bowl combine sour cream, horseradish and mashed egg yolk. In a separate small bowl, whip the cream until it forms soft peaks. Fold it into the sour cream mixture. Season with paprika, salt and pepper. Makes 1 1/2 cups.

QUICK & ELEGANT CRAB SALAD

Sweet and succulent crabmeat makes this cold salad a plain and simple hit.

EASY • SERVES 4-6

1 pound crabmeat, preferably lump or backfin
1/2 cup mayonnaise
1 1/2 tablespoons chili sauce
2 teaspoons lemon juice
1 tablespoon capers, chopped

Place crabmeat in a large bowl. By hand, delicately remove any shells from crabmeat. In a small bowl, combine mayonnaise, chili sauce, lemon juice and capers. Stir carefully into crabmeat. Refrigerate until ready to serve. Serve with small crackers or spoon onto celery.

NOTE: If you're entertaining, this recipe easily doubles and triples. Arrange 10 lettuce leaves individually on a platter. Spoon crabmeat onto each leaf and garnish with chopped parsley. Place a large spoon near serving platter so guests can easily serve themselves.

PINE NUT CHEESE PUFFS

Pine nuts and Gruyère cheese make these puffs special. They are a variation on a savory cream puff. They are best served hot. If made ahead, simply reheat for 4-5 minutes in a 400° oven. They also freeze well; simply thaw, heat and serve.

AVERAGE • MAKES 3-4 DOZEN

1/2 cup milk
1/2 cup water
5 tablespoons butter
3/4 cup flour
1/4 teaspoon crushed red pepper
1/4 teaspoon white pepper
4 eggs
1/2 cup grated Gruyère cheese, lightly packed
1/3 cup grated Parmesan cheese, plus 2 tablespoons more for sprinkling on top
1/2 cup pine nuts

Preheat oven to 400°.

Combine milk, water and butter in a medium saucepan. Bring just to a boil over medium heat. Remove pan from heat and add flour, red pepper and white pepper. Stir vigorously with a wooden spoon until smooth and shiny. Beat in eggs 1 at a time, blending well after each one. Fold in the Gruyère, Parmesan and pine nuts.

Drop by heaping teaspoonfuls onto a lightly greased cookie sheet. Sprinkle a pinch of Parmesan cheese on top of each. Bake for about 20 minutes until puffed and well-browned. Do not open the oven door until done.

Pâté in "Pastry" Shells

Quick and easy "pastry" shells can be made from sliced bread and miniature muffin pans. The shells are brushed with butter and toasted in the oven. Many different fillings can be used as in the variation below. If you don't have time to make your own pâté, specialty grocers sell a wide variety of pâtés, many of which are vegetarian.

EASY • YIELDS 24 HORS D'OEUVRES

- • **Easy Bread Shells**
- 1/2 **pound good quality liver sausage, such as Kahn**
- 1 **tablespoon butter**
- 3/4 **cup sliced green onions**
- 1/4 **cup port**
- 1/2 **teaspoon freshly ground pepper**
- 1/4 **teaspoon thyme**
- • **small parsley sprigs**

Make bread shells.

To make pâté filling: place liver sausage in food processor and run until fairly smooth. Melt 1 tablespoon butter in medium skillet over medium heat. Add green onions and sauté until tender, 2-3 minutes. Add port to pan and boil to reduce by about half. Add to food processor, scraping out all of the liquid. Add pepper and thyme. Process until well combined and fairly smooth. Chill. There will be about 1 cup of filling.

Mound about 2 teaspoons filling in each bread cup and top with a tiny sprig of parsley.

Easy Bread Shells

- 24 pieces firm, homestyle bread, such as Pepperidge Farm Sandwich Bread
- 3 tablespoons butter, melted

To make shells: preheat oven to 400°. Using a fluted (or round) 2 - 2 1/2" cookie cutter, cut 1 circle from each slice of bread. Flatten each circle slightly with your fingers. Brush both sides lightly with melted butter and press into mini muffin pans. Bake in preheated 400° oven for about 10 minutes until browned. Cool on racks.

Chutney and Brie Bites

Use the same method for easy "pastry" shells to create another appetizer for your next gathering.

EASY • YIELDS 24 HORS D'OEUVRES

- • **Easy Bread Shells**
- 24 **pieces whole wheat bread**
- 3 **tablespoons melted butter**
- 1 **8-ounce jar mango chutney**
- 5-6 **ounces Brie, rind removed**

Preheat oven to 400°. Make bread shells according to recipe above using whole wheat bread.

Spoon about 1 teaspoon chutney into each bread cup. Top with a small piece of brie. Return to oven long enough to warm the chutney and melt the brie, about 5 minutes.

Carolina Bouillabaisse

Bouillabaisse is a French stew of fresh seafood, herbs, tomatoes and garlic. Though there are many variations, it was first made on the beaches of Provence by fishermen who used large cauldrons to cook the fish least suitable for market. ***Taste Full****'s Carolina version, scented with thyme, garlic, and orange rind, adds extra tomatoes to thicken the broth. Stir a dollop of Aïoli – a Provençal, very garlicky mayonnaise – into the Bouillabaisse immediately before serving to enhance the flavors. Serve the stew with a mix of fresh salad greens and a crisp, light white wine such as a Pinot Grigio for a perfect Sunday supper.*

Average • Serves 8

- 1 pound shrimp, peeled with shells removed and reserved
- 1 pound sea scallops
- 2 pounds firm white fish such as grouper, swordfish, or tile, cut into bite-sized pieces
- 24 clams or mussels, cleaned
- 2 large yellow onions, 1 coarsely chopped, 1 finely chopped, divided
- 3 carrots, coarsely chopped
- 3 stalks celery, coarsely chopped
- 4 sprigs fresh thyme or 1 teaspoon dried
- 4 sprigs fresh parsley
- 1 bay leaf
- 1 tablespoon black peppercorns
- 6 garlic cloves, 4 whole, 2 minced, divided
- 1 teaspoon fennel seeds
- 2 tablespoons orange zest
- 10 cups water
- 1 tablespoon unsalted butter
- 1 35-ounce can whole tomatoes with the juice
- 1 teaspoon salt
- 1 teaspoon pepper
- • Aïoli
- 1 cup good quality Parmesan cheese, shaved or grated

Aïoli

- 5 large garlic cloves
- 1 teaspoon Dijon mustard
- 2 large egg yolks
- 1/2 teaspoon cayenne pepper
- 1/2 teaspoon salt
- 1/2 cup extra virgin olive oil

Place all ingredients except oil into a blender. Pulse to combine. With motor running, slowly add oil to mixture. Place in small serving bowl. Cover and refrigerate immediately. Makes 1 cup.

Wash and prepare seafood. Refrigerate until ready to add to stew. Set aside reserved shrimp shells for making fresh stock for stew.

In a soup pot, combine the 1 coarsely chopped onion, carrot, celery, thyme, parsley, bay leaf, peppercorns, 4 whole garlic cloves, fennel seeds, zest, reserved shrimp shells and water. Bring ingredients to a boil, then reduce heat to low and simmer for 45 minutes. Strain stock through a fine mesh sieve, discarding solids and setting stock aside. Reserve soup pot.

In reserved soup pot over medium heat, melt butter. Add 1 finely chopped onion and cook for 5 minutes. Add tomatoes and 2 cloves minced garlic and simmer for 30 minutes. Strain mixture through a fine mesh sieve, reserving solids and liquid. Place solids in food processor and puree. Return liquid and reserved fish stock to soup pot. Stir in purée. Add salt and pepper. The broth may be made up to 2 days ahead.

About 45 minutes before serving, bring broth to a boil. Add all seafood reducing heat to warm. Cook, covered for 12-15 minutes until all seafood is just tender.

Divide soup into 8 bowls. Stir a tablespoon of Aïoli into each and sprinkle with Parmesan cheese. Serve crusty bread on the side.

Crabmeat Vichyssoise

This delightful cold soup is very rich and makes a wonderful lunch or a great appetizer for any dinner.

Easy • Serves 4-6

1 leek, sliced
1 medium onion, sliced
1/4 cup butter
1 medium potato, peeled and diced
2 cups chicken broth
1 teaspoon salt
1/2 teaspoon white pepper
1 cup crabmeat (about 1/2 pound)
2 cups heavy cream
1/4 cup freshly chopped chives

In a medium saucepan, sauté leek and onion in butter. When onions are soft, add potato and chicken broth, and simmer until the potato is done, about 20 minutes. Purée mixture in a food processor or blender for one minute or until smooth. Pour purée into a large bowl. Season with salt and pepper and cool.

Pick through the crabmeat for shells. Add crab to soup along with cream. Refrigerate covered for 4 hours. Garnish with fresh chives and serve.

Karen's Green Chile Squash Soup

*Karen Evans of Weslaco, Texas, shared this recipe with the publisher's father J.K. Norfleet. Good recipes are hard to keep a secret in the Norfleet family, and luckily Evans was game to share this delicious soup with **Taste Full**'s readers.*

Easy • Serves 8

2 1/2 pounds zucchini/yellow squash, sliced
1 14 1/2-ounce can chicken broth
1/2 cup water
3-4 chicken bouillon cubes
1/2 medium onion, finely chopped (2/3 cup)
1 4-ounce can chopped green chiles
1 1/2 tablespoons butter
1/8 teaspoon pepper
1/2 cup sour cream
1/4 cup chopped cilantro
• julienne strips of squash for garnish

Simmer squash in chicken broth, water and bouillon cubes in covered pot for 15-20 minutes or until squash is soft. Add onion and green chiles and cook 5 minutes more.

Put mixture through food processor in batches, but do not puree completely. Flecks of green and yellow should remain.

Add butter, pepper, sour cream and cilantro. Serve either hot or cold. The soup can be made ahead and reheated or served cold. Garnish with julienne strips of the squash if desired.

VIDALIA ONION SOUP WITH FRESH THYME

The Amontillado sherry and fresh herbs give life to this rich and flavorful soup shared by Executive Chef Jon Hofland of the Eseeola Lodge in Linville, North Carolina. This charming, rustic lodge, built in 1926 in the shadow of Grandfather Mountain in the Blue Ridge Mountians, remains as popular today as a summer resort as it did when it first opened. Eseeola (e-see-ola) is the American Indian term for "cliffy river."

AVERAGE • SERVES 4-6

6	**large Vidalia onions (about 6 cups)**
1	**cup unsalted butter, divided**
2	**tablespoons minced shallots**
1/2	**cup dry white wine**
1/2	**cup flour**
4	**cups chicken stock**
•	**small piece of cheesecloth and cotton string**
5	**cloves peeled garlic**
2	**teaspoons whole black peppercorns**
10	**sprigs fresh thyme**
1	**bay leaf**
1	**cup heavy cream**
1/2	**cup Amontillado sherry**
•	**juice of 1 lemon**
•	**salt and white pepper to taste**
•	**fresh thyme leaves**

Thinly slice the Vidalia onions. Melt 1/2 cup of the butter in a heavy-bottomed soup pot over medium heat until hot but not browned. Add onions and sauté stirring often until slightly caramelized (about 12 minutes). Add shallots and cook 1 minute more. Pour in white wine and simmer until liquid is completely absorbed (about 5 minutes). Stir in flour with a whisk and cook 2 minutes more. Gradually add chicken stock, whisking briskly to blend with flour.

To make a bouquet garni: lay cheesecloth out flat and fill with garlic, peppercorns, thyme sprigs and bay leaf. Tie tightly with piece of cotton string.

Add bouquet garni to soup pot and bring soup to a boil, then lower heat and simmer for 30 minutes. Stir frequently to prevent soup from sticking to bottom of pan. Add heavy cream and cook 20 minutes more. Stir in sherry, lemon juice, salt and white pepper. Whisk in remaining 1/2 cup butter, 1 tablespoon at a time. Remove bouquet garni. Ladle soup into bowls and garnish with fresh thyme.

Makes 6 1/2 cups.

The last frost has passed. It's time to plant the daisies. Warm up for the chore with Curried Asparagus Soup served in an earthenware crock.

Curried Asparagus Soup

This first-course soup will gently spur the appetite. If you like a little heat, the regular curry may be replaced with 1/2 tablespoon or more of madras (or hot) curry.

Easy • Serves 4

1	**pound asparagus**
1	**tablespoon butter**
1/2	**cup chopped onion**
3	**cups chicken broth**
1/4	**teaspoon white pepper**
1 1/2	**tablespoons curry**
1/2	**cup heavy cream**

Break off the woody ends of asparagus and discard. Cut stalks into 1" pieces. Set the tips aside.

In a soup pot, melt butter and sauté onions over medium heat for 3 minutes. Add asparagus stalk pieces with the chicken broth. Bring soup to a boil and simmer 1/2 hour. Meanwhile, blanch the asparagus tips in a small amount of boiling water for 2-3 minutes. Drain and set aside.

Purée simmered soup in a blender or food processor until smooth; return to the soup pot. In a small bowl, add white pepper and curry to the heavy cream; add cream to the soup. Reheat soup until warmed through. Add asparagus tips just before serving.

Italian Tomato Pasta Soup

This recipe was shared by the former Regulator Café in Hillsborough and was originally published in one of ***Taste Full*** *magazine's earliest issues. This delightful soup is a part of Elizabeth's permanent recipe file.*

Easy • Serves 4 to 6

1	**onion, diced**
1	**green pepper, diced**
2	**garlic cloves, diced**
1	**zucchini, diced**
4	**tablespoons olive oil**
1	**teaspoon dried basil**
1/2	**teaspoon dried thyme**
1/4	**teaspoon dried oregano**
4	**cups water**
3	**cups fresh tomatoes, diced (or diced, canned tomatoes with juice)**
1/2	**cup red wine**
1/4	**cup umeboshi vinegar (plum vinegar, available in natural food stores)**
1/4	**cup clear soya sauce (A light soy sauce. Do not substitute with regular soy sauce.)**
2	**cups pasta, cooked (bow tie, macaroni, or orzo)**
•	**salt and pepper to taste**
•	**freshly grated Romano cheese**

In large stovetop dutch oven, sauté onion, green pepper, garlic and zucchini in olive oil until onion is transparent. Sprinkle basil, thyme, and oregano on vegetables and add water, tomatoes, red wine, umeboshi vinegar and clear soya sauce. Simmer on low heat for 20-30 minutes. Add cooked pasta. Season to taste. Garnish with freshly grated Romano cheese.

Spring Salad with Strawberries

Several years ago Elizabeth's husband hunted turkeys at Fort Lewis Lodge, a full service country inn at the heart of a 3200-acre mountain estate near Millboro, Virginia. Caryl Cowden, who with her husband John operates the lodge, shared this recipe that is delicious served with grilled steak or chicken.

Easy • Serves 4-5

1	pound mixed fresh greens (romaine, leaf or spinach)
1	pint fresh strawberries, hulled and halved
1/2	cup sugar
2	tablespoons sesame seeds
1	tablespoon poppy seeds
2	teaspoons minced onion
1/4	teaspoon paprika
1/4	teaspoon Worcestershire sauce
1/2	cup vegetable oil
1/4	cup cider vinegar

Wash greens and tear into bite-size pieces. Combine with strawberries in a large salad bowl. Cover and refrigerate. Combine remaining ingredients in blender or food processor; process for 30 seconds at low speed until well combined. Shortly before serving, drizzle dressing over greens and strawberries; toss gently.

Blue Penne Pasta Salad with Prosciutto and Olives

Tangy blue cheese and prosciutto are at the heart of this salad.

Average • Serves 8

•	Penne Dressing
1/2	pound penne pasta
2/3	cup chopped red onion
1	cup chopped red bell pepper
1/2	cup chopped black olives
1/4	pound prosciutto, sliced thin
1/4	pound blue cheese (or if you prefer, gorgonzola)
1/4	cup chopped fresh parsley

Prepare dressing. In a large pot of boiling water, cook penne until *al dente*; drain and rinse under cold water and cool.

In a large bowl, combine cooked pasta with red onion, red pepper and olives. Cut prosciutto into thin strips and crumble the blue cheese. Add to the salad with the chopped parsley. Toss salad with dressing. Chill thoroughly and serve.

Penne Dressing

2/3	cup mayonnaise
1	tablespoon balsamic vinegar
1	tablespoon red wine vinegar
1/2	teaspoon basil
1	teaspoon salt
1/2	teaspoon black pepper

Whisk all ingredients together until smooth.

A cloudless May afternoon, a spirited game of badminton – now serve up a Spring Salad with Strawberries.

Warm Madras Spinach Salad

This salad has unbelievable flavor and variety.

Easy • Serves 6

- • Madras Dressing
- 2 packed cups coarsely shredded fresh spinach
- 1 bunch watercress
- 1 pound small new potatoes
- 1 cup shredded radishes
- 1/2 cup minced green onions
- • salt and pepper to taste
- 1 head green or red leaf lettuce
- 2 tablespoons fresh chopped mint, for garnish
- 2 tablespoons fresh chopped cilantro, for garnish
- 1/4 cup chopped roasted peanuts, for garnish

Prepare dressing. Wash and dry spinach and watercress. In medium pot of salted boiling water, cook potatoes until tender, 10-12 minutes.

Combine spinach, watercress, radishes, and onions with dressing.

Halve warm potatoes. Add to salad. Add a little salt and pepper to taste. The potatoes will slightly wilt the spinach. Serve warm over whole lettuce leaves. Garnish with mint, cilantro and peanuts.

Madras Dressing

- 2 tablespoons lime juice
- 2 tablespoons rice vinegar
- 1 teaspoon mango chutney
- 2 minced garlic cloves
- 2 teaspoons sugar
- 1 teaspoon chili oil

Combine all ingredients in a bowl and mix well.

Olive Pesto macaroni salad

Tiny grape tomatoes are a nice addition to this easy, delicious pasta salad.

Easy • Serves 6-8

- 1 pound macaroni
- 1 1/2 cups (12 ounces) pesto, purchased or homemade
- 1-1 1/2 cups pitted calamata olives
- 1 pound grape tomatoes, whole

Cook pasta according to package directions. Drain and rinse under cold water. Stir in pesto, combining well. Carefully stir in olives and tomatoes. Serve at room temperature.

CAROLINA BLUEFISH CAESAR SALAD

Smoked bluefish adds a taste of Carolina to this salad favorite.

EASY • SERVES 6

- **3** **cups Garlic Croutons**
- **•** **Carolina Caesar Dressing**
- **1** **large head romaine lettuce**
- **1/2** **cup grated Parmesan cheese**
- **•** **freshly ground black pepper**

Make Garlic Croutons and Carolina Caesar Dressing ahead.

Wash lettuce and break into bite-size pieces, removing ribs from the larger leaves. Eight to 10 cups of loose lettuce will provide ample salad for 6. Place lettuce in a large bowl. Stir in croutons; add dressing 1/3 cup at a time as needed. Toss to lightly coat, not laden lettuce. Sprinkle with Parmesan and pepper. Toss again and serve.

Garlic Croutons:

- **3** **tablespoons butter**
- **1** **tablespoon olive oil**
- **1** **tablespoon minced garlic**
- **3** **cups 1/2" cubed dry French or Italian bread**
- **1** **tablespoon chopped parsley**

Melt butter and olive oil in a skillet with garlic. Heat until you smell garlic. Toss bread cubes in a large bowl with butter/oil mixture and parsley. When absorbed and well-coated, return bread cubes to skillet and cook on medium-high heat tossing to brown on all sides. Remove from pan and cool.

Carolina Caesar Dressing:

- **3** **ounces smoked bluefish**
- **1** **tablespoon minced garlic**
- **1** **egg yolk, see note**
- **1/2** **teaspoon Dijon mustard**
- **2 1/2** **tablespoons lemon juice**
- **1/3** **cup olive oil**

Flake bluefish into bowl of food processor with garlic, egg yolk, mustard and lemon juice. Process to blend. When smooth, slowly pour olive oil through spout while processor is running; the dressing will thicken. Refrigerate but bring to room temperature before serving. Makes 1 cup.

Editor's Note: There has been some concern of late regarding the use of raw eggs. If you are concerned, either omit or look for pasteurized eggs, which are becoming more available in the marketplace.

Bobbers, 1999

Black and White Pasta with Creole Scallops

Colorful and spicy, this is a beautiful dish to serve a lively group of friends. If you don't wish to make your own Creole Seasoning from your own spice shelf, it's available at the grocery store. Serve with Vincenzo's Salad on page 104.

Average • Serves 6

3/4	cup olive oil
1/3	cup lemon juice
3	tablespoons honey
3	tablespoons soy sauce
1/4	cup Creole Seasoning
12	ounces black fresh-dried fettuccine
12	ounces plain fresh-dried fettuccine
2	pounds bay scallops
1/4	cup chopped fresh parsley

Make the Creole Seasoning first and set aside.

In a large sauté pan, heat olive oil over medium heat. Add lemon juice, honey and soy sauce and blend well. Stir in Creole Seasoning and let sauce simmer 2 minutes. Set sauce aside until you are ready to cook the pasta.

Please note, the longer it sits, the hotter the spice will become.

Mix black and white pastas together and cook according to the package directions. While the pasta is cooking, bring sauce back to a simmer over medium-high heat. Add scallops and parsley; cook for about 5 minutes until just cooked, tossing lightly to coat scallops with seasoning. With a slotted spoon, remove scallops from sauce and keep them warm. When pasta is cooked *al dente*, drain and immediately toss with the sauce in a bowl. Divide pasta among six plates. Next, divide the scallops. Spoon sauce over each serving, but not so much that it pools on the bottom of the plate.

Creole Seasoning

1	tablespoon salt
1/2	teaspoon black pepper
1 1/2	teaspoons cayenne pepper
1	teaspoon white pepper
1 1/2	teaspoons garlic powder
2	teaspoons onion powder
1 1/2	teaspoons thyme
1	teaspoon oregano
1/4	teaspoon mace
1/2	teaspoon nutmeg

In a small bowl, mix all ingredients together. Store in airtight spice jar.

A loaf of crusty bread, a jug of wine – gather a group of friends and serve them this Black and White Pasta with Creole Scallops.

FONTANA
COLLI

Hazel's Shrimp Scampi

*Scampi with a Caribbean flavor was shared with **Taste Full** in 1994 by Hazel Burnette of St. Lucia when she was a visiting chef at King Neptune Restaurant in Wrightsville Beach, North Carolina.*

Easy • Serves 4

2	pounds fresh medium or large shrimp
1/2	cup butter
1	tablespoon minced garlic
1	tablespoon minced shallots
1	bunch green onions, chopped
1	cup julienned red pepper
1	cup julienned green pepper
1/4	cup fresh chopped parsley
1/2	cup white wine
1/2	teaspoon black pepper
•	salt to taste

Peel and devein shrimp. In a large skillet or sauté pan, melt butter over high heat and sauté shrimp with garlic for 1-2 minutes. Add shallots, green onions, peppers, parsley, white wine, black pepper and salt. Lower heat and simmer for 3 minutes. Serve over orzo or a seasoned rice.

Catfish Fillets with Horseradish Crust

*This delicious recipe comes from the folks at Carolina Classics Catfish in Ayden, North Carolina. **Taste Full** added a Mediterranean Tartar Sauce.*

Easy • Serves 4

4	green onions
1/4	cup prepared horseradish
1/3	cup dry bread crumbs
4	tablespoons butter at room temperature
4	catfish fillets, about 1 1/3 pounds
•	salt
•	Mediterranean Tartar Sauce

Heat broiler. Slice green onions and combine them with horseradish, bread crumbs and soft butter. Sprinkle the fillets on both sides with salt and put them on a lightly buttered broiler pan. Press a quarter of the crumb mixture onto the top of each fillet. Broil the fish 6"-8" from the heat source until the crumbs are brown and crisp, about 8 minutes.

Serve immediately.

Mediterranean Tartar Sauce

1/4	cup olives, finely minced
1/4	cup red onion, finely minced
1/2	cup sour cream
1/2	cup mayonnaise
2	tablespoons lemon juice
1	tablespoon capers, chopped

Combine ingredients in bowl until well blended. Let stand at room temperature for 1 hour, then refrigerate. Makes 3/4 cup.

SOFT-SHELL CRABS WITH LIME HOLLANDAISE

A delightful entrée. The crab flavor explodes from the hint of lime in the hollandaise. Serve with Wild Basmati Rice on page 183 and a green vegetable.

AVERAGE • SERVES 8

16	**soft-shell crabs, see note**
•	**seasoned flour for dredging**
2	**tablespoons vegetable oil, divided**
2	**tablespoons butter, divided**
•	**Lime Hollandaise**

Clean crabs. Dredge in flour. Heat 1/2 the oil and butter in each of 2 large sauté pans or skillets. Cook the floured crabs 4-5 minutes on each side until brown and crisp. If you need to cook crabs in shifts, keep the cooked crabs warm in a 300° oven. Serve with Lime Hollandaise drizzled over the top.

NOTE: If the crabs have not been cleaned at the fish market, do so. To clean soft-shell crabs, rinse under cold water. Cut off their faces by making a parallel slice 1/4" behind the eyes. Lift the body flap on each side of the back and remove the fibrous gills. Turn the crab over and remove the triangular apron on its stomach. Pat them dry.

Lime Hollandaise:

3/4	**pound butter, clarified**
9	**egg yolks**
•	**juice of 3 limes**
•	**salt and pepper to taste**

Clarify butter in a heavy saucepan by melting over medium heat and cooking until most of the bubbles subside. The milky fat will stick to the bottom of the pan, so the clarified butter (clear liquid) can be carefully ladled off the top.

Place egg yolks in a blender. At medium speed, slowly pour in the hot clarified butter. Continue running the blender until the sauce is thick. Add lime juice, salt and pepper.

If the hollandaise sauce should curdle or separate, remove the hollandaise to another bowl and clean the blender. Put in another egg yolk and repeat the process by slowly adding the curdled mixture back in, until the sauce thickens. Then add lime juice and seasonings, if necessary. Yields 1 1/2 cups.

Island Crab, 1981

Trout Blue with Parsley Butter

Trout for this recipe from Chef Jerri Broyles were caught from a stream across the road from her original Frog and Owl Restaurant in the old Buck Creek Mill near Highlands, North Carolina. The precarious nature of the mill's location near the stream forced the restaurant to relocate to nearby Franklin. Chef Broyles explained why this classic French recipe is so named. When fresh, whole trout not more than several hours old are poached with vinegar, a film forms in the poaching water that turns the skin of the trout blue. Gut the trout before cooking, but leave the head on. Serve with Pecan Scallion Rice on page 183.

Average • Serves 2

- 2 quarts water
- 1/2 cup cider vinegar
- 1 bay leaf
- 1 teaspoon salt
- 1 small onion, skinned but whole
- 2 fresh trout, 12" with heads on or 1-pound trout fillets
- 1 1/2 tablespoons butter
- 1 cup grated carrots
- • parsley butter

In a poaching pan or large pot bring water, vinegar, bay leaf, salt and onion to a boil. Reduce heat and simmer poaching liquid 10 minutes. Drop in fish and poach 4-5 minutes or until done. Meanwhile, in a small saucepan or sauté pan, melt butter and cook carrots for 2-3 minutes. Spoon 1/2 cup carrots on each of 2 dinner plates; place cooked trout on bed of carrots. Top with parsley butter.

Parsley Butter

- 1/2 stick unsalted butter
- 1/4 cup fresh parsley, chopped

Over medium heat, brown the butter. Add chopped parsley when butter is the desired brown. Watch for spitting oil when the parsley is added.

"It cleans like glass" promised early ads for the white-spattered enameled dishware in blue, red, green, yellow or white. Since it was inexpensive and durable, agateware became immensely popular both in the kitchen and around the campfire. On southern farms in the early-to-mid-1900's, the enameled pitchers held buttermilk in an icebox, and the sturdy plates and mugs were carried to the field hands at lunchtime. An optimistic boy might take a plate with him to the trout stream. Eventually, around the nicks and dents, the paint chipped off. It was then that agateware plates and pitchers did duty under a flowerpot, as a vase for cut flowers, or catch-all for nails and screws or buttons. Over the years, these collectibles have also added color and character to Bob Timberlake's paintings.

Vegetable Curry Whistles Dixie

Black-eyed peas combine with garden fresh vegetables, Asian spices and hot curry paste to create a memorable vegetarian dinner.

Average • Serves 6

1/4	cup vegetable oil
1	medium carrot, sliced 1/2" thick
1	red bell pepper, chopped
1	cup chopped onion
1	cup sliced celery
1 1/2	cups cauliflower florets
1 1/2	cups broccoli florets
1	cup peeled turnip, 1/2" dice
1	cup peeled butternut squash, 1/2" dice
8	ounces mushrooms, sliced
1	cup thin red cabbage ribbons
1	teaspoon cumin
1/2	teaspoon ground coriander
1/2	teaspoon caraway seeds
1	14-ounce can coconut milk
1/2	cup tomato juice
1 1/2	tablespoons Thai red curry paste
1	16-ounce can black-eyed peas, drained and rinsed
•	salt and pepper to taste

In a high-sided sauté pan, heat oil on medium high. Add carrots, pepper, onion and celery, and cook for 5 minutes. Add cauliflower, broccoli, turnip and squash; sauté until vegetables are almost tender, about 6-8 minutes. Add mushrooms, red cabbage, cumin, coriander and caraway and cook 2 minutes more.

In a small bowl, blend coconut milk, tomato juice and red curry paste. Stir this mixture into vegetables. Fold in black-eyed peas. Cover and cook 5 minutes more or until vegetables are tender and sauce thickens. Season with salt and pepper to taste. Spoon over cooked brown rice.

Easter Baked Ham with Orange-Honey Glaze

Baked ham is always welcome on any buffet. Rich with flavor, this preparation is a cinch.

Easy • Serves 16

1	**6- to 8-pound smoked, fully cooked ham**
•	**whole cloves**
1/2	**cup unsweetened orange juice**
1/3	**cup orange marmalade**
1/4	**cup firmly packed brown sugar**
2	**tablespoons honey**
1	**tablespoon Dijon mustard**
1/2	**teaspoon ground ginger**

Preheat oven to 425°. Trim fat from ham. Score outside of ham in a diamond pattern, and stud with cloves. Place ham on a rack in a shallow roasting pan.

Combine orange juice and next 5 ingredients in a bowl. Stir well and brush mixture over surface of ham. Bake for 5 minutes. Reduce heat to 325°, and bake 1 hour or until meat thermometer registers 140°. Baste ham once or twice with orange juice mixture. Let ham stand 15 minutes before slicing.

Bowties with Country Ham & Sugar Snaps in Vodka Sauce

An exciting exchange between southern staples and Italian goodness.

Average • Serves 2-4

2	**tablespoons olive oil**
2	**tablespoons minced garlic**
1/3	**cup vodka**
1/4	**pound country ham, julienned**
2	**cups fresh plum tomatoes, peeled and chopped**
1/2	**teaspoon crushed red pepper**
1	**cup heavy cream**
1/4	**cup grated Parmesan cheese**
1/2	**pound blanched sugar snap peas**
•	**salt to taste**
1/2	**pound bowtie pasta, cooked *al dente***
•	**chopped parsley**

Heat olive oil in a large sauté pan and cook garlic until almost brown. Add vodka and carefully ignite with a match. Let fire burn until vodka has almost completely cooked off. Blow out flame. Add country ham and tomatoes and simmer 5 minutes. Stir in red pepper and heavy cream and cook until sauce thickens slightly. Stir in cheese and sugar snaps. Season with salt and heat through. Toss cooked pasta in sauce and garnish with parsley. Serve immediately.

Pecan Chicken with Citrus Beurre Blanc

A wonderful, make-ahead chicken entrée. Prepare the tangy citrus sauce close to serving time and keep warm.

Easy • Serves 6

6	boneless chicken breast halves
1 1/2	cups coarsely ground pecans
1/3	cup chopped parsley
1	teaspoon paprika
3/4	teaspoon thyme
1/2	teaspoon marjoram
3/4	teaspoon salt
1/4	teaspoon black pepper
2	eggs
2	tablespoons milk
3	tablespoons flour for dredging
•	Citrus Beurre Blanc

Cut any fat or sinew from chicken breasts; set aside.

In a large shallow dish, mix the pecans with parsley, paprika, thyme, marjoram, salt and pepper. In second dish, whisk together eggs and milk. In a third dish place flour.

To assemble recipe, lightly grease a baking sheet. Dredge each chicken breast lightly in flour, dip into the egg mixture, and finally into the pecan mixture. Pat gently to coat both sides with pecans. Shake off any excess coating and arrange comfortably on the baking sheet. Cover and refrigerate if you make the recipe ahead. The chicken breasts may be prepared to this point up to 4 hours in advance.

Preheat oven to 375°. Bake chicken breasts uncovered for 35-45 minutes, depending on size and thickness. Serve with a generous tablespoon of Citrus Beurre Blanc over the top.

Citrus Beurre Blanc

1/4	cup lemon juice
1/4	cup orange juice
1	teaspoon lemon zest
1	teaspoon orange zest
3	tablespoons minced shallots
3/4	cup chilled butter, or 12 tablespoons, cut in pieces
•	salt and pepper to taste

In a medium-sized saucepan over medium heat, simmer the citrus juices with lemon zest, orange zest and shallots. When the liquid has been reduced to about 1 tablespoon, turn heat down to low. Whisk in chilled butter, 1 tablespoon at a time. Be sure each butter piece is well blended before making the next addition. This is important for a beurre blanc sauce. Season with salt and pepper to taste. Keep sauce warm for up to 20 minutes in a double boiler over hot water.

Native to the North American continent, the pecan – the most valuable of nuts – quickly became an item of commerce for the American colonists. Even before George Washington and Thomas Jefferson planted pecan trees in their gardens, Native Americans fermented the nuts to produce an intoxicating drink called "Powcohicora."

ROASTED CHICKEN WITH DRIED FIG AND FENNEL RICE STUFFING

Nutty flavors emerge in a brown rice stuffing featuring dried figs, fennel and fresh garlic.

AVERAGE • SERVES 4-5

•	**Dried Fig and Fennel Rice Stuffing**
4	**carrots, sliced**
1	**bunch fresh cilantro, washed**
1	**4-pound chicken**
•	**olive oil**
•	**salt**
•	**freshly ground pepper**
•	**coriander**
4	**fresh figs, chopped**

Make rice stuffing. Allow to cool.

Preheat oven to 450°. In roasting pan place carrots and cilantro. Spoon cooled stuffing into chicken cavity and place bird on top of carrots and cilantro. Rub beneath and on top of skin with olive oil, salt, pepper and coriander. Place in oven for 15 minutes, then reduce heat to 350° and cook for 1 hour and 15 minutes. Add fresh figs and cook 15 more minutes. Let rest 15 minutes before serving. Remove stuffing to a bowl. Cut chicken into serving pieces, then serve with carrots, figs and stuffing.

Dried Fig and Fennel Rice Stuffing:

6	**dried figs**
1/2	**cup chicken stock**
2	**tablespoons olive oil**
4	**cloves garlic, minced**
1/2	**cup chopped onions**
1/2	**cup fresh fennel or celery, chopped**
1/2	**teaspoon crushed coriander seed**
1 1/2	**cups cooked brown rice**

Chop figs and place in microwave-safe bowl with chicken stock. Microwave on high for 1 minute. Set aside to steep for 20 minutes. Heat a medium skillet over medium heat. Once hot, add olive oil then sauté garlic, onion, celery and coriander about 5 minutes. Add figs and chicken stock and cook another

Roast Duck with Strawberry Rhubarb Sauce

Game birds add a flavorful dimension to Spring entertaining, and when served with a Rhubarb Strawberry Sauce, no main course could be more seasonal. The method used to prepare the duck is adapted from one Laurey Masterton of Asheville shared of her late mother's, Elsie Masterton. Together her parents owned Blueberry Hill, an inn in Goshen, Vermont. The ducklings are mostly steamed then browned in a hot oven. If you prepare the duck during the winter months, try the Sun-Dried Cherry and Port Sauce.

AVERAGE • SERVES 4

- 2 whole ducks about 5-6 pounds each
- • salt and pepper to taste
- 1 teaspoon ground ginger
- 1 teaspoon ground cloves
- 2 cups chicken stock

Rub each duckling thoroughly inside and out with salt and pepper. In a small bowl combine ginger and cloves, and rub on the outside of both ducks. Place ducks on a rack in a large roasting pan with a cover. Tilt birds toward you, fixing it so each cavity remains slightly tilted upward. Pour chicken stock into each cavity. Add enough water to fill the pan 1/4" deep. Cover tightly and place on a top burner. Bring to a boil (you'll hear it), reduce heat and cook slowly for about 2 hours or until very tender, testing from time to time. Be very careful when you remove the lid of the roaster. The steam may burst out at you, so go easy. Turn each duck once, after about an hour, letting chicken stock pour into pan.

Preheat oven to 500°. When ducks are so tender you can move drumsticks easily, and a fork goes in and comes out smoothly, remove from pan. Place in hot oven until skin is crisp and brown, about 15 minutes.

Strawberry Rhubarb Sauce:

- 2 tablespoons minced shallots
- 1 tablespoon butter
- 1/3 cup Triple Sec or Cointreau
- 1 cup cooked rhubarb (see note below)
- 1 cup strawberries, stemmed and washed
- 1 cup duck or chicken stock
- 1 cup fresh orange juice
- 1 teaspoon brown sugar
- 1/2 teaspoon ground ginger
- 1/4 teaspoon cinnamon
- 1/4 teaspoon allspice
- 1/8 teaspoon ground cloves

In a medium saucepan, sauté shallots in butter over medium heat until soft but not browned. Add liqueur; stir and cook until syrupy. While sauce is reducing, purée cooked rhubarb (see below) and strawberries in a food processor or blender. Add fruit purée to pan with the remaining ingredients. Simmer uncovered, stirring occasionally until sauce is the thickness of heavy cream. This will take 30 minutes or longer. Remove from heat. Refrigerate if made in advance and reheat on low.

NOTE: To prepare 1 cup of cooked rhubarb: If using fresh, cook 3 cups, sliced in 1" pieces, in 1 1/2 cups water for 20 minutes. If using frozen, cook 2 cups in the same amount of water for 10 minutes. Drain and sprinkle with 1 teaspoon sugar.

Sun-Dried Cherry and Port Sauce

- 1 tablespoon butter
- 1/4 cup minced onion
- 1/2 cup dried cherries
- 1/4 cup golden raisins
- 1 cup port
- 1 tablespoon rice wine vinegar
- 2 tablespoons sugar
- 1/2 cup chicken stock

In a medium saucepan, melt butter over medium high heat and sauté onions 3 minutes. Add remaining ingredients; bring to a boil. Reduce heat and simmer over low heat until the sauce is like thin gravy. Carve ducks and spoon sauce over.

Four of a Kind, 1981

From childhood

Bob Timberlake roamed the woods of Piedmont North Carolina and hunted the variety of game to be found there. Timberlake has a special fondness for well-crafted duck decoys and owns an extensive collection.

Provençal Beef Stew

Marinating the beef in tarragon vinegar gives the meat a delicately tangy taste. The thin slice of orange peel gives this stew an authentic French flair.

Average • Serves 6

4 1/2	pounds chuck steak, cut into 1" chunks
•	tarragon vinegar, enough to soak
2	dried bay leaves
5	whole cloves garlic, peeled
2-3	cups all-purpose flour
4	tablespoons unsalted butter, divided
1	large onion, peeled and julienned
3	medium carrots, peeled and sliced
1/2	cup frozen peas
2	cups dry red wine
1	tablespoon brandy
1	thin slice of orange peel, about 1" long
•	salt and pepper to taste
•	egg noodles
2	tablespoons chopped parsley
2	cups grated Gruyére cheese

In a non-reactive bowl, toss beef lightly with tarragon vinegar, bay leaves and garlic cloves. Refrigerate for 6 hours. Remove beef from vinegar, reserving garlic cloves. Lightly coat beef with flour.

Preheat oven to 325°. In a large skillet, melt 2 tablespoons butter over medium heat. Working in batches, brown the beef adding more butter as needed. With a slotted spoon remove to an ovenproof casserole and set aside. In the same skillet, sauté onions until soft; stir into beef. Stir carrots, peas, wine, brandy and orange into casserole and season with salt and pepper. Cover tightly with foil and place in oven for 1 1/2 hours. Serve over egg noodles garnished with chopped parsley and grated Gruyère cheese over each portion.

Pork Tenderloin with Port and Prunes

A classic recipe shared by an English inn visited by Pat Storie Polk, a long time ***Taste Full*** *magazine subscriber.*

Easy • Serves 4

1 1/2	pounds pork tenderloin
1	tablespoon olive oil
8	pitted prunes
2	tablespoons prune juice
1/2	cup port
1	cup heavy cream
•	salt and white pepper to taste

Preheat oven to 325°. Trim fat and silver strings from tenderloin. Coat meat with olive oil. Roast for 20 minutes. Meanwhile slice prunes into long, thin strips and set aside. Remove pork from oven when meat thermometer reads 145° and cover with foil and keep warm. Pour pan juices into a sauté pan. Heat over medium-high heat and add prunes, prune juice and port. Boil 2 minutes until liquid is slightly reduced, then lower heat. Stir in heavy cream, simmering until sauce thickens. Season with salt and white pepper. Cut tenderloin into 1/2" thick medallions. Spoon sauce over and serve.

Oven-Barbecued Lamb Shanks

The aroma of these oven-baked shanks will draw everyone into the kitchen. This is a cozy supper to serve to family or good friends.

Easy • Serves 4

4	lamb shanks
2	tablespoons olive or vegetable oil
2/3	cup ketchup
1	cup beef broth or water
1	tablespoon Worcestershire Sauce
1/2	cup red wine vinegar
2	tablespoons firmly packed brown sugar
•	dash of hot pepper sauce
1	teaspoon salt or to taste
1/4	teaspoon freshly ground pepper
2	medium onions, sliced
5	medium carrots, peeled and sliced 1/2" thick (2 cups)

Trim excess fat from shanks. Heat oil in large deep skillet.

Preheat oven to 350°. Brown lamb shanks about 12-15 minutes over medium heat. Remove excess fat with baster or spoon. In a small bowl combine ketchup, broth, Worcestershire sauce, vinegar, sugar, hot sauce, salt and pepper. Add onions and carrots. Pour over lamb shanks. Cover and bake for 1 1/2 -2 hours until meat is fork-tender.

Chocolate Strawberry Pecan Torte

This cake is testimony to why the gods made chocolate – and strawberries!

Involved • Serves 16

Chocolate Torte Layers:

12 ounces semi-sweet chocolate
3/4 cup unsalted butter, at room temperature
2 cups sugar
8 eggs
2 tablespoons vanilla extract
1/4 teaspoon salt
3 1/2 cups pecans, finely chopped
- Strawberry Buttercream
- Chocolate Silk Icing
- 9 strawberries for garnish
- 16 whole pecans for garnish

Lightly grease four, 9" round cake pans. Line bottoms with wax paper.

Preheat oven to 350°. Melt chocolate in top of double boiler; set aside to cool.

With a mixer, cream butter and sugar. Add eggs 1 at a time, beating after each. Continue to beat for 5 minutes until mixture is light and fluffy. Add vanilla and salt. Beat in melted chocolate and chopped pecans. Divide the batter evenly among the prepared pans. (A kitchen scale is helpful for evenly dividing.) Bake for 20 minutes. Cool 5 minutes, then turn out onto cardboard cake circles for easy handling. Peel off any remaining wax paper. Cool and then chill before assembly.

Prepare Strawberry Buttercream and the Chocolate Silk Icing. To assemble torte, delicately place 1 layer of cake on a serving plate. Put 1/3 (1 cup) of Strawberry Buttercream on cake layer; spread evenly. Repeat this twice and add the top layer, uncovered. Trim any edges, if needed. Ice entire torte with Chocolate Silk Icing.

To garnish torte, slice 8 washed and stemmed strawberries in half. Alternate placing strawberries with whole pecans on the outside rim of cake. Fan 1 more strawberry and place in center of torte.

Note: This cake is very delicate to handle. If it cracks it can be easily patched together with Strawberry Buttercream. The secret is to refrigerate cakes, once cooled, before assembling.

Chocolate Silk Icing

3 ounces semi-sweet chocolate
6 tablespoons butter
1/2 cup hot water (You could use water from bottom of double boiler.)
1/2 cup plus 2 tablespoons sugar
3/4 cup cocoa, sifted
3 tablespoons vegetable oil

In a double boiler melt chocolate with butter. In separate bowl mix together hot water and sugar; stir in cocoa. Add chocolate mixture, then vegetable oil stirring until smooth. Let cool to room temperature. (Do not refrigerate to cool or the icing will lose its shine.)

Strawberry Buttercream:

1 cup fresh sliced strawberries
1 1/2 cups (3 sticks) unsalted butter, softened
2 cups confectioners' sugar
1/4 cup strawberry preserves

Purée fresh strawberries in food processor or blender. You should have about 3/4 cup strawberry purée. With a mixer, cream butter and sugar. Gradually beat in puréed strawberries and preserves. Refrigerate until of spreading consistency. Makes 3 cups.

This atmospheric canoe painting from Bob Timberlake's private collection with plates from his "Late Snow At Riverwood" dinnerware pattern reflect his passion for the outdoors and set the perfect stage for delicious Chocolate Strawberry Pecan Torte.

SOUR CREAM BLUEBERRY PIE

*A recipe shared by **Taste Full** magazine subscriber, Ted Sloan of Sanford. This pie is luscious and rich, and, best of all, easy to prepare. Please note the second filling recipe is for a deep dish pie plate. The crust recipe is ample for both standard and deep dish pies.*

EASY • SERVES 6-8

- 2 9" pie crusts
- 3 cups blueberries
- 1 cup sour cream
- 1 cup sugar
- 3 tablespoons cornstarch
- 1 teaspoon melted butter
- 1 tablespoon sugar

For a deep dish pie, increase recipe as follows:

- 4 cups blueberries
- 1 1/4 cups sour cream
- 1 1/4 cups sugar
- 4 tablespoons cornstarch
- 1 teaspoon melted butter
- 1 tablespoon sugar

Preheat oven to 350°. Line a pie plate with 1 crust and arrange blueberries evenly on bottom. In a medium bowl, mix sour cream, sugar and cornstarch together and pour over blueberries. Cover top with second crust and seal. Brush top of crust with butter and sprinkle with sugar. Bake at 350° for 45-50 minutes.

Pie Crust

YIELDS 2 CRUSTS FOR ONE 9" PIE

- 2 1/2 cups flour
- 1 teaspoon salt
- 1/2 cup vegetable shortening
- 1/4 cup unsalted butter
- 4-5 tablespoons ice water

In a medium bowl combine flour and salt. Cut up shortening and butter and add to bowl. Cut in with pastry blender or fork until consistency of coarse meal. Sprinkle water over and stir gently to combine. Gather into 2 balls. Cover and chill 15-30 minutes.

Flatten 1 ball and roll into circle on floured pastry cloth. Line pie plate, and trim even with edge of pie, then moisten with a bit of water. Put filling in crust. Roll out second ball and gently fold circle in half and make 4 or 5 cuts with a sharp knife for vents. Place on top of pie and unfold. Press to seal edges.

CRÉME CELESTE WITH STRAWBERRIES

Tangy, velvety rich, unbelievable flavor! A dessert for the more sophisticated palate – make this!

EASY TO AVERAGE • SERVES 6

- 1 teaspoon unflavored gelatin
- 1/4 cup cold water
- 1 cup sugar, divided
- 2 cups heavy cream
- 2 cups sour cream
- 1/4 cup brandy
- 1 pint strawberries, hulled and sliced thin
- 1/4 cup fresh lemon juice

In a small bowl sprinkle the gelatin over cold water and let stand 5 minutes. In a saucepan combine 3/4 cup sugar with heavy cream; cook over medium heat, stirring until the sugar is dissolved. Add the gelatin mixture; cook, constantly stirring, until gelatin is dissolved. Set aside.

In a large bowl, whisk together the sour cream and brandy; slowly pour in the heavy cream mixture. Let crème cool; pour into an 8" x 8" glass baking dish and chill, covered, 3-4 hours.

In a small bowl combine sliced strawberries, the remaining 1/4 cup sugar and lemon juice. Chill until ready to serve. Spoon the cream mixture into 6 dessert glasses; top with sliced strawberries.

Brown Sugar Pound Cake with Peach Frosting

Brown sugar and poppy seeds impart texture and flavor to this rich pound cake. The peach frosting makes the perfect accent. This cake holds at room temperature which makes it a perfect "travelling" cake.

Easy • Serves 14 to 16

- 1 cup softened butter, plus 2 tablespoons melted butter
- 2 1/3 cups firmly packed light brown sugar
- 6 eggs
- 3 cups sifted all-purpose flour
- 1/4 teaspoon baking soda
- 1/2 teaspoon salt
- 1 cup yogurt, divided
- 2 teaspoons vanilla extract
- 1/3 cup poppy seeds
- • Peach Frosting

Preheat oven to 325°. Use a pastry brush to grease 10" tube or bundt pan with 2 tablespoons melted butter. Set aside.

In a bowl of electric mixer, cream 1 cup softened butter and add sugar. Cream until light and fluffy, about 10 minutes. Use a rubber spatula to scrape down sides of bowl. Add eggs 1 at a time, mixing well. Scrape down sides. In a medium bowl combine flour, baking soda and salt. Add 1/3 flour mixture to batter and mix to combine. Add 1/2 cup yogurt and mix well. Repeat steps, ending with flour. Stir in vanilla and poppy seeds and blend well.

Pour batter into prepared pan. Bake 1 hour and 10 minutes, or until a sharp knife inserted comes out clean. Remove from oven, transfer to a cooling rack and cool for 10 minutes. Unmold cake onto rack and cool completely. Spread icing over cooled cake and serve.

Peach Frosting

- 1/2 cup butter, softened
- 1/4 cup peach preserves
- 1/4 cup peach yogurt
- • pinch of salt
- 2 1/2 cups powdered sugar, sifted

In small bowl of electric mixer, cream butter until smooth. Add preserves, yogurt and salt. Cream well. With mixer on low, add powdered sugar one cup at a time. Mix to blend well. Spread over cooled cake.

"U Pick Em." "Pick your own." Signs such as these dot the landscape of farm country in the Atlantic coastal south. Take the family for a journey to a strawberry patch, and the evening's reward could be a churn brimming with homemade strawberry ice cream, or maybe a strawberry pie or strawberry shortcake wearing a top hat of whipped cream.

Strawberries, 1980

Chocolate Chip Coconut Crisps

This cookie is a variation of the cookie jar favorite – chocolate chip. Rice Krispies add crunch, and coconut adds wonderful flavor. Perfect for a child's outdoor tea party.

Easy • Yields 3 dozen

- 1/2 cup butter, softened
- 1/3 cup brown sugar, firmly packed
- 1/3 cup granulated sugar
- 2 eggs
- 1 cup all-purpose flour
- 1/2 teaspoon baking powder
- 1/4 teaspoon salt
- 1/2 teaspoon vanilla
- 2 cups semi-sweet chocolate chips
- 1 cup Rice Krispies
- 3/4 cup coconut

Preheat oven to 375°. Cream butter and sugars until light and fluffy. Add eggs. Beat until fully incorporated. Add flour, baking powder, salt and vanilla. Stir until blended. Add remaining ingredients. Mix well. Place level tablespoons of dough 2" apart on lightly greased cookie sheets. Bake for 6-8 minutes in upper level of oven. Cool on wire rack.

Black Bottom Cupcakes

*A knockout shared by **Taste Full** magazine subscriber Edie Spinks of Winston-Salem. These cupcakes freeze well after baking. Kids will flock to your house.*

Easy • Yields 15 cupcakes

- • Cream Cheese Filling
- 1 1/2 cups all-purpose flour
- 1 cup sugar
- 1/4 cup cocoa
- 1 teaspoon baking soda
- 1/2 teaspoon salt
- 1 cup water
- 1 tablespoon cider vinegar
- 1/3 cup vegetable oil
- 1 teaspoon vanilla
- • cupcake liners

Cream Cheese Filling

- 1 8-ounce package cream cheese, softened
- 1 egg, beaten
- 1/3 cup sugar
- 1/8 teaspoon salt
- 1 cup semi-sweet chocolate chips

In a medium bowl, beat together cream cheese, egg, sugar and salt. By hand, fold in chocolate chips. Set aside.

Make the cream cheese filling and set aside.

Preheat oven to 350°. In a large bowl, sift together the flour, sugar, cocoa, baking soda and salt. Stir in water, vinegar, oil and vanilla; beat batter well. Place cupcake liners into 2 3/4" x 1 3/8" (scant 1/2 cup) muffin tins. Fill liners 2/3 full with batter. Add 1 tablespoon cream cheese filling to the top of each cupcake. Bake at 350° for 15 minutes.

Spring means the return of outdoor play. Chocolate Chip Coconut Crisps were the request for this doll tea.

Almond Crescent Cookies

Enjoy these simple, delicate, rich cookies perfect with fresh fruit or ice cream.

Easy • Makes sixty $1^1/2$" crescents

6	ounces slivered almonds
$1^3/4$	cups unsifted all-purpose flour
1	cup butter, softened
$^1/3$	cup sugar
2	cups powdered sugar

Place almonds in food processor. Grind. Transfer to a bowl and add flour.

In bowl of electric mixer, cream butter. Add sugar and beat until light and fluffy. On low speed, add flour and nut mixture. Cover bowl and chill for 1 hour.

Preheat over to 325°. Spray 3 sheet pans with cooking spray. Dust clean work surface with flour. Divide dough into 6 portions. With floured fingertips, roll each portion back and forth on work surface to shape long pieces about $^1/2$" in diameter. Cut each portion in 1" lengths. Shape into crescents with slightly tapered ends. Place on baking sheets. Bake for 12-15 minutes. Cookies will be golden around the edges. Place baking sheet on wire rack. Sift powdered sugar over warm cookies.

Cool. Store in airtight containers up to 1 week at room temperature or freeze up to 1 month.

Edinburgh Shortbread

This delicious shortbread has a delightfully soft cake-like texture.

Easy • Makes 36

1	cup unsalted butter, softened
$^1/2$	cup sugar
1	teaspoon vanilla extract
$^1/2$	teaspoon almond extract
$1^3/4$	cups all-purpose flour
$^1/4$	cup cornstarch
$^1/4$	teaspoon baking powder
$^1/4$	teaspoon salt

Cream butter and sugar until light and fluffy. Add vanilla and almond flavorings and mix well. In a small bowl combine flour, cornstarch, baking powder and salt. At low speed, add dry ingredients to butter mixture until well blended. Transfer dough to waxed paper and chill for 1 hour.

Spray a sheet pan with cooking spray. On floured surface, roll dough into a $^1/2$" thick rectangle. Cut into $2^1/2$" x $1^1/2$" rectangles, and transfer to prepared sheet pan. Using a fork, prick each cookie 3 times. Chill for 15 minutes. Preheat oven to 375°.

Bake for 15-18 minutes, until lightly browned. Remove from oven; cool for 10 minutes. Transfer to a wire rack and cool completely. Store in an airtight container until ready to serve. The dough may also be rolled out and cut with cookie cutters.

Spirited Ambrosia

In Greek mythology, ambrosia meant "immortality." In the South, ambrosia is a chilled fruit dessert made with simply cut oranges (and sometimes bananas) and grated coconut. This version is "immortalized" with the addition of Grand Marnier.

Easy • Serves 6

4	**navel oranges**
1	**4-ounce package frozen grated coconut**
1/2	**cup Grand Marnier (4 ounces)**
1/4	**cup confectioners' sugar**

Peel oranges and remove all white pith (underskin). Slice oranges very thinly. Arrange alternate layers of orange slices and coconut in a glass bowl. Sprinkle each layer with Grand Marnier and confectioners' sugar. End with top layer of coconut. Chill overnight.

White Chocolate Raspberry Cheesecake

There are no words to describe this delicious, incredibly sinful recipe.

Average • Serves 16

- • Graham Cracker Crust
- 5 8-ounce packages cream cheese, softened
- 3/4 cup sugar
- 2 tablespoons vanilla extract
- 4 egg yolks
- 4 whole eggs
- 1/4 cup sour cream
- 3/4 cup raspberry preserves, divided
- 4 ounces white chocolate, melted

Prepare graham cracker crust.

Preheat oven to 400°. In a mixing bowl, cream the cheese and sugar until blended. Add vanilla and egg yolks and mix well. Add the whole eggs, sour cream and 1/2 of the preserves. Stir until well blended, but do not over-mix. Never over-mix cheesecake. Add the melted white chocolate quickly, or it will solidify. Swirl in the remaining preserves to leave a marble design. Pour into prepared crust.

Place a pan of water on the bottom rack of oven; this will add moisture while the cheesecake bakes. Bake on the middle rack for 10 minutes. Lower temperature to 275° and cook for 1 hour and 20 minutes. Turn the oven off. Open oven door slightly and let the cheesecake cool completely in oven. Cover with plastic and refrigerate until well chilled. Remove springform mold and slice. Garnish plates with fresh raspberries.

Graham Cracker Crust

- 1 1/2 cups graham cracker crumbs
- 1/2 cup melted butter

Grease bottom and sides of a 10" springform pan. Mix the cracker crumbs and butter together in a bowl; press into the bottom of springform pan and 2" up the sides. Bake at 325° for 10 minutes. Cool completely.

Fig Crumble

A wonderful way to use fresh figs, particularly those that are so easily bruised or broken.

Easy • Serves 6-9

- 1 1/2 cups flour
- 1 1/4 cups rolled oats (oatmeal)
- 2/3 cup brown sugar
- 1 1/4 teaspoons ground ginger, divided
- 1/2 teaspoon plus a dash nutmeg, divided
- 1/2 teaspoon salt
- 12 tablespoons butter (1 1/2 sticks), slightly softened
- 3 cups figs
- 1 tablespoon lemon zest
- 1/4 cup sugar

Preheat oven to 350°. In small bowl combine flour, oats, brown sugar, 1 teaspoon of the ginger, 1/2 teaspoon of the nutmeg, and salt. Mix in butter with a fork until combined and crumbly. Divide in half. Press one half into the bottom of a lightly greased 8" x 8" square pan. Bake until lightly brown, about 15 minutes. Cool about 10 minutes. Meanwhile, wash figs and remove stems, cut in halves or quarters if they are big ones. In small bowl combine lemon zest, sugar, remaining 1/4 teaspoon ginger and dash of nutmeg. Carefully toss with figs. Arrange figs with sugar on top of baked crust; crumble remaining crust mixture over the top of the figs. Return to oven and bake another 20-25 minutes until top is golden and figs are tender.

Summer
Bob Timberlake

Cool And Capered Shrimp

Marinated shrimp have never tasted better – another winner to add to your favorite hors d'oeuvres. Buy twice as much shrimp as you think you will need. No one can stop eating these.

Easy • Serves 10

3-3 1/2 pounds large shrimp
1 cup celery, chopped
3/4 cup green onions, chopped
1 tablespoon garlic, minced
1/4 cup capers
1/2 cup ketchup
1 cup mayonnaise
1/2 cup Dijon mustard
1 tablespoon Worcestershire sauce
1/4 cup lemon juice
2 tablespoons finely chopped fresh parsley

Cook shrimp in batches. Let each batch come to a boil and when shrimp begin to rise to the top, pull out with a slotted spoon. Let shrimp cool in shell (they will cook slightly longer). Next, peel and devein. Place shrimp in a large bowl.

Combine the remaining ingredients. Pour over shrimp, coating well with marinade. Refrigerate overnight. To serve, line a large shallow bowl with large lettuce leaves – use green leaf or red-tipped lettuce. Place generous amount of shrimp on top; replenish as needed. Have container with toothpicks nearby.

sweet & savory Swiss Pie with Kiwi

Kiwi adds a twist to this quiche. Serve as an hors d'oeuvre sliced in thin wedges, or prepare as an unusual luncheon entrée.

Easy • Serves 6-8

2 cups grated Swiss cheese
1 tablespoon flour
1 pre-baked 9" pastry pie shell
4-5 kiwi, sliced into rounds
3 eggs
1 cup milk
• ground pepper to taste

Preheat oven to 400°. Toss grated Swiss cheese with flour. Spread in pie shell. Place 6-8 kiwi slices over cheese. Mix eggs with milk. Add ground pepper to taste. Pour over kiwi. Add more kiwi slices on top. Bake 15 minutes, then reduce to 325°. Bake about 25 minutes or until knife inserted in center comes out clean. This can be made ahead and frozen unbaked.

Previous page *Gilley's Well*, 1982

Blue Cornmeal Appetizer Muffins

The inspiration for this recipe comes from a favorite restaurant in Minneapolis, Minnesota, where wonderfully delicious blue corn sticks are served hot and crisp from the oven. Blue corn is native to the American Southwest, and was ground into meal by the Pueblo Indians of the area. It can be found in specialty food stores; however, if unavailable, try these corn muffins using yellow corn meal. The secret to their great flavor is a purée of cilantro, garlic and jalapeño peppers mixed into the batter – delicious flavor bites to serve hungry company. Stuff each hot muffin with a bit of Swiss cheese if desired, for a great hors d'oeuvre.

Average • Makes 3 dozen

6 tablespoons butter
1/4 cup fresh cilantro, lightly packed
1 clove garlic
2 jalapeño peppers, seeded
1 egg
1 cup milk, at room temperature
1 cup blue corn meal
3/4 cup flour
2 tablespoons sugar
1 tablespoon baking powder
1 teaspoon salt

Preheat oven to 400°. Lightly grease 3 mini-muffin pans.

Melt butter; set aside to cool. In food processor, combine cilantro, garlic and jalapeños. Process until fairly smooth, scraping down as needed. Add egg; process again until smooth. Add melted butter and milk; process to combine. In separate bowl, combine blue corn meal, flour, sugar, baking powder and salt. Make a well in center of dry ingredients. Pour in mixture from food processor and stir just to combine.

Spoon into prepared pans using about 1 1/2 tablespoons per muffin cup. Bake until well-browned, about 18-20 minutes.

Red, White & Blue Nachos

Party nachos – baked tortilla chips covered with prosciutto and creamy blue cheese. A sure crowd pleaser. Make these!

Easy • Serves 10

2 9-ounce bags baked tortilla chips
1/2 pound thinly sliced Prosciutto ham
1 cup sliced banana peppers
1 cup sliced green onions
2 cups chopped tomatoes
3 cups grated Monterey Jack cheese
1 cup crumbled blue cheese

Preheat oven to 350°. Line 2 sheet pans with foil. Spray with cooking spray. Spread a bag of tortilla chips over each pan. Coarsely chop ham and layer over chips. Sprinkle with peppers, green onions, and tomatoes. Top each batch with 1 1/2 cups Monterey Jack and 1/2 cup blue cheese. Bake one pan for 20 minutes. Reserve the second pan. Using a large spatula, transfer nachos to serving platter. Serve with lots of napkins. Cook the second batch while guests are enjoying the first.

NC3446G

Smoked Salmon Tortilla Roll-ups

These roll-ups using flour tortillas can be put together in a snap. They slice more easily if made a day ahead. Many different fillings could be used. Here are two.

Easy • Yields 10-12 spirals

1	9-10" flour tortilla
2	tablespoons cream cheese, softened
1	tablespoon Dijon mustard
1	tablespoon chopped fresh dill
1	teaspoon grated lemon zest
2	ounces thinly sliced smoked salmon

Lay tortilla on flat surface. In small bowl combine cream cheese and mustard. Spread evenly on tortilla. Sprinkle with dill and lemon zest. Spread salmon in 1 layer on top, leaving about a 3" margin on top edge for sealing. Starting at bottom edge, roll tightly. Wrap tightly in plastic wrap seam side down; twist ends tightly to seal. Refrigerate several hours or overnight. Slice and serve.

Roasted Pepper Roll-ups

Easy • Yields 10-12 spirals

1	9-10" flour tortilla
3	tablespoons cream cheese, softened
1	tablespoon fresh oregano, coarsely chopped
4	ounces roasted pepper (about 1/3 of a jar)
•	thinly sliced Fontina cheese

Lay tortilla on flat surface; spread evenly with cream cheese. Sprinkle with oregano. Drain peppers on paper towels; cover with wax paper and pound lightly with a meat mallet to flatten. Lay on tortilla leaving about a 3" margin on the top edge for sealing. Lay thinly sliced Fontina cheese on top. Roll, starting at bottom end and seal with section that only has cream cheese and oregano. Wrap, seam side down, tightly in plastic wrap, twisting ends to seal. Refrigerate for several hours or overnight. Slice and serve.

This old rowboat has yarns to tell – of sons and grandsons who watched the sun rise and set over the Atlantic, baited fishing lines and dropped them over her side, of memories made, of trust, respect and friendship, of lessons learned, of love strengthened and expanded. Bob Timberlake's paintings capture the character of inanimate objects. Look and listen. They'll tell you a story.

NC3446G, 1999

Black-Eyed Pea Salsa

A refreshing appetizer with a Southern twist. Serve with your favorite corn chips.

Easy • Makes 4-5 cups

2 cups tomatoes, peeled, seeded, cubed
2 cups cooked black-eyed peas
1 yellow bell pepper, stemmed, seeded, chopped
2 garlic cloves, minced
1 onion, chopped
2 tablespoons basil, fresh
1/2 cup olive oil
1/4 cup red wine vinegar
• juice of 1/2 lime
• salt and pepper to taste

Prepare all ingredients and combine. Salt and pepper to taste. Let sit for 4 hours or refrigerate overnight.

Fresh Tomato Thyme Salsa

Delicious as a dip with plunging tortillas, or use alongside grilled chicken or fish.

Easy • Makes 3 cups

2 large ripe tomatoes, diced (about 2 cups)
1/2 cup green pepper, finely diced
3 green onions, finely chopped
1/4 cup light olive oil
1 tablespoon red wine vinegar
1 large garlic clove, minced
1 tablespoon fresh thyme leaves (or 1 teaspoon dried thyme)
1 tablespoon fresh parsley, chopped
1/2 teaspoon salt
• freshly ground pepper to taste

Combine ingredients in bowl until well blended. Let stand at room temperature for 1 hour, then refrigerate.

A verdigris bunny can only dream of diving into this Black-Eyed Pea Salsa. Lucky you gets to actually dip into it!

Although it's thought of as a Southern delicacy, watermelon has an ancient history. Native to tropical Africa, this succulent fruit of the gourd family is a cousin of the cucumber. There is a Sanskrit word for watermelon, and the fruits were depicted by early Egyptian artists, indicating an antiquity in agriculture of more than 4,000 years.

Sunny Corn Soup

We call this soup sunny because it captures summer's golden color and the season's fresh tastes of corn and yellow peppers.

Average • Serves 4-6

6	**ears of corn, uncooked (or 3 cups frozen)**
4	**tablespoons butter**
3	**medium leeks, sliced**
2	**tablespoons minced shallots**
1	**yellow bell pepper, chopped**
3	**cups chicken stock**
1	**teaspoon salt**
1/2	**teaspoon white pepper**
1	**cup heavy cream**
•	**chopped parsley and red pepper cut in slivers for garnish**

Cut corn from uncooked cob to yield about 3 cups. Melt butter in a large saucepan. Sauté corn, leeks and shallots in butter for 5 minutes. Add yellow pepper and cook another 3 minutes. Stir in chicken stock and simmer for 30 minutes.

Purée soup in small batches in a food processor or blender. Return soup to saucepan and season with salt and white pepper. Add heavy cream and heat until soup thickens.

Garnish with chopped parsley and red pepper.

Chilled Honeydew Watermelon Soup

Refreshing! Transport as a great summer picnic soup, or serve as a first course before a meal of grilled seafood.

Easy • Serves 6

2	**large ripe honeydew melons**
1 1/4	**cups dry white wine**
2	**tablespoons fresh lemon juice**
1/4	**cup lime juice**
2	**teaspoons ground ginger**
1/4	**cup fresh mint, chopped**
1 3/4	**cups watermelon, seeded and cut into 1/2" dice**
•	**fresh mint for garnish**

Cut the honeydew in half and scrape out all seeds and strings. Scoop out flesh and purée in blender or food processor. There should be about 6 cups purée. Combine honeydew flesh with wine, lemon and lime juices, ginger and chopped mint; blend well. Chill covered for 1 hour before serving. Garnish with diced watermelon and fresh mint.

Black Bean Gazpacho

Vary this cold soup recipe with what you have on hand, for example in a pinch you may substitute diced cold potatoes for the black beans. Cilantro may be used as a substitute for basil in other seasons.

Easy • Serves 6-8

2 cucumbers, peeled, coarsely chopped
1 green pepper, seeded, coarsely chopped
4-5 green onions, coarsely chopped
1 large clove garlic, crushed
1/4 cup basil leaves, or more
2 tablespoons parsley tops
2 14.5-ounce cans diced tomatoes, or 3 cups diced fresh tomatoes
3 tablespoons red wine vinegar
3 tablespoons olive oil
2 teaspoons salt
1 teaspoon ground pepper
2 cans black beans, rinsed and drained
1 cup vegetable stock

In bowl of food processor, pulse cucumbers, pepper, onion, garlic, basil and parsley on and off until mixture is coarsely chopped. Empty into a large bowl.

Process tomatoes in same manner until just broken up. Add to vegetable mixture with remaining ingredients. Mix well, adjust seasonings and chill. This soup will keep several days in the refrigerator.

Red Pepper Soup with Herbed Croutons

This coral-colored soup, enhanced by flavorful croutons, may be served hot or cold. Serve with Baked Herb Crouton Sticks on page 189.

Easy • Serves 8

3 pounds red bell peppers
1 cup chopped onion
2 tablespoons butter
4 cups chicken stock
1 cup heavy cream
1 teaspoon salt
1/2 teaspoon white pepper

Roast the peppers under the broiler or on a grill until charred on all sides. (Charring will be easier if the peppers are split and lightly flattened.). Run under cold water and remove the skin, seeds and ribs. Cut peppers into quarters.

In a small pan, sauté onions in butter over medium heat until soft. Purée onions and peppers in a food processor or blender until smooth. Place pepper purée in a 3-quart saucepan and add chicken stock, cream, salt and pepper. Simmer 10 minutes over low heat. If serving the soup warm, ladle into bowls, add a few croutons and serve. If serving cold, let the soup cool and then chill in the refrigerator for 3 hours. Do not let this soup chill for too long as the texture thickens.

Traditionally a winter warm-up, soup is more than a cold-weather meal. Chilled soups are the perfect food in summer's heat and can be made ahead. Give the stove a rest and enjoy summer's harvest in a delicious soup.

A Rosy Summer Salad with Toasted Walnut Dressing

When raspberries are ripe for the picking, you want to eat them in everything. Try this green salad with a rosy hue; it's full of red — red onion, radishes, red lettuce and raspberries.

Easy • Serves 4

- 1 cup red lettuce leaves
- 1 cup green lettuce leaves
- 1 cup arugula leaves
- 1 pound asparagus tips, blanched
- 1/2 cup thinly sliced red onion
- 1/2 cup thinly sliced radishes
- 3/4 cup raspberries
- • Toasted Walnut Dressing

Prepare salad greens by tearing into bite-size pieces. Combine all ingredients except berries in large salad bowl. Toss with dressing moments before serving. Scatter berries in salad.

Toasted Walnut Dressing

- 2 tablespoons walnuts
- 2 tablespoons white wine vinegar
- 1/3 cup walnut oil
- • pinch dry mustard
- • pinch sugar
- 1/2 cup raspberries
- 1 tablespoon grated orange peel

Toast walnuts in 350° oven for 10 minutes and chop. In a medium-sized bowl, whisk together vinegar, oil, mustard and sugar. Add raspberries and crush them with the whisk. Stir in walnuts and orange peel. Serve at room temperature over salad. Makes 3/4 cup.

Scallops and Cantaloupe with Citrus Vinaigrette

A refreshing mixture of summer's sweet bounty, this composed salad presents an attractive and colorful plate.

Average • Serves 4

- 1 pound scallops, see note
- • juice of 1 lemon
- • juice of 2 limes
- 1 small cantaloupe
- 1 small Vidalia onion
- 1/2 pound sugar snap peas
- 1/4 cup fresh chopped parsley
- 2 cups croutons
- • Citrus Vinaigrette
- 1 pound fresh spinach, washed and stemmed
- 12 cherry tomatoes or 2 medium tomatoes

Citrus Vinaigrette

- 1/4 cup lime juice
- 1/4 cup raspberry vinegar
- 1/2 cup salad oil (safflower or canola)
- 1/4 teaspoon salt
- • freshly ground black pepper to taste

Whisk together vinaigrette ingredients. Set aside.

Combine scallops with lemon and lime juices. Cover and marinate in refrigerator for 3 hours, tossing occasionally.

Dice cantaloupe and thinly slice Vidalia onion. Blanch sugar snap peas in boiling water for 2 minutes. Drain and cool.

Drain and discard juices from scallops and combine with cantaloupe, onion, sugar snaps, parsley and croutons. Toss scallop mixture with vinaigrette.

Make a bed of spinach leaves on each plate. Arrange salad atop the spinach. Garnish with tomato wedges or halved cherry tomatoes.

Note: If the scallops are bay scallops, marinate them whole. If sea scallops are used, cut in half or quarters to 1/2" pieces.

Fiesta Salad

Everyone raves over this salad which features summer corn and cherry tomatoes. The cumin in the dressing gives this salad zing and makes it a knockout accompaniment to any meal. Perfect for picnic or potluck.

Easy • Serves 6

- 6 ears corn or 4 cups cooked corn
- 18 cherry or grape tomatoes, quartered
- 3/4 cup chopped red onion
- 1/3 cup chopped parsley
- 2 cloves garlic, minced
- 1/2 cup crumbled feta cheese
- • Tangy Dressing

Boil the fresh corn in salted water for 8 minutes. Remove from water, cool and cut the kernels from the ears. Combine with tomatoes, onion, parsley, garlic and feta cheese. Toss with dressing. Refrigerate for at least an hour. This salad will keep for several days in the refrigerator.

Tangy Dressing

- 1/4 cup vegetable oil
- 1/3 cup olive oil
- 2 tablespoons red wine vinegar
- 1 tablespoon balsamic vinegar
- 1 tablespoon lemon juice
- 1 tablespoon Dijon mustard
- 1 teaspoon salt
- 1 teaspoon ground black pepper
- 1 teaspoon cumin

Whisk together all the ingredients until well-blended.

Shrimp Cobb Salad

Why not adapt that standard recipe to a coastal catch? The blend of shrimp with red onion, bacon, avocados and tomato is a delight to dig into.

Average • Serves 6

- 1 1/2 pounds shrimp
- • Cobb Dressing
- 1/2 red onion, sliced thinly
- 1/2 pound bacon
- 3 avocados
- 3 tomatoes
- 7 cups mixed lettuce (romaine and bibb)
- 1 cup watercress

Bring 2" water to boil in a large pot. Drop in shrimp and when water returns to boil, drain and ice down. When cool, peel and devein. Make Cobb Dressing and toss shrimp and red onion with 1/2 cup dressing. Cover and refrigerate at least 30 minutes. Cook bacon, drain, and when cool, crumble. Peel, pit, and dice avocados. Slice tomatoes in wedges. Wash, dry and break up lettuce and watercress. In a large bowl, layer greens, shrimp with red onion, tomatoes, avocados and bacon pieces. Toss carefully with remaining dressing and divide among plates.

Cobb Dressing

- 1 cup olive oil
- 1/3 cup vegetable oil
- 1/3 cup white wine vinegar
- 3 tablespoons minced shallots
- 1 teaspoon salt
- 1/2 teaspoon freshly ground black pepper

Whisk ingredients together in a small bowl.

Pan-Seared New York Strip Steak Salad

This attractive and delicious salad plate combines down-home flavors with easy elegance. A recipe shared by Walter Royal of The Angus Barn in Raleigh, North Carolina, all the steps may be prepared ahead and simply tossed and served at meal time.

EASY • SERVES 4 DINNER SALADS

To prepare steak:

- **2** **cloves garlic**
- **2** **tablespoons fresh thyme leaves**
- **2** **teaspoons extra virgin olive oil**
- **1** **teaspoon balsamic vinegar**
- • **salt and pepper to taste**
- **1** **large New York Strip steak (1 pound)**

With mortar and pestle, crush garlic and thyme together until they form a paste. Add oil, a few drops at a time, until the paste is the consistency of a thick sauce. Add balsamic vinegar; the amount of oil and vinegar can be adjusted according to taste. Rub steak with mixture and sear in a heavy skillet to medium rare. Allow to cool to room temperature. Slice thinly on the bias. Reserve.

NOTE: Ask for a steak 2" thick, at least 1 pound.

For salad base:

- **1** **large red onion, sliced 1/4" to 1/2" thick**
- • **balsamic vinegar and oil to taste**
- **1** **pound mixed salad greens (hearts of romaine, bibb, radicchio, arugula, etc.)**
- **2** **medium tomatoes, diced in 1/2" cubes**
- **1** **red bell pepper, diced in 1/4" to 1/2" cubes**

Dress onion slices with a bit of oil and vinegar and sear along with the steak. Combine the salad greens, onions, tomatoes and red bell pepper in a large bowl. Toss with Walter's Vinaigrette. To plate salad: rim each with the black-eyed peas, recipe above. Mound the salad green mixture in the middle of each plate. Add slices of strip steak around the side. Garnish with sprigs of fresh thyme.

Walter's Vinaigrette:

- **2** **tablespoons balsamic vinegar**
- **6** **tablespoons extra virgin olive oil**
- • **salt and pepper to taste**
- • **fresh thyme for garnish**

Whisk together ingredients and pour over salad greens.

Black-eyed Peas

- 1/4 pound dried black-eyed peas (about 2/3 cup)
- 1/4 cup small diced carrots
- 1/4 cup small diced celery
- 1/4 cup small diced onion
- 1 ham hock
- 2 cups chicken stock, fresh or canned

Soak black-eyed peas according to package directions. Sauté carrots, celery and onions in medium saucepan until translucent. Add black-eyed peas, ham hock and enough stock to cover peas by 1". Simmer over medium-low heat until peas are done, about 1/2 hour. Do not overcook; peas should retain shape. Cool to room temperature.

Summer's Tomato Pizza with Buffalo Mozzarella

This classic Italian pizza – tomatoes, fresh mozzarella and basil – will become a standard in your recipe repertoire. The easy-to-prepare crust is made in a food processor in less than 10 minutes.

Easy • Serves 4

- • **pizza crust**
- 3 **tablespoons extra virgin olive oil**
- 3 **large fresh ripe tomatoes (2 1/2-3 lbs. cut in 1/4" slices)**
- 1 **tablespoon balsamic vinegar**
- • **coarse salt and freshly ground pepper**
- 1/2 **cup packed fresh basil leaves**
- 1 **pound fresh buffalo mozzarella, cut in 1/4" slices**

Prepare pizza crust.

Preheat oven to 500°. Brush a large 16" pizza pan with some of the olive oil. For an evenly cooked, crisp but chewy crust, we cannot emphasize enough the benefits of a vented pizza pan. The air-bake ones prevent burning.

On a floured surface, press the ball of dough into a flat circle. Place dough on pizza pan. With heels of hands continue to press and stretch dough to fit pan. Crimp a 1/2" rim around edge of crust. Brush crust with half the remaining olive oil.

Place tomato slices evenly over dough. Brush with remaining oil and balsamic vinegar. Sprinkle with salt and pepper to taste. Roll up basil leaves and slice into thin strips. Sprinkle basil over tomatoes. Place cheese slices evenly over tomatoes. Bake in oven until dough is browned and cheese is bubbling, about 10 minutes.

Note: If fresh mozzarella is unavailable, use packaged mozzarella.

Pizza Crust Dough

- 1 envelope dry yeast
- 1 teaspoon sugar
- 1 cup warm water (105°-115°)
- 3 cups unbleached flour
- 1/4 teaspoon salt
- 1 teaspoon olive oil

Dissolve yeast and sugar in water in glass measuring cup. Let stand until foamy, 5-10 minutes. Combine flour and salt in food processor. Add olive oil to yeast/water mixture. With processor running, pour yeast mixture through feed tube. Process until dough forms a ball and is smooth and elastic. Remove dough; let rest for 10 minutes.

Silver Queen & Black Bean Pizza

Summery, delicious and meatless for one of those nights you just want to eat light.

Easy • Serves 4

- 1 **pizza crust, recipe above**
- • **Silver Queen Corn Salsa**
- 1 **16-ounce can black beans**
- 1/2 **pound Monterey Jack cheese**

Prepare pizza dough according to instructions above. Prepare salsa.

Drain and rinse black beans. Thinly slice cheese. Spread salsa on each pizza. Scatter with black beans. Top with cheese slices. Bake in a 500° oven until dough is browned and cheese is bubbling, about 10 minutes.

Silver Queen Corn Salsa

- 6 ears Silver Queen corn
- 24 cherry tomatoes, quartered
- 2/3 cup chopped red onion
- 1/4 cup chopped parsley
- 2 tablespoons chopped cilantro
- 2 cloves garlic, minced
- 1/4 cup olive oil
- 2 tablespoons red wine vinegar
- • salt and pepper to taste

Cook corn, drain and cool. Cut kernels from cobs. Combine with tomatoes, onion, herbs, garlic, oil and vinegar. Season to taste.

Native Americans introduced corn to the world. Even in Columbus' day there were varieties of red, blue, pink and black kernels in addition to the well-known yellow. A favorite Southern corn for over 30 years is a hybrid white variety called Silver Queen, a sweet corn with a crunchy texture whose sugar lingers about a week after picking instead of the normal few days.

Silver Queen Crab Cakes

Crab, corn and onion flavors blend for a sweet diversion from spicy seafood. Use white bread for the cakes as whole wheat doesn't cut it with crab. Serve with sugar snap peas and Fiesta Salad, page 64.

Easy • Serves 4

- 1 tablespoon butter plus 1/4 cup, divided
- 2 cups finely chopped onion
- 3 slices white bread
- 1/4 cup milk
- 2 eggs, lightly beaten
- 2 ears Silver Queen corn
- 1 tablespoon chopped parsley
- 1/2 teaspoon hot paprika
- 1/2 pound fresh crabmeat, picked
- 1 teaspoon salt
- 1 teaspoon pepper
- • seafood breader mix
- • Chili Tartar Sauce

In large skillet, melt 1 tablespoon butter over medium heat. Add onion. Sauté until soft and translucent. Set aside.

In large bowl, tear bread into small pieces. Add milk and soak 2 to 3 minutes. Stir in onion and eggs. Cut corn kernels from cobs and add to egg mixture along with parsley, paprika, crab, salt and pepper. Mix well. Cover and refrigerate for 1 hour. Mold into 8 cakes. Pour breader mix onto a large plate; coat cakes.

Heat remaining butter in large skillet over medium-high heat. Cook cakes, a few at a time, 3-4 minutes per side. Keep warm in 200° oven. Transfer to a warm serving platter. Top each with tartar sauce.

Chili Tartar Sauce

- 1 1/2 cups mayonnaise
- 2 teaspoons chili garlic paste
- 1 teaspoon minced jalapeño pepper
- 1 tablespoon chopped red pepper

In small serving bowl, combine all ingredients. Store in refrigerator.

Skewered Shrimp with Green Chile Salsa

A spicy entrée for an outdoor gathering. Serve with rice or orzo.

Average • Serves 6

- 1 1/2 pounds large shrimp (at least 30), shelled and deveined

Marinade:

- 2 cloves garlic, minced
- 2 tablespoons chopped fresh cilantro
- • juice of 2 limes
- 2 tablespoons lemon juice
- 1/4 cup olive oil

Combine marinade ingredients. Marinate the shrimp for 30 minutes. (The marinade may be made in advance and the shrimp marinated up to 4 hours if kept in the refrigerator.) Remove the shrimp and thread on skewers. Grill or broil 2 minutes on each side. Garnish with cherry tomatoes and serve with Green Chile Salsa on the side.

Green Chile Salsa

- 7 tomatillos
- 1 jalapeño pepper, seeded and minced
- 1/2 red onion, chopped
- 2 cloves garlic, minced
- 1/2 teaspoon salt
- 1 tablespoon lemon juice
- 2 tablespoons chopped fresh cilantro

Put the tomatillos in a saucepan with water to cover and bring to a boil. Simmer 10 minutes, drain and cool. Remove core; chop in a food processor with a metal blade. Combine with the other ingredients, mix well and chill. Take the salsa out of the refrigerator 1/2 hour before serving. Makes 2 cups.

Paella Carolina

Country ham and fresh okra give this Valencian-style paella a decidedly Southern flair. A festive one dish meal, paella is a Spanish dish named for the wide, shallow pan in which it is prepared and served. The essential ingredient for this peasant invention is saffron-flavored rice. Add meats and vegetables of your choice – even leftovers – to your paella. Wonderful for casual gatherings or large family suppers. Serve with Simple Blue Salad on page 142.

Average • Serves 8-10

4 1/2 cups chicken broth
1/2 teaspoon saffron threads
1/4 cup olive oil
1 large Spanish onion, chopped
3/4 pound country ham, cut in bite-sized pieces
3/4 pound spicy sausage such as chorizo, cut in 1/4" slices
4 cloves garlic, minced
2 bay leaves
1 teaspoon paprika
1/2 teaspoon salt
1/2 cup white wine
2-3 pounds chicken legs and thighs
2 cups arborio rice
3/4 pound medium shrimp, peeled
1/2 pint shucked oysters
2 14 1/2-ounce cans diced tomatoes, drained
2 cups fresh okra, blanched
1 cup frozen peas
2 lemons cut into 8 wedges

Combine chicken broth and saffron threads in a medium saucepan and warm over low heat for 10 minutes.

Meanwhile, heat oil in a high-sided cooking (or sauté) pan; sauté onion, ham and sausage for 3-4 minutes. Add garlic, bay leaves, paprika, salt, wine, reserved broth and chicken. Cover and simmer for 15 minutes. Chicken will be partially cooked. Add rice into mixture. Bring to a boil and simmer for 5 minutes.

Transfer to a 4-quart shallow ceramic or other ovenproof pan. Push shrimp and oysters down into mixture. Strew tomatoes, okra and peas over top; do not stir. Place in 350° oven for 15-20 minutes, until liquid is absorbed and rice is cooked. Remove from oven and cover loosely with foil. Let sit for 10 minutes before serving. Garnish with lemon wedges.

Bob Timberlake's seashore retreat overlooks the sound – where egrets fish among the reeds, crabs hide in the damp sand and the sunsets are spectacular. This is where fishermen live, where they dock their boats and find safe harbor from the sea winds. It's also where artist-fishermen such as Timberlake find inspiration.

Docked, 1999

Sesame-Crusted Flounder with Pineapple Ginger Sauce

A crisp, crunchy sesame crust gives way to tender flounder, perfect for grilling. Topped with a tangy pineapple and ginger sauce, this dish is a knockout. Mushroom soy sauce, 5-spice powder and pickled ginger may be purchased in the specialty food sections of supermarkets or at an Oriental market.

Easy • Serves 4

- 2 large flounder
- 1/2 cup mushroom soy sauce
- 1 cup sesame seeds
- 1/2 teaspoon Chinese 5-spice powder
- • Pineapple Ginger Sauce

Have fish market fillet flounder and cut each into 2 pieces, yielding 4 servings. Place soy sauce in a large resealable bag, add fillets and marinate in refrigerator for 30 minutes.

Meanwhile, spread sesame seeds on baking sheet. Toast in 300° oven for 20 minutes. Place sesame seeds and Chinese spice powder in another resealable bag. Shake each flounder fillet in seed bag, coating completely. Place on flat tray. Cover and refrigerate for 1 hour.

To grill flounder: Place flounder on a medium high grill. Grill 5-6 minutes per side. Remove to a warm platter and spoon sauce over fillets.

Pineapple Ginger Sauce

- 1/4 cup shredded carrot
- 1 cup crushed pineapple
- 1/2 cup pineapple juice
- 1 tablespoon crunchy peanut butter
- 2 tablespoons rice vinegar
- 1 tablespoon mushroom soy sauce
- 1/2 tablespoon pickled ginger, chopped
- 1 tablespoon honey
- 2 teaspoons cornstarch

Mix ingredients in a microwavable bowl. While fish is on grill, heat on high in microwave for 3 minutes, stirring at 1-minute intervals.

Shrimp Tonight

This simple yet elegant cold pasta salad features shrimp and snow peas. Make it in the morning to allow the salad to absorb the herbal essences by suppertime.

EASY • SERVES 10

$4^1/_2$	cups water
$1^1/_2$-2	pounds unpeeled fresh shrimp
$^1/_2$	pound snow peas
1	16-ounce package fusilli or rotini
6	green onions, chopped
4	medium tomatoes, peeled, chopped and drained
$^1/_4$	cup chopped fresh parsley
$^1/_2$	cup wine vinegar
1	teaspoon oregano
$1^1/_2$	teaspoons basil
$^1/_2$	teaspoon garlic salt
$^1/_2$	teaspoon coarsely ground black pepper
$^3/_4$	cup olive oil

In large stockpot, bring water to a boil; add shrimp and cook 3-5 minutes until shrimp turn pink. Do not overcook. Drain well; rinse with cold water. Chill. Peel, devein and set aside. Bring large pot of salted water to a boil. Add snow peas and blanch 1-2 minutes; remove with slotted spoon and run under cold water or put in ice water. Cook pasta according to package directions and drain. Rinse with cold water and drain again.

In a mixing bowl, combine shrimp, snow peas, cooked pasta, onions, tomatoes and parsley, tossing gently. In separate small bowl, whisk together vinegar, oregano, basil, garlic salt and pepper. Gradually whisk in olive oil. Toss with pasta mixture. Cover and chill at least 2 hours.

Steamy August days in the South turn into sultry August nights – so hot that they can simply rob a body of its appetite. When you're eating for sustenance, you might as well make it delicious. A pasta salad to cool summer's heat is Shrimp Tonight. Make it at dawn, before it gets too hot to think about cooking. At suppertime, serve it on the veranda accompanied by a mint julep and the music of crickets and katydids.

Stuffed Eggplant Roulades

*We adapted a sausage and rice filling recipe from Emeril Lagasse's **Louisiana Real and Rustic**, (Morrow, 1996), and rolled it into slices of grilled eggplant called roulades. The combination is a tastebud knockout.*

AVERAGE • SERVES 6

Sausage Rice Stuffing:

1	medium eggplant, peeled, cut into 1/2" cubes
4	cups cooked long grain rice
1	pound mild Italian sausage, casing removed
1	cup chopped onion
1/2	cup chopped bell pepper
1/2	cup chopped celery
1	teaspoon salt
1/4	teaspoon cayenne pepper
3/4	cup water
3	tablespoons chopped parsley

Chunky Tomato Sauce

3	14.5-ounce cans diced tomatoes
1	cup chopped onion
4	cloves garlic, minced
2	tablespoons olive oil
1	15-ounce can tomato sauce
1	cup chopped fresh basil
•	pinch of sugar
•	salt and pepper to taste

Place tomatoes in a sieve to drain; reserve juice. In medium saucepan, slowly sauté onion and garlic in olive oil about 8-10 minutes. Add tomatoes with 1 cup of reserved juice, tomato sauce, basil, sugar, salt and pepper. Bring to boil, then simmer 15 minutes. Makes 1 quart.

Place cubed eggplant in colander and salt lightly. Let drain for 30 minutes. This removes the bitterness from the eggplant. Rinse and dry on paper towels. Prepare rice according to package instructions.

In a skillet, brown sausage and drain off all but 4 tablespoons of fat. Sauté onion, pepper and celery until tender. Stir in salt, cayenne, eggplant and water. Stir constantly over medium heat until eggplant has almost dissolved into sausage mixture; mash eggplant with spoon as you stir, about 10-12 minutes. Add cooked rice and parsley. Adjust seasoning as necessary. Yields 4-5 cups.

Eggplant Roulades:

2	large eggplants
1/2	cup olive oil, or more as needed
2	cups Chunky Tomato Sauce

Cut eggplants lengthwise into 1/2" slices. Stack in a colander and salt lightly. Let drain for 30 minutes. Rinse and dry with paper towels. Brush both sides of eggplant slices with olive oil and grill or broil until golden brown. (On a gas grill, cook eggplant slices 2-3 minutes over medium heat.) Let cool.

Spoon about 1/3 cup Sausage Rice Stuffing into the center of the larger eggplant slices; scale back filling as needed for smaller slices. Roll up and place in one 9" x 12" Pyrex baking dish, seam side down. (Secure with toothpicks if needed.) Just before baking, spoon tomato sauce over roulades. Cover with foil and bake at 300° for 20-30 minutes, or until sauce bubbles and roulades are warmed through. Makes 14-16 roulades.

Variation: If the roulade sounds too complicated, layer grilled eggplant slices and spoon stuffing over top. Place in a buttered casserole dish. Top with shredded Parmesan cheese and bake until golden.

Classic Grilled Tenderloin

This recipe utilizes a meat marinade from J.K. Norfleet, the publisher's father. An easy make ahead entrée for a sit down dinner or buffet supper, serve with Tomato Rosemary Rolls (page 189) – the sun-dried tomatoes and rosemary are perfect complements to the tenderloin.

Easy to Average • Serves 6-8

- **4-5** **pounds of beef tenderloin, fully trimmed, see note**
- **•** **J.K.'s Meat Marinade**

Make marinade. Place tenderloin in roasting pan. Salt and pepper the meat. Rub marinade generously over tenderloin and refrigerate at least 8 hours, periodically rubbing marinade over meat.

Prepare grill. Place meat over coals, turning meat over so that it browns on all sides. Cook meat until it reaches an internal temperature of 120° for medium rare, about 10-12 minutes. Remember, the meat will continue to cook after it is taken off the fire.

To serve for a buffet: Thinly slice tenderloins about 45 minutes before your party begins and arrange on a platter. Garnish platter edge with fresh rosemary stems. Have 2 large, decorative forks to aid serving. Place basket of sliced rolls and a dish of mustard next to platter. For a seated dinner: Slice tenderloin just before serving. These slices will be a little thicker, about 1/4" or more. Serve with Au Gratin Potatoes and Tomatoes Rockefeller found in Completing the Menu.

Note: When you buy tenderloin, make sure it's fully trimmed of fat and that the silverskin is removed. You may want to leave with 3-4 pounds of meat, waste removed. When grilling meat, you lose 20% in the cooking process. The cooked meat will weigh 2 1/2-3 1/2 pounds.

JK's Meat Marinade

- 1/3 cup Dijon mustard
- 2-3 tablespoons red wine vinegar
- 2 tablespoons soy sauce
- 1/4 cup dry white wine
- 2 cloves minced garlic
- 2 tablespoons olive oil
- 1 teaspoon dried rosemary
- 1 teaspoon dried thyme
- • salt and pepper to taste

Mix all the ingredients *except* olive oil and herbs. Pour in the olive oil in a slow steady stream; whisk until well blended. Stir in herbs. Rub the marinade over up to 2 tenderloins. Makes 3/4 cup.

Derby Down Fried Chicken

Featured in a Derby Party menu, this fried chicken is the equal of any Kentucky favorite.

Easy to Average • Serves 8

- **2** **whole chickens, cut into pieces**
- **2** **eggs**
- **2** **cups milk**
- **2** **cups flour**
- **2** **teaspoons salt**
- **2** **teaspoons black pepper**
- **2** **teaspoons paprika**
- **2** **cups shortening**
- **3** **tablespoons bacon grease**

Pat chicken pieces dry. Beat eggs with the milk in a bowl. In a strong paper bag, combine flour, salt, pepper and paprika. Dip each piece of chicken in egg and milk. Shake each piece separately in the flour bag until well-coated. Let the floured pieces of chicken rest on a rack 5 minutes before frying. In a heavy skillet or cast iron pan, melt shortening with bacon grease over medium heat. The cooking oils should sizzle but not smoke. Place chicken pieces in hot frying oil; do not crowd your skillet. Fry each piece for 12 minutes on each side until golden brown.

Grilled Chicken Pitas

A sandwich perfect for casual company. Full of tangy flavor. Quick and easy to assemble and so good to eat. Serve with Dilled Cucumber with Tomatoes on page 177 and Homemade French Fries on page 181.

Easy • Serves 2-3

4	**boneless chicken breast halves**
1/2	**cup plus 3 tablespoons olive oil, divided**
1	**clove garlic, minced**
2	**sprigs fresh thyme**
1	**large Bermuda onion**
3	**tablespoons balsamic vinegar**
1	**tablespoon Dijon mustard**
•	**salt and pepper to taste**
2-3	**large pita pocket loaves, halved**

Wash chicken and pat dry. Combine 1/2 cup of the olive oil with the garlic and thyme leaves, pulling the leaves off the stem. Pour over chicken breasts and marinate overnight.

Slice onion into thick 1/2" rings. In a small skillet over medium-high heat, combine 3 tablespoons olive oil and balsamic vinegar. Add sliced onion and cook until onions are translucent. Add mustard, then continue cooking over low heat 3-5 minutes. Season with salt and pepper. Meanwhile, grill marinated chicken breasts until done. Once cooked, keep warm until you are ready to assemble sandwiches.

To serve, cut grilled chicken breasts into strips and place generous portions inside pita bread halves. Add cooked onions, and voilà, a delicious sandwich.

Skinny Pork Barbecue

Straightforward and easy, this is Elizabeth's father's leaner way to prepare chopped barbecue. Choose a good onion roll or kaiser roll from your local bakery and pile it on! The recipe calls for Scott's Barbecue Sauce, a vinegar-based, Eastern North Carolina blend from Goldsboro. Developed by Adam Scott in the early 1940s, this sauce was further developed by his son, Martel, and bottled for retail sales in 1948. It has been on the shelves of the Norfleet family since then. Serve with J.K.'s Cole Slaw on page 181.

Easy • Serves 8

1	**3-3 1/2 pounds boneless pork loin, fat removed**
•	**salt and pepper to taste**
•	**Scott's Barbecue Sauce to taste (about 11-12 tablespoons)**
8-12	**hamburger rolls**

Heat coals or a gas grill to a low 200°. For a smoky flavor, add hickory chips to the fire. Place pork loin on a grill and cook slowly with the top down for 45 minutes to 1 hour. Turn several times. When a meat thermometer inserted into the thickest part of the loin reads 145°-150°, remove from grill.

Cut pork loin into large 3"-4" chunks. Put into a food processor a few chunks at a time, grinding the meat to a size between peas and popcorn. Do not overprocess. Transfer pork to a medium saucepan. Season lightly with salt and pepper. Add Scott's Barbecue Sauce to taste. The suggested amount of Scott's Sauce in the recipe will produce barbecue that has a little bite. Guests may want to add more once it hits the plate or sandwich. Heat through and keep warm until ready to serve.

Grilled Chicken in pita makes a perfect picnic pick-up.

Teff Spoonbread with peaches and coconut

Teff, one of the more unusual grains available, has been used for centuries to make the national bread of Ethiopia, a crepe-like bread called Injera. Its addition to this Southern classic creates an unusual yet delicious spoonbread.

Average • Serves 6-8

- 3/4 cup golden raisins
- 1/2 cup dark rum
- 3/4 cup coconut
- 1 cup whole teff (not teff flour), available at natural food stores
- 2 large peaches
- 1/2 cup peach juice (or substitute apple juice)
- 5 tablespoons honey
- 2 tablespoons softened butter
- 3 eggs, separated
- 1/2 teaspoon ground cinnamon
- 1/2 teaspoon ginger
- 2 teaspoons baking powder
- 1/4 teaspoon salt
- • fresh peaches, berries and whipping cream, optional

Soak raisins in rum for 30 minutes. Toast coconut in 300° oven for 10-15 minutes, stirring occasionally until golden brown. Increase oven to 350°. Butter a 2-quart casserole and set aside. In a medium saucepan, bring 3 cups water to a boil. Add whole teff, reduce heat, cover and simmer 15 minutes until liquid is absorbed. This should yield 3 cups cooked teff. Set aside to cool.

Peel and coarsely chop peaches. In a large bowl, stir together teff, raisins with rum, and peach juice. Add chopped peaches, coconut, honey, butter, egg yolks, cinnamon, ginger, baking powder and salt.

In a separate bowl, beat egg whites until they form stiff peaks; gently fold into batter. Pour into prepared casserole and bake at 350° for 1 hour and 30 minutes or until a knife inserted in center comes out clean. Serve warm or cold with fresh peaches, berries and whipped cream.

Mango Crisp

A simple, tropical fruit dessert for your buffet. For easy preparation, mangos are available in jars in the refrigerated section of supermarkets.

Easy • Serves 10-12

- 6 cups chopped mango
- 4 ounces candied ginger, divided
- 3 cups all-purpose flour, plus 3 tablespoons, divided
- 1 1/2 cups unsalted butter
- 1 cup granulated sugar

Preheat oven to 350°.

Mix mango with 2 ounces of ginger and 3 tablespoons flour in large bowl. Place butter, sugar, 3 cups flour and remaining 2 ounces ginger in food processor. Pulse until crumb consistency (or mix by hand with a pastry blender). Butter and flour a 9" x 12" glass baking dish. Spread mangos in dish. Top generously with crumbs. Bake 1 hour. Best served warm right out of the oven.

"As pretty as a Georgia peach." This Southern compliment to a young lady may have begun in colonial days, when Georgia led the colonies in peach production. Today, the leading peach producer of both freestone and clingstone varieties is California, followed by South Carolina. Georgia is a distant third, but never mind. Georgia peaches are still as pretty as Southern women.

Saucy Peach Gingerbread

Tangy sweet peaches enhance this gingerbread from top to bottom. Literally! You may need to adjust the sugar in the sauce depending on the sweetness of the peaches.

Average • Serves 10

Gingerbread:

- 1/2 cup butter, softened
- 3/4 cup light brown sugar
- 1/2 cup molasses
- 1 egg
- 1 3/4 cups flour
- 1/2 teaspoon salt
- 1 teaspoon baking powder
- 1 1/2 teaspoons ground ginger
- 1 teaspoon cinnamon
- 3/4 cup buttermilk
- 4 peaches, peeled and sliced

With mixer, cream softened butter with brown sugar. Add the molasses and egg and blend well.

Combine the dry ingredients in a separate bowl and add to the batter alternately with buttermilk. Grease an 8" x 11" x 2" baking dish and line the bottom with the peach slices. Spread the batter evenly over the peaches and bake in a 350° oven for 45 minutes.

Peach Sauce

- 3 cups sliced peaches
- 1/2 cup water
- 3 tablespoons sugar
- 1 tablespoon cornstarch
- 1 tablespoon lemon juice
- 2 tablespoons chilled butter, cut in pieces

Peel and slice peaches and cut into large chunks. In a small saucepan, bring the peaches, water and sugar to a boil. Lower heat and simmer until peaches are tender. Mix cornstarch with lemon juice in a small bowl and stir until smooth. Add cornstarch to peaches and simmer, stirring until thick. Remove from heat and whisk in the butter, piece by piece. Serve warm, and generously, over gingerbread. Makes 5-6 cups.

Raspberry Brownies

This is based on a recipe shared by Sharon and Todd Brenner of the former Brenner's Restaurant in Wilmington. The ganache was changed to feature white chocolate.

Easy to Average • Yields 24

- 1 cup unsalted butter, room temperature
- 1 1/4 cups sugar
- 1/2 cup brown sugar, firmly packed
- 4 large eggs
- 1/2 cup unsweetened cocoa powder
- 1 teaspoon vanilla extract
- 1/4 teaspoon salt
- 1 1/4 cups all-purpose flour
- 1 1/2 pints fresh raspberries (use frozen if necessary)

Preheat oven to 325°. Grease a 9" x 13" pan. Beat butter, sugar and brown sugar in large bowl until fluffy. Add eggs 1 at a time, beating well after each addition. Stir in cocoa, vanilla and salt. Gently mix in flour. Pour batter into prepared pan. Sprinkle raspberries evenly over batter. Bake until tester inserted into center of brownies comes out clean, about 30-35 minutes. Cool completely in pan on wire rack.

White Chocolate Ganache

- 1/4 cup whipping cream
- 3-4 ounces white chocolate, cut into small pieces

Prepare ganache by heating whipping cream in saucepan until scalding. Remove from heat. Add white chocolate pieces and mix with spoon until smooth. Dip fork into glaze and drizzle over brownies decoratively. Let stand until glaze sets. The ganache can be prepared 8 hours ahead. Cover and store at room temperature.

Red-White-And-Blue Ice Cream Cake

Ice cream and the Fourth of July are almost inseparable. Roll up classic sponge cake with raspberry sorbet and vanilla ice cream for a colorful spiral. Top it with whipped cream and Fresh Blueberry Sauce, and you are sure to delight the whole crowd.

Average • Serves 10

- • Classic Sponge Cake
- 1 pint raspberry sorbet
- 3 cups vanilla ice cream
- • Fresh Blueberry Sauce
- • Sweetened Whipped Cream

Bake the Classic Sponge Cake in a jellyroll pan.

Put sorbet and ice cream into refrigerator for about 15 minutes to soften slightly. Unroll cake and spread about 1/3 of the surface with raspberry sorbet, and remaining 2/3 of the cake with vanilla ice cream.

Starting with the raspberry end, roll up cake like a jellyroll. Put into freezer to harden for several hours or overnight. Prepare Fresh Blueberry Sauce and Sweetened Whipped Cream and chill.

Slice cake with sharp knife. (Hint: To warm knife for easy cutting, dip in hot water, then dry.) Put onto serving plate; top with a dollop of whipped cream and blueberry sauce. Garnish with fresh mint.

Classic Sponge Cake:

- • parchment paper
- 6 eggs, separated
- 1/2 cup sugar
- 1 teaspoon vanilla extract
- • pinch of salt
- 1/2 cup all-purpose flour
- • confectioners' sugar
- • tea towel

Preheat oven to 350°. Lightly butter a 17" x 12" jellyroll pan. Line with parchment paper or wax paper; butter and flour lightly, tapping out excess.

In medium bowl, with electric mixer, beat egg yolks, sugar and vanilla until thick and light yellow in color; set aside. In separate bowl with clean beater, beat egg whites with a pinch of salt until stiff peaks form when batter is lifted. Fold gently into egg yolk mixture. Put flour in sifter or sieve and gradually sift and fold gently into batter. Pour into prepared pan, spreading evenly.

Bake in 350° oven for 15 minutes. Run a knife around edge of pan, then cool 5 minutes. Meanwhile, sift a thin layer of confectioners' sugar onto a tea towel. Turn cake out onto the towel. Carefully remove parchment paper; immediately, while still hot, roll up in the towel. Cool completely. (Hint: To store overnight before continuing, put cake, towel and all, into large plastic bag.)

Fresh Blueberry Sauce

- 2 cups blueberries
- • zest of 1 lemon
- 1 tablespoon lemon juice
- 1/2 cup sugar
- 1 tablespoon water
- 3 tablespoons blueberry liqueur or brandy

In medium saucepan, combine all ingredients except the liqueur. Cook over medium heat, stirring frequently until the sauce is fairly thick, about 8-10 minutes. Remove from heat; stir in liqueur. Cool and chill. Makes 1 1/2 cups.

Sweetened Whipped Cream

- 1 cup whipping cream
- 1 teaspoon vanilla extract
- 2 tablespoons confectioners' sugar
- • fresh mint sprigs, optional

Whip about 1 cup of cream to soft peaks; flavor with vanilla and confectioners' sugar.

Thornless blackberries are a modern development. Throughout history, in order to enjoy this summer fruit, man has endured torture from this prickly bush that grows in abundance in north temperate regions of the world. Its black or red-purple fruits, each consisting of numerous drupelets adhering to a juicy core, are a fairly good source of iron and vitamin C. But the best thing about blackberries is the preserves, conserves, jams, jellies, cobblers and pies that are made from this delicious fruit.

Nanette's Fresh Blackberry Cake

This recipe from Nanette Langhorne of Langhorne Blueberry Hill Farm in Gibsonville uses summer blackberries that grow wild along southern roadsides.

Easy • Serves 8-12

1 cup butter or margarine, softened
2 cups sugar
3 eggs
3 cups flour
1 tablespoon baking soda
1 teaspoon salt
1 teaspoon nutmeg
1 teaspoon cinnamon
1 teaspoon cloves
1 cup buttermilk
1/2 cup chopped pecans or walnuts
1/2 cup raisins
2 cups fresh blackberries

Preheat oven to 350°. Grease and flour a 10" bundt pan.

In a large mixing bowl, cream butter and sugar until light and fluffy. Beat in eggs 1 at a time. In separate small bowl, combine flour, baking soda, salt, nutmeg, cinnamon and cloves. Add to creamed mixture alternating with the buttermilk. Stir in nuts, raisins and blackberries.

Spoon batter into prepared pan. Bake at 350° for 55-60 minutes or until toothpick inserted in center of cake comes out clean. Cool in pan 10 minutes, then turn out on rack or plate.

Chocolate Chip Pound Cake

Make this yummy cake in a bundt pan and it comes out small enough for hands to hold. No plates needed.

Easy • Serves 10-12

1/2 cup unsalted butter, softened
1 1/2 cups sugar
3 eggs
1 teaspoon vanilla extract
1/4 cup sour cream
1/4 cup vegetable oil
1 1/2 cups flour
1/2 teaspoon salt
1/4 teaspoon baking soda
1/4 cup cocoa (unsweetened)
1 cup chocolate chips

Preheat oven to 350°. Cream butter with the sugar, then beat in the eggs 1 at a time. Add vanilla, sour cream and vegetable oil, blending well after each addition. Combine the dry ingredients together and then mix them into egg mixture. Beat well. Fold in chocolate chips. Pour into a well-greased and floured bundt pan. Bake for 1 hour at 350°. When cool, turn out onto a plate and slice.

Carolina Melon with Blackberry Thyme Salsa

Cool and refreshing, sweet ripe melon with fresh berries and thyme is the perfect finish to a summer meal.

Easy • Serves 6-8

2 cups fresh blackberries
1 tablespoon chopped fresh thyme
1 tablespoon sugar
1 tablespoon honey
1 tablespoon lemon juice
1 large cantaloupe

Two hours before serving, gently combine blackberries, thyme, sugar, honey and lemon juice in a medium bowl. Set aside at room temperature. At dessert time, slice and peel melon. Arrange slices on a platter or on individual plates. Spoon fresh berry salsa over melon and serve.

Lemon Balm Shortbread

An earthy variation of the classic Scottish cookie featuring fresh lemon balm and shredded carrots.

Easy • Makes 28 cookies

1/2 cup grits, divided
1/2 cup packed lemon balm leaves
1/2 cup shredded carrots
1 cup unsalted butter, softened
1 cup brown sugar
2 1/2 cups plain flour
1/2 cup cornmeal
1 teaspoon vanilla extract

Preheat oven to 325°.

Sprinkle 1/4 cup grits on each of 2 non-stick cookie sheets. Set aside.

Place lemon balm and carrots in food processor and chop finely. Add butter and brown sugar and process until well blended. Add flour and cornmeal and process until smooth. Add vanilla and process.

Place dough in heaping tablespoons on cookie sheet. Flatten with fork tines to a thickness of 1/2". Bake for 18 minutes. Serve with melon.

These easeful days,
The dreamless nights;
The homely sounds of plain delights;
The calm, unambitioned mind,
The simple stuff of summertime.
–Aster Austin Dobson

Fall

Curried Pecans

Make and keep on hand to serve at any impromptu gathering.

Easy • Makes 2 cups

2 cups pecan halves
2 tablespoons margarine, melted
1/2 teaspoon seasoned salt
1/2 teaspoon curry powder
1/8 teaspoon ground cumin
• dash of ground red pepper

Preheat oven to 350°. Place pecan halves in a bowl. Drizzle with melted margarine.

Combine remaining ingredients in a small bowl. Sprinkle mixture over nuts, tossing gently to coat. Spread nuts on a shallow roasting pan. Bake for 15 minutes or until golden, stirring occasionally. Cool completely, and store in an airtight container.

Sherried Pecans

A somewhat candied pecan with a zing of sherry and a zest of orange. A nice hostess gift!

Easy • Makes 2 cups

2 cups pecan halves
1 cup brown sugar
1 tablespoon white vinegar
1 tablespoon grated orange zest
1 tablespoon sherry
1/2 teaspoon salt
3/4 cup water

Toast pecans in a heavy skillet until they begin to smell toasted. Stir frequently. Add remaining ingredients and bring to caramel stage. Pour onto a greased baking sheet and spread pecans out to cool. Store in an airtight container.

Southerners adore pecans. We chop pecan meat for muffins, cookies, cakes and icing, and add it to chicken salad. We toast them with butter and salt, or simply leave a bowl of whole nuts with a nutcracker and pick by an easy chair.

Previous page *Best Friends*, 1994

COLD DEVILLED SHRIMP

Everyone loves cold shrimp, and the tangy lemon sauce brings out the devil in this recipe. Serve as an hors d'oeuvre with toothpicks, or over a bed of greens as a first course.

EASY • SERVES 6-8

2	**pounds shrimp, cooked, shelled, deveined**
1	**red onion, thinly sliced**
1	**lemon, thinly sliced**
1/3	**cup black olives, pitted, sliced**
•	**Devil Sauce**

Prepare shrimp. Ready the onion, lemon and olives.

Make Devil Sauce. Combine with shrimp, onion, lemon and olives in a large glass or plastic bowl. Marinate in refrigerator for 2 hours, turning the shrimp over in the sauce occasionally. Do not leave in marinade for too long or shrimp will be too lemony and have an overcooked texture.

Devil Sauce

2/3	cup lemon juice
2	tablespoons white wine vinegar
1/3	cup olive oil
1	tablespoon minced garlic
•	freshly ground pepper
1	teaspoon salt
1/2	bay leaf, crumbled
1	tablespoon chopped fresh parsley

Combine all ingredients in a small bowl.

BRATWURST ROUNDS IN MUSTARD SAUCE

This recipe was inspired by food stylist Janet Grennes' late sister, Virginia, who lived in Wisconsin where eating bratwursts are practically a way of life. She found that first grilling the brats, then simmering them in beer made them especially tasty, plump and juicy. These are great just slathered with mustard and popped into a bun. However, for an hors d'oeuvre, cutting the brats into bite-sized pieces and heating them in a mustard sauce makes an irresistible flavor treat.

EASY • MAKES ABOUT 64 ROUNDS

8	**bratwursts (or Italian sausage)**
12	**ounces beer**
1 1/2	**cups water (or a bit more to barely cover brats)**
1	**bay leaf**
1/2	**cup reserved cooking liquid**
1/4	**cup spicy brown mustard**
1	**tablespoon horseradish**

Grill bratwursts over medium heat for about 15 minutes, turning often. (If grill is unavailable, brown the brats in a skillet over medium-low heat.)

In a medium saucepan, combine beer, water and bay leaf. Bring to a boil; add grilled bratwurst and return to a boil. Reduce heat to low, cover and simmer until plump and juicy, about 10 minutes. Leave in the liquid until ready to continue with the recipe. If making the day before, refrigerate in the cooking liquid.

Shortly before serving, drain brats; reserve 1/2 cup of the cooking liquid. Cut into 1/2" rounds. Place in a large heavy skillet along with the reserved 1/2 cup cooking liquid. Bring to a boil and cook, reducing the liquid to about 2-3 tablespoons. Turn heat to low. In a small bowl, combine mustard and horseradish. Add to skillet, stirring well. Cook until rounds are well-coated and hot, 2-3 minutes. Serve with toothpicks.

Indian Summer, 1993

Black Bean Hummus

The Mediterranean meets the Southwest in this crowd-pleaser shared with ***Taste Full*** *by Barley's, a beer hall and pub in Asheville, North Carolina. Naturally, this is a perfect snack with a cold brew.*

Easy • Makes 3 1/2 cups

3	cups canned black beans, drained and rinsed
4	tablespoons tahini (ground sesame)
1/4	cup lemon juice
3	tablespoons olive oil
1	tablespoon salt
1	tablespoon black pepper
2	tablespoons minced garlic
1	tablespoon paprika
1 1/2	teaspoons cumin
1 1/2	teaspoons chili powder
1/2	teaspoon cayenne

Blend ingredients in a food processor to the consistency of a thin peanut butter. If too thick, add a small amount of water until a smooth, spreadable consistency is reached. Serve with sliced pita bread wedges or sliced pieces of red or yellow peppers.

Tailgate Caponata

Caponata is a fusion of wonderful Mediterranean flavors – eggplant, onions, tomatoes, capers, olive oil and herbs. There are many recipes for this popular side dish but this one is particularly good. Serve with bread, crackers or pita bread points.

Average • Serves 12

2 medium eggplants (6 cups diced)
1 1/2 teaspoons salt
1/2 cup olive oil, divided
1 pound mushrooms, sliced
2 cups chopped onions
1 medium green pepper, chopped
1 1/2 cups sliced celery
4 cloves garlic, minced
1 1/2 teaspoons basil
1 1/2 teaspoons oregano
1/2 teaspoon freshly ground pepper
2 14.5-ounce cans diced tomatoes, drained
1 cup calamata olives, pitted, coarsely chopped
1 3.5-ounce jar capers
1/2 cup chopped Italian (flat-leaf) parsley
1/3 cup balsamic vinegar
6-8 pieces pita bread, cut into 8 wedges each

Peel eggplants and cut into 3/4" dice. Place in colander and toss with salt. Let sit 30-40 minutes to drain. Dry on paper towels.

Heat 2 tablespoons olive oil in large Dutch oven over medium-high heat. Add sliced mushrooms and sauté, stirring occasionally, about 5 minutes until mushrooms release liquid and it evaporates. Remove mushrooms from pan and set aside.

Heat remaining olive oil in Dutch oven. Add onions, green pepper, celery, garlic and reserved eggplant. Cook over medium-low heat 10-15 minutes until vegetables are almost tender. Add basil, oregano, and pepper; cook about 2 minutes. Add drained tomatoes, reserved mushrooms, olives and capers. Cook, stirring occasionally, another 15 minutes until tender. Remove from heat. Stir in parsley and vinegar. Serve at room temperature with pita wedges.

Fall has arrived. The first frost nips the garden, the temperature drops, and you light the first fire of the season. That's when Mother Nature delivers a surprise gift – a few perfect days called "Indian Summer."

Smoked Fish Pâté

Choose a flavorful smoked fish to make your pâté – one that is dense with no small bones, such as smoked trout, bonito, salmon, bluefish or king mackerel.

Easy • Serves 4-6

- 1/2 pound smoked fish
- 6 tablespoons butter, softened
- 1/2 cup heavy cream
- 1/2 teaspoon salt
- 1 teaspoon brandy
- 1 tablespoon lemon juice
- • freshly ground pepper
- 1/2 cup black olives, pitted and chopped

Purée the smoked fish in a food processor until it is smooth and creamy. Slowly add the butter and cream and continue to process. Season with salt, brandy, lemon juice and pepper. Put into a greased crock or ramekin and chill until firm. Turn out onto a plate if desired or leave in the crock. Top with chopped olives and serve with crackers or small French bread toasts.

Phyllo Chévre Tart

Old World flavors of salami and chévre — goat cheese — baked in a flaky crust. Cut into slender wedges and serve as a great appetizer. This also would be a delicious luncheon entrée served with a fresh fruit salad and French bread.

Average • Serves 6

- • Phyllo Crust
- 1 tablespoon butter
- 1/2 cup chopped green onions
- 1 cup chopped shiitake or oyster mushrooms
- 1/2 pound hard salami, julienned
- 1/2 pound goat cheese
- 2 tablespoons sour cream
- 2 eggs, beaten
- 1/2 cup fresh chopped basil leaves

Make phyllo crust and let cool slightly. Turn oven down to 350°.

In a large sauté pan, melt butter. Cook green onions, mushrooms and salami 5-7 minutes until onions are soft. In a medium bowl, combine chèvre, sour cream and eggs. Add fresh basil and salami/mushroom mixture. Spoon into the pre-baked phyllo crust. Bake 30 minutes or until lightly browned and puffy.

Phyllo Crust

- 1/2 cup unsalted butter, melted
- 5 sheets phyllo dough, see note
- 1/3 cup toasted pine nuts, chopped
- 1/3 cup toasted breadcrumbs
- 1/2 teaspoon crushed red pepper

Preheat oven to 425°. Using melted butter, brush 8" round glass dish and line with a sheet of phyllo dough. Brush with more butter and sprinkle with some of the pine nuts, breadcrumbs and red pepper. Repeat with remaining 4 sheets of phyllo. Bake for 5-8 minutes.

Note: Making rectangular shaped phyllo sheets fit into a round pan can be tricky. Fold the edges over on themselves and brush with melted butter to make them stick.

Italian Sausage Diamonds

Stromboli is usually made more like a loaf, but this one is made flat for easy serving. This delicious stuffed bread is great cut in small diamonds or squares for hors d'oeuvres. It could also be cut in larger pieces and served with a salad for a light lunch. If made ahead, reheat in 400° oven for about 10 minutes.

Average • Makes 25-30 Appetizer servings

Crust:

- **1 cup water (105°-115°)**
- **1 envelope dry yeast**
- **1/2 teaspoon sugar**
- **3 cups flour**
- **1/2 cup Parmesan or Romano cheese, divided**
- **1 teaspoon salt**
- **3 tablespoons olive oil**

Filling:

- **1 pound Italian Sausage, removed from casing**
- **1 large onion, coarsely chopped**
- **3 cloves garlic, minced**
- **• about 18 whole basil leaves**
- **• about 1/4 pound coarsely grated Fontina cheese**
- **1 egg beaten with 1 tablespoon water**
- **1 teaspoon coarse salt**

Place water, yeast and sugar in a small bowl, stirring to dissolve yeast. Set aside for about 5 minutes to proof. It should foam up.

Place flour, 1/4 cup of the Parmesan (save rest for the top) and salt into bowl of food processor. Process to combine, about 5-10 seconds. Add olive oil and start processor. With motor running, add yeast mixture through the feed tube. Process to combine, scraping down sides as needed. Then process about 15 seconds more to begin the kneading. Turn out on lightly floured surface and knead 2-3 minutes until smooth. Place in oiled bowl, turning dough to oil surface. Cover with a towel and put in a warm place to rise for 45-60 minutes until doubled in bulk.

Meanwhile, place sausage, onion and garlic into large skillet over medium heat. Sauté, stirring to break up the sausage until sausage is cooked and onions are tender, about 10 minutes. Drain in a sieve to remove any grease. Set aside.

Punch dough down and divide into 2 pieces. Roll one into a 15" x 9" rectangle and place on lightly greased baking pan. Spread sausage mixture evenly over the dough, leaving about a 1/2" margin all around. Distribute basil leaves over the sausage; top with grated Fontina cheese.

Roll remaining piece of dough into another 15" x 9" rectangle. In a small bowl, mix egg with 1 tablespoon water. Brush egg wash on edges of lower crust. Set other dough on top, stretching to fit if necessary. Pinch edges to seal. With a sharp knife, score top dough in a lattice pattern. (Do not cut through to the meat.) Brush top with egg wash and sprinkle with 1 teaspoon coarse salt. Let rise for about 15 minutes.

Preheat oven to 425°. Bake for 15 minutes. Sprinkle remaining 1/4 cup Parmesan cheese on top of the stromboli, and bake until golden brown, about 10 minutes more. Serve hot cut into diamonds or squares.

Bruschetta with fresh tomatoes

Bruschetta is made by toasting crusty Italian bread, rubbing it with garlic, then drizzling good Italian olive oil over the top. It can be eaten plain, or with flavorful cheese and vegetable toppings. The tomato topping in this recipe takes full advantage of the fresh tomatoes of early fall. However, for a flavor treat the rest of the year, well-drained, diced canned tomatoes make a very satisfactory substitute. This bruschetta makes a great hors d'oeuvre, or serve it in larger portions for a delicious lunch or supper along with a salad. Fresh sage provides a delicious flavor experience that is really quite different from the dried version.

Average • Makes 16 servings

- **1 loaf crusty Italian bread**
- **2 cloves garlic, unpeeled**
- **4 tablespoons extra virgin olive oil, divided**
- **4 ounces soft goat cheese, at room temperature**
- **1/4 cup chopped fresh sage**
- **1/2 teaspoon freshly ground pepper**
- **• Mediterranean Tomato Topping**

Make Tomato Topping first.

Preheat broiler. Cut Italian bread in half to make 2 long flat pieces about 1" thick. Toast under broiler, watching carefully. Cut a garlic clove in half and rub cut edge on toasted surfaces. As garlic becomes dry, replace with another 1/2 clove. Drizzle toast with about 2 tablespoons olive oil.

In small bowl, mix goat cheese with the remaining 2 tablespoons olive oil, fresh sage and pepper. Spread evenly on the toast halves. Put back under the broiler briefly to lightly melt cheese. Spoon on Mediterranean Tomato Topping. Cut each piece into about 8 pieces. Serve immediately.

Mediterranean Tomato Topping

- 1 1/2 cups peeled, chopped and drained tomatoes (about 2 large fresh tomatoes or a 14.5-ounce can of drained diced tomatoes)
- 1 clove garlic, minced
- 2 tablespoons chopped fresh sage
- 1/2 cup coarsely chopped calamata olives
- 2 tablespoons capers, rinsed and drained
- 1 tablespoon balsamic vinegar

Combine all ingredients in a small bowl. For best flavor, let sit at room temperature for 30-60 minutes. The topping can be made ahead, but bring back to room temperature before using.

"The first tomato of summer is like a benediction."

– Bob Timberlake

Because the tastiest are homegrown, most Southerners have at least one tomato plant in their yard or garden, even if it's only a potted patio tomato. A half-dozen beefsteak tomato plants in your garden will provide enough fruit to fill your pantry with canned jars of sauce and soup. Refrigeration kills the flavor and makes the tomato's flesh pulpy, and excessive heat will split their tender skin. Store ripe tomatoes at room temperature, out of direct sunlight and use within a day or two. To ripen tomatoes, put them with an apple in a perforated paper bag and leave them on the kitchen counter for a few days. This old wives' tale works magic.

Succotash Chowder

The taste of late summer corn and baby limas are captured in this soup. Succotash is a Southern dish made of lima beans and corn with a little red or green pepper cooked into them. The name is from the Narragansett Indian word msickquatash, meaning "boiled whole kernels of corn."

AVERAGE • SERVES 6-8

3-4 ears corn (2 cups)
1/2 pound shelled baby limas
4 tablespoons butter
2 cloves garlic, minced
1 yellow bell pepper, diced small
2 medium potatoes, peeled and diced
1/4 cup flour
1 teaspoon paprika
4 cups chicken or vegetable broth
1/2 cup heavy cream
1/2 cup half & half
1 teaspoon salt
1/2 teaspoon white pepper

Cook corn in boiling water 4-6 minutes. Remove; let cool enough to handle. Cut kernels from cobs to yield 2 cups and set aside. Shell lima beans, if necessary, and boil in unsalted water 10-15 minutes. Test for tenderness. Remove from heat, drain and set aside.

In large soup pot, melt butter over medium high heat and sauté garlic, pepper and potatoes 10 minutes, stirring occasionally. Stir in flour and paprika and cook 2 minutes. You are making a *roux* which will thicken the soup. Add broth slowly while whisking to blend evenly. Bring to a boil. Let simmer 5 minutes; then test potatoes for doneness. Cook a little more if necessary. Add cream, half & half, salt, white pepper, reserved corn and limas. Simmer 5 minutes more to heat through. Adjust seasoning and serve.

Kapusta – Polish Cabbage Soup

A recipe shared by Gary H. Bachara of Wilson, North Carolina. This is an old Polish recipe he remembers his grandmother making on Christmas Eve as part of a 12-course special meal served before going to Midnight Mass.

EASY • SERVES 4-6

1 leftover pork roast with bone and drippings
1 pound fresh sauerkraut, thoroughly rinsed
1 14.5-ounce can diced tomatoes
1 8-ounce can whole mushrooms and liquid
1 cup beef broth
4 cups chicken broth
1 3 3/4-ounce can fish steaks in oil, drained

Put all ingredients in large soup pot. Simmer 45 minutes. In the Polish tradition, this would be served with rye or pumpernickel bread and a sweet wine such as Mogen David.

Sweet Potato, Corn & Jalapeño Chowder

This soup, adapted from a recipe shared by Louise Turner of Lulu's Café in Sylva, North Carolina, reflects a spectrum of autumn flavors. Now Lulu's On Main, this popular restaurant is a highlight in the friendly mountain town.

Easy • Serves 4-6

2	large sweet potatoes (2 cups)
1/2	cup finely diced onion
2	tablespoons unsalted butter
1	quart vegetable or chicken stock
2	cups whole kernel corn (fresh or frozen)
2	teaspoons minced jalapeño pepper
1/2	cup heavy cream
1	teaspoon salt
1/2	cup chopped green onions

Peel sweet potatoes and cut into large chunks. Boil until soft. When cool, place in blender and pulse briefly to purée.

Meanwhile, sauté onion in butter until soft. Add puréed sweet potato and stock. Bring to boil, reducing liquid slightly. Add corn, jalapeños, heavy cream and salt. Simmer soup for 5 minutes. Garnish with green onions and serve.

Carolina Peanut Bisque

This unusual soup featuring peanut butter and a hint of jalapeño was adapted from a Caribbean recipe by Hazel Burnette of St. Lucia.

Average • Makes 5 cups

4	tablespoons butter
1/2	cup chopped celery
1	medium onion, chopped
1	teaspoon minced garlic
2	teaspoons minced fresh ginger
1	jalapeño pepper, seeds removed, minced
1/4	teaspoon oregano
4	cups vegetable broth
1	cup water
1 1/2	cups (12 ounces) creamy peanut butter
1	teaspoon salt
1/2	teaspoon white pepper
1	tablespoon finely chopped fresh cilantro
1/2	teaspoon paprika
3	tablespoons sherry

Melt butter in a soup pot over medium heat. Sauté celery, onion, garlic, ginger, jalapeño pepper and oregano for 5 minutes until onions and celery are soft. Add vegetable broth and water and bring to a boil. Stir in peanut butter, blending until smooth. Simmer 5 minutes. Add salt, white pepper, cilantro and paprika. Simmer on low heat 5 minutes more. Add sherry, and adjust seasoning to taste. Ladle 1/2-cup portions into bowls. Garnish with more chopped cilantro.

Favorite fall vegetables, warmed with the tang of jalapeño peppers, chase away autumn's chill in this robust chowder.

Brunswick Stew

This hearty stew shared by Elizabeth's mother, Peggy Stockton, is a Southern favorite that originated in Brunswick County, Virginia. Like barbecue, there are all sorts of variations: Some regions prefer a mixture of chicken and pork, others claim to add a little squirrel meat. Many add potatoes to their Brunswick stew, but in all honesty, folks, you can't beat this recipe. Whenever there's a homecoming, Elizabeth's mother always makes a big pot of this slowly simmered one-dish meal.

AVERAGE • SERVES 6-8

1	**hen or roaster plus 2 chicken breasts**
•	**salt and pepper to taste**
6	**small onions, peeled and chopped**
2	**28-ounce cans of tomatoes**
1	**15-ounce can tomato soup**
2 1/2	**cups fresh or frozen okra**
2 1/2	**cups fresh or frozen lima beans**
2 1/2	**cups fresh or frozen corn**
1/3	**cup Worcestershire sauce**
1/2	**teaspoon sugar**

Place hen in pot of water with enough water to just cover it. Add salt and pepper and chopped onions to flavor the stock. Cook for 1/2 hour and add the chicken breasts. When the hen is tender, take out of pan to cool. The chicken will be more tender if it is not cooked too fast. Reserve stock, skimming fat from the top. When hen is cooled, take meat off bones and cut up into large chunks. (Be sure not to leave any skin.) Put chicken back into the stock. Add the tomatoes, soup, okra and lima beans.

Cook over medium-high heat until vegetables are cooked down, about 1 hour. Don't let the stew boil. Add corn and cook 30 minutes or more. Season with Worcestershire sauce and sugar. Continue stirring so none of the ingredients stick. The mixture should be fairly thick.

Freddy Lee's Pumpkin Soup

Thick and delicious, this smooth soup is an appetite teaser from Freddy Lee of Bernardin's restaurant in Winston-Salem. Serve as a first course for your Thanksgiving feast. *Serve with Baked Herbed Crouton Sticks on page 189.*

AVERAGE • SERVES 8

1	**small onion**
1	**medium potato**
2	**tablespoons butter**
1	**tablespoon minced garlic**
5	**cups chicken stock, divided**
4	**cups peeled, coarsely chopped pumpkin**
1	**cup heavy cream**
1	**teaspoon ground nutmeg**
1/2	**teaspoon mace**

Chop onion and peel and dice potato. In a large saucepan or soup pot, melt the butter. Add onion, potato and garlic and sauté over medium heat for 4-5 minutes. Add 4 cups of the chicken stock and pumpkin. Bring to a boil and simmer 30 minutes until pumpkin is tender. Remove pan from heat and cool 10 minutes.

Purée pumpkin mixture in a blender or food processor in batches, then return soup to the original pan. On medium heat, pour in the remaining 1 cup stock, heavy cream, nutmeg and mace. Simmer, stirring 5-10 minutes more until blended and smooth. Ladle soup into bowls.

Down East Clam Chowder

An easy chowder that can be made with fresh or canned clams. If using fresh clams, open with a knife and remove meat from shells, or place clams in freezer and the shells will pop open once they are frozen.

Easy • Makes 10 cups

- **1/4 pound fatback, bacon or streak of lean, diced**
- **1 1/2 quarts clams in the shell or four 10-ounce cans whole clams**
- **2 cups small diced onion**
- **2 cups small diced celery**
- **2 small potatoes, peeled and diced**
- **3 cups half & half**
- **salt and pepper to taste**
- **2 tablespoons cornmeal (optional)**

In a large soup pot, cook fatback or bacon over low heat until it renders fat covering the bottom of the pan. Open fresh clams and rinse with water to remove grit. If using canned, drain clams and reserve liquid.

Sauté clams, onion and celery in fat until clams are just cooked. Add reserved liquid and/or water to make 8 cups and bring to a boil. Add potatoes and cook until tender about 10-15 minutes. Stir in half & half. Season with salt and pepper and thicken with cornmeal (mixed in a little hot liquid) if desired. Heat through and serve.

Studies of Figure 8, 1980

Black-Eyed Pea & Chicken Gumbo

Now that the weather is turning cool, weekday meals can feature hearty one-pot suppers such as this gumbo. Serve with a fruit salad such as Mixed Cherry, Kiwi and Oranges on page 141 and good bread.

Average • Serves 6

2 pounds boneless chicken breasts
• garlic powder
• salt and freshly ground pepper to taste
3 pounds frozen black-eyed peas
1 1/2 pounds fresh okra or two 10-ounce packages frozen chopped okra
1/2 cup vegetable oil
3/4 cup flour, divided
2 teaspoons minced garlic
1 medium onion, chopped
1 green pepper, chopped
1 red pepper, chopped
1 cup chopped celery
5-6 cups chicken broth
1 tablespoon paprika
1 1/2 teaspoons cayenne pepper
1 teaspoon gumbo filé, see note

Rub both sides of chicken breasts with garlic powder, salt and pepper. Cover and let rest in the refrigerator 30 minutes.

Cook black-eyed peas according to the directions on the package. Drain and set aside. Slice fresh okra into 1/2" pieces and steam in 2" of water or in a steamer, until tender (about 6-8 minutes). If using frozen okra, cook according to package directions, drain and set aside.

In a heavy skillet, heat oil over medium-high heat. Dredge chicken breasts in 1/4 cup flour and brown in oil about 4 minutes per side. Remove chicken from pan; drain on paper towels. To make a dark *roux* (a secret to good gumbo): Scrape brown particles up from the bottom of the pan, and gradually add remaining 1/2 cup flour to hot oil in the skillet. Cook over medium-high heat whisking constantly until the *roux* turns dark brown to black. Do not burn. Add garlic, onion, peppers and celery to the *roux* and sauté about 5 minutes, stirring constantly until vegetables are soft.

In a large soup pot, bring chicken broth to a boil. Add vegetables and roux to the stock in large spoonfuls, whisking to blend. When stock comes back to a boil, reduce heat to a simmer. Finely dice reserved chicken breasts and add to gumbo along with the black-eyed peas and okra. Season with paprika, cayenne pepper and gumbo filé. Salt and pepper to taste. Simmer 30 minutes, adding more chicken stock if the gumbo becomes too thick.

Note: The Choctaw Indians from the bayou country in Louisiana first used this seasoning made from ground, dried leaves of the sassafras tree. Now an integral part of Creole cooking, look for filé powder in the spice section of most large supermarkets.

Mountain Apple Salad

Cindy Zinser of Old Stone Inn in Waynesville, North Carolina – the heart of apple-growing country – shared this twist on the classic Waldorf Salad.

Easy • Serves 4

- 3 large MacIntosh apples
- 1/2 cup chopped celery
- 1/2 cup chopped dates
- 3 tablespoons fresh orange juice
- 1/2 cup sour cream
- 1 tablespoon mayonnaise
- 2 tablespoons heavy cream
- • pinch sugar
- 1/2 cup chopped pecans

Wash apples; remove seeds and dice (do not peel). In a medium bowl, combine apples, celery, dates and orange juice. Blend well to coat evenly. In a separate bowl, whisk together sour cream, mayonnaise, heavy cream and sugar. Stir into apple mixture until thoroughly mixed. Chill for several hours. Add nuts just before serving.

Potato Salad with Cheddar & Green Olives

Delicious. A hint of ginger and soy lends this red potato salad bold flavor. The green olives toss in a hint of the Mediterranean.

Average • Serves 4-6

- 1 1/2 pounds small red potatoes
- • Ginger Soy Dressing
- 1/2 cup sliced green olives, well-drained
- 1/2 pound sugar snap peas
- 6 ounces extra sharp cheddar cheese, cut into 1/2" cubes

Scrub potatoes and put in saucepan with salted water to cover. Bring to a boil, covered; reduce heat and boil gently about 15 minutes until just tender. Drain and run under cold water. As soon as you can handle them, cut into quarters or eighths.

While potatoes are cooking, make dressing. Toss the dressing with the potatoes while they are still hot. Add the olives, cool and then chill.

Cut the sugar snap peas in half, and soak in ice water 20-30 minutes to crisp. When potatoes are cold, add the sugar snap peas and cheese cubes. Chill several hours or overnight.

Ginger Soy Dressing

- 1/4 cup rice vinegar
- 1 tablespoon soy sauce
- 2 teaspoons honey
- 2 tablespoons Dijon mustard
- 1 clove garlic
- 1 tablespoon fresh ginger, finely chopped
- 1 teaspoon dried ginger
- 1/4 teaspoon salt
- 1/2 teaspoon freshly ground pepper
- 1/2 cup peanut oil

In bowl of food processor put vinegar, soy, honey, mustard, garlic, fresh and dried ginger, salt and pepper. Process until well-combined. With motor running, add peanut oil in a thin stream through feed tube and process until emulsified (milky texture).

An Avocado, Tomato, Cucumber Dice

A side salad that you can serve on its own or tuck into a pita. Originated by Elizabeth's father, J.K. Norfleet.

Easy • Serves 8-10

- 4 tomatoes, diced
- 2 avocados, diced
- 3 small red onions, chopped fine
- 3 small cucumbers, diced
- 1 jalapeño pepper, minced
- • Mustard Vinaigrette

Prepare vegetables and place in serving bowl. Put enough dressing over chopped vegetables to thoroughly blend.

Mustard Vinaigrette

- 2 tablespoons red wine vinegar
- 2 tablespoons balsamic vinegar
- 1 1/2 tablespoons Dijon mustard
- 2 cloves garlic, minced
- • salt and pepper to taste
- 1 cup olive oil

In a small bowl, combine red wine and balsamic vinegar, mustard, garlic, salt and pepper. Gradually whisk in olive oil. (The vinegars can be substituted with 1/4 cup lemon juice.)

Black Bean Confetti

A south-of-the-border salad.

Easy • Serves 8

- 2 pounds cooked black beans, rinsed and drained (2 cans)
- 3 cups cooked white corn
- 1 cup chopped green pepper, 1/4" dice
- 1/2 cup chopped red onion
- 12 cherry tomatoes, quartered (2 cups)
- 2 tablespoons chopped parsley
- 1 cup Cumin Vinaigrette

In a medium bowl, combine black beans with vegetables and parsley. Toss gently with Vinaigrette and let sit at least 30 minutes in the refrigerator. Serve cold.

Cumin Vinaigrette

- 1/2 cup olive oil
- 1/4 cup vegetable oil
- 2 tablespoons balsamic vinegar
- 2 tablespoons lemon juice
- 1 teaspoon Dijon mustard
- 1/2 teaspoon salt
- 1/2 teaspoon black pepper
- 1/2 teaspoon cumin

Combine all ingredients in a small bowl. Whisk until blended. Makes 1 cup.

On a beautiful fall day, leave your journal and take a walk or play in the leaves. Then enjoy an armchair picnic starring a perfectly ripe avocado.

Vincenzo's Salad

This recipe features arugula, an aromatic salad green that has a peppery mustard-like flavor.

Easy • Serves 4

- 2 cups arugula
- 4 cups red leaf lettuce
- 2 navel oranges
- 1/2 red onion
- • Lemon Dressing

Wash and dry the arugula and red leaf lettuce. Peel and section oranges; cut each orange section into bite-size pieces. Slice red onion into thin rounds; separate into rings. Combine the arugula, lettuce, oranges and red onion in a medium-size salad bowl. Pour dressing over salad. Toss lightly and serve.

Lemon Dressing

- 1 tablespoon balsamic vinegar
- 2 tablespoons lemon juice
- 1/4 teaspoon salt
- 1/4 teaspoon pepper
- 3/4 cup extra virgin olive oil

Whisk together the vinegar, lemon juice, salt and pepper. Gradually whisk in olive oil.

Wild Rice Salad with Lemon Honey Mustard Dressing

Wild rice, a truly American product, makes a great salad. If asparagus are not available, substitute sugar snap peas. If serving a smaller group, save the rest for later. It is even better the next day.

Average • Serves 10

- 1/2 cup wild rice
- 1/2 cup long grain rice
- 1 pound zucchini, about 3 small or 2 medium
- 1/2 teaspoon salt
- 1 pound asparagus
- 1 red or green bell pepper, chopped
- 1/2 cup chopped green onions
- 1 cup sliced green olives
- • Honey Mustard Dressing
- 3-4 Roma tomatoes

Prepare wild rice and long grain rice separately according to package directions; cool.

While rice is cooking, shred zucchini. (A food processor works well.) Toss with 1/2 teaspoon salt and set aside.

Remove and discard tough ends of asparagus; cut asparagus into 1 1/2" pieces, keeping tender tips separate. Bring a large pot of salted water to a boil. Add stem pieces and boil 2 minutes; add tips and boil 2 minutes more. Drain and refresh under cold water.

In large bowl, toss together cooled wild rice and long grain rice, grated zucchini, bell pepper, green onions and olives. Stir in Honey Mustard Dressing. Carefully toss in asparagus. Slice Roma tomatoes into thin wedges and place on top of salad. Serve at room temperature.

Honey Mustard Dressing

- 1/2 cup fresh lemon juice
- 1/3 cup honey mustard
- 1/2 teaspoon salt
- 1/2 cup extra virgin olive oil

Whisk together lemon juice, mustard and salt. Gradually whisk in olive oil; set aside.

A simple salad of lettuce greens, red onion and citrus reposes in a very old, perhaps Native American, hand-carved wooden bowl. One of Bob Timberlake's collectibles, the bowl is testimony to his eye for craftsmanship and rustic beauty.

Smothered Pork Chops with Gingered Applesauce

This is an updated version of Humphrey Bogart's pork chops and applesauce. Balsamic vinegar, cider and rosemary impart a distinct flavor to the pork chops. This is a memorable meal, sure to bring smiles.

Average • Serves 4

- 1/3 cup olive oil
- 4 thick-sliced pork loin chops
- 6 medium shallots, slivered
- 3/4 cup apple cider
- 1 tablespoon fresh rosemary
- • salt and pepper to taste
- 1 tablespoon balsamic vinegar
- • Gingered Applesauce

Prepare applesauce ahead.

Heat olive oil over high heat in large heavy-bottomed sauté pan. Sear pork chops on both sides in hot oil until lightly browned. Remove from pan and reserve. Add shallots and sauté over medium heat until translucent. Add cider, rosemary, salt and pepper. Return chops to pan. Cover and cook on medium heat until done, about 25 minutes. Remove chops with a slotted spoon from pan and keep warm.

Add balsamic vinegar to the liquid in the pan. Reduce until thickened and almost syrupy. Pour over chops and serve. Accompany with Gingered Applesauce.

Gingered Applesauce

- 2 cups apple cider
- 3 medium Rome apples, unpeeled, cored and sliced thickly
- 1 tablespoon fresh ginger
- 3 tablespoons cognac or brandy
- 2 teaspoons molasses

Place cider, apples, ginger and brandy in medium saucepan. Simmer for 25-30 minutes over low heat. Apples will still be somewhat firm, but beginning to give up skin. Add molasses and serve warm with chops. Makes 4 cups.

Milledge Road Crabcakes

These crabcakes are moist and delicious. Use claw crabmeat; it is more flavorful, and less expensive to boot.

Easy • Makes 8-10 cakes

- 1 pound crabmeat
- 2 cups crumbled saltines
- 2 teaspoons Dijon mustard
- 1 egg
- 1/2 cup real mayonnaise
- 1 cup minced green pepper
- 1 cup minced celery
- 1 tablespoon butter
- • cayenne pepper to taste
- • oil for cooking

Combine the crabmeat, saltines, mustard, egg and mayonnaise in a bowl. Sauté the green pepper and celery in the butter until soft. Mix it with the crabmeat. Season with cayenne. Mold into cakes and cook in 1 tablespoon oil over medium-high heat, 8 minutes on each side.

Smoked Turkey And White Bean Ragoût

A spicy, warming dish to thaw any autumn chill.

Average • Serves 8

20	ounces Great Northern white beans, washed and picked over
4	sprigs parsley
4	cloves garlic, peeled and whole
3	whole cloves
1 1/2	teaspoons salt
•	water to cover (about 10 cups)
3	ears corn, fresh or thawed if frozen
•	olive oil
1	cup diced onion
2	cloves garlic, minced
4	ribs celery, diced
1	Anaheim chili, seeded and diced, see note
2	Chipotle peppers, rehydrated, seeded and diced, see note
1	red bell pepper, diced
2	cups reserved cooking liquid from beans
1	tablespoon chili powder
1	tablespoon cumin
1	teaspoon dried thyme
1/2	teaspoon salt
1/2	teaspoon pepper
1	pound smoked turkey, cut into 3/4"-1" dice

In large stockpot, cook beans with parsley, garlic, cloves and salt, plus water to cover, about 10 cups. Bring to a boil, then simmer, partially covered, until beans are tender, about 1-1 1/2 hours. Add more water if needed. Drain, reserving 2 cups of cooking liquid. Remove parsley, garlic, and cloves.

Meanwhile, brush corn with olive oil and roast in preheated 400° oven, turning occasionally, about 20 minutes or until lightly browned. Cool; cut from cob with a sharp knife. Set aside.

In a large pot, heat 2 tablespoons olive oil until hot but not smoking over medium heat. Sauté onion, garlic, celery, Anaheim, Chipotle and red peppers until vegetables are soft. Add cooked beans and 2 cups of reserved cooking liquid from beans. Add chili powder, cumin, thyme, salt and pepper. Stir in diced turkey and roasted corn. Adjust seasonings. Simmer, covered, for 30 minutes.

Note: Anaheim chilies are found fresh or canned and have a somewhat sweet taste with just a little bite. Chipotle chilies are really smoked jalapeño peppers, and can be found dried, or diced and canned; they'll impart a smoky heat to the ragoût.

Barbecued Turkey

This recipe was a long-ago prize winner at the annual North Carolina Turkey Federation's Turkey Contest in Raeford, North Carolina. Developed by Ruby Ingram of Kernersville, it makes a great weeknight supper.

Easy • Serves 4

- 1/2 boneless, skinless turkey breast (1 pound) cut into 1" thick steaks
- 1/2 cup soy sauce
- 1/2 cup red wine
- • Barbecue Sauce

Place turkey steaks in a glass dish or self-closing plastic bag. Mix soy sauce and wine. Pour over steaks and marinate 4 hours or overnight, turning 2 or 3 times. Dip meat in barbecue sauce and grill over medium-high heat 10 minutes, or until no longer pink in center. The heat source should be 4-6 inches directly under the turkey. Baste with additional sauce while cooking.

Barbecue Sauce

- 1 cup ketchup
- 2/3 cup water
- 1/4 cup brown sugar
- 1/3 cup chopped onions
- 1/2 teaspoon salt
- 1/2 teaspoon black pepper
- 1 teaspoon mustard
- 1 tablespoon Worcestershire sauce
- • juice of 1 lemon

Mix all ingredients in a saucepan and simmer 10 minutes.

Baked Chicken Breast with Herbed Cheese Stuffing

Savory stuffing gives the chicken a mild herb flavor. This entrée may be assembled earlier in the day and refrigerated.

Average • Serves 4-6

- 1 cup ricotta cheese
- 8 ounces cream cheese, softened
- 3/4 cup Parmesan cheese
- 2 teaspoons thyme
- 1 teaspoon basil
- 2 tablespoons chopped parsley
- 6 bone-in chicken breast halves with skin on
- • salt and pepper to taste

Sauce:

- 1/2 cup white wine
- 3 green onions, chopped fine
- 2 tablespoons lemon juice

Combine ricotta and cream cheeses with the Parmesan, thyme, basil and parsley.

Preheat oven to 400°. Separate the skin from the chicken breast on one side keeping it attached along the edges. Press spoonfuls of the stuffing under the skin distributing it evenly among the chicken breasts. Tuck skin under the chicken and place in a baking pan. Salt and pepper the tops to taste. Bake for 10 minutes. Reduce heat to 375° and bake for 30 minutes more or until golden brown. Remove the chicken to plates.

Deglaze the roasting pan with the white wine. Pour juices from the roasting pan into a small saucepan. Add green onions and lemon juice. Cook 4-5 minutes, stirring often. Drizzle a little sauce over each chicken breast.

Cider Chicken Over Apple Potato Cakes

A perfect meal for brunch or home-style supper. Tart apple cider sauce surrounds the chicken and tops crunchy potato-apple cakes.

AVERAGE • SERVES 6

1 pound boneless chicken breasts
• Cider Cream Sauce
1/4 cup sliced green onions
6 slices bacon
1 cup small diced onion
1 cup small diced leeks
1 cup small diced celery
2 Rome apples, peeled, cored and shredded
3 cups shredded or grated, peeled potatoes
2 eggs, lightly beaten
1 tablespoon flour
1 teaspoon salt
4 tablespoons butter, divided

Poach chicken breasts in boiling water about 10 minutes or until done. Cut into medium pieces and reserve. Make Cider Cream Sauce and stir in chicken and green onions. Keep warm while you make the apple-potato cakes.

In a large skillet, cook bacon until crisp. Remove, crumble and add to Cider Cream Sauce. In same skillet with reserved bacon droppings, sauté onion, leeks and celery until translucent. Add apples and cook until just soft.

Combine the above in a bowl with grated potatoes; mix in eggs, flour and salt. Form the potato mixture into 2"-3" patties. In a large skillet, melt 2 tablespoons butter over medium-high heat. Sauté cakes until golden brown and crisp on both sides. Repeat with remaining butter and cakes. Plate and serve with Cider Chicken spooned over the top.

Cider Cream Sauce

1 1/2 cups chicken stock
1 1/2 cups apple cider
1/4 cup half & half
4 tablespoons butter
3 tablespoons flour
1/2 teaspoon salt
• pepper to taste
• scant 1/8 teaspoon nutmeg
1/2 teaspoon dried basil

In small saucepan, heat chicken stock, cider and half & half. Do not boil. In medium saucepan over medium heat, melt butter. Add flour, stirring constantly, and cook until golden brown to make a *roux*. Slowly add heated stock, salt, pepper, nutmeg and basil to roux. Cook over low heat until thickened and all taste of flour is gone. Keep warm.

If making ahead, let cool then place wax paper directly on sauce to cover and refrigerate. This prevents condensation from diluting the sauce and a skin from forming on the surface.

An apple a day keeps the doctor away. Chicken soup can cure anything. That's what folks say. Maybe they're right. When you're down and out, cover all your bases. Add *pomme de terre* to your *pomme* and some cream to that chicken soup. Stir in a few more ingredients, and in no time you'll have Cider Chicken Over Apple Potato Cakes – a sure cure for anything that ails you.

Grilled Tuna with Niçoise Olives

Several years ago the former 23 Page in Asheville, North Carolina shared a recipe for Grilled Grouper with Niçoise Olives and Lemon Buerre Blanc. We adapted the olive topping and paired it with an easy grilled tuna.

Average • Serves 4

- •	**Olive Compote**
- 4	**fillets fresh tuna, about 1/2 pound each and 1" thick**
- 1-2	**tablespoons olive oil**

Prepare olive compote recipe 1 week ahead.

Lightly brush fillets with olive oil and grill until tuna's flesh is easily flaked but not overdone. To serve, top tuna with a spoonful of olive compote and garnish with a sprig of thyme.

Olive Compote

- 1/3 pound Niçoise olives, pitted and chopped
- 1 cup olive oil
- 1/2 lemon, cut into chunks
- 1 clove garlic, peeled and crushed
- 1/2 teaspoon cumin seeds
- 1 sprig fresh thyme
- 1/4 teaspoon hot pepper flakes
- 1/2 teaspoon black peppercorns

Combine all the ingredients in a 1-quart jar; the olive oil should cover olives. Marinate for at least 1 week (or up to 2 months). The olive oil will gradually be absorbed. Makes 2 cups.

Seared Tuna Sandwiches with Honey Ginger Glaze

Celebrate the sea with these hearty burgers. Fresh yellowfin tuna is one of the culinary pleasures of coastal North Carolina. Its steak-like consistency molds into a perfect patty. The tangy flavors of ***Taste Full****'s Asian Sweet and Sour Slaw on page 180 are a complement to the zesty seasoning of the tuna burgers.*

Easy • Serves 4

- •	**Honey Ginger Glaze**
- 2	**pounds yellowfin tuna**
- 1	**tablespoon minced garlic**
- 1	**egg**
- 2	**tablespoons Dijon mustard**
- 1/2	**teaspoon cayenne pepper**
- 1/2	**teaspoon black pepper**
- 1	**teaspoon salt**
- 1/2	**cup olive oil, divided**
- 4	**gourmet hamburger buns with sesame seeds**
- 2	**tablespoons butter, melted**

Prepare Honey Ginger Glaze. Remove any gristle from tuna. With a large knife, shred tuna to hamburger consistency. Place in medium-sized mixing bowl. Set aside.

In another small bowl, combine garlic, egg, mustard, cayenne pepper, black pepper and salt. Add to tuna and mix well. Using slightly wet hands, form mixture into 4 burgers. Cover and refrigerate until ready to sauté.

In a large skillet, heat 1/4 cup olive oil over medium heat. Add 2 of the burgers. Cook for 4 minutes per side for medium burgers, or 6-7 minutes per side for more well done. Transfer to a warm plate and tent with foil. Repeat with 2 remaining burgers.

While burgers are cooking, preheat the broiler. Brush tops of buns with melted butter and toast until golden. Top burgers with Honey Ginger Glaze and serve on buns with Asian Sweet and Sour Slaw.

Honey Ginger Glaze

- 1/2 cup soy sauce
- 2 teaspoons minced fresh ginger
- 1 teaspoon minced garlic
- 2 tablespoons honey
- 1 tablespoon Dijon mustard

In a heavy-bottomed saucepan, combine all ingredients. Bring to a boil, reduce heat and simmer for 4-5 minutes. Cover and keep warm until ready to use.

A member of the mackerel family, there are several varieties of tuna, but the mildest flavored are albacore and yellowfin. Albacore, popular in Chile and along the Pacific coast of South America, is a white meat tuna with a hint of pink. Yellowfins, larger than albacores, abound along the Mid-Atlantic coast and have pale pink flesh.

Golden Cornmeal & Country Ham Dumplings

Natural sugars in the onion and carrot make them perfect for caramelizing with the cabbage. Best made in an 11" skillet, cook the cabbage first then drop the dumplings on top, cover and cook a little longer for an easy and tasty meal. A fruit salad would round out the meal.

Average • Serves 4

6	tablespoons bacon fat or vegetable oil
1	cup chopped onion
4	carrots, peeled and thinly sliced
1	head green cabbage, chopped (6 cups)
2	cups chicken stock
1	cup chopped fresh parsley
•	salt to taste
3/4	teaspoon pepper, divided
3/4	cup yellow plain cornmeal
3/4	cup plain flour
1	teaspoon sugar
1 1/2	teaspoons baking powder
2	tablespoons butter
1 1/4	cups milk
1/2	teaspoon Tabasco sauce
1 1/2	cups cooked country ham, minced (about 1/3 pound)

In an 11" skillet, heat fat or oil over medium heat. Add onions and carrots and sauté 2-3 minutes. Add cabbage and cook, stirring, 5-7 minutes. Stir in chicken stock and parsley. Cover, reduce heat to medium and cook another 8-10 minutes. Salt to taste, and add 1/2 teaspoon of pepper. While cabbage is cooking, mix up the dumplings.

In a medium bowl, stir together cornmeal, flour, sugar, 1/4 teaspoon of salt, 1/4 teaspoon of pepper, and baking powder. Cut in butter to a coarse meal mixture. Stir in milk, Tabasco and country ham. Remove lid from cabbage and drop dumplings into skillet on top of cabbage mix, using a scant 1/3 cup per dumpling. Cover and cook 15-20 minutes more. Test dumplings for doneness with toothpick. Serve immediately. Makes 7 dumplings.

Pastor Moore's Shrimp Creole

A tangy taste on an old favorite. This recipe is compliments of Bob Timberlake's good friend Pastor Lamar Moore.

Easy • Serves 4-6

2	pounds shrimp
1	medium onion
2	stalks celery
1	green bell pepper
1/3	cup vegetable oil
1	15-ounce can tomato sauce
1	tablespoon sugar
1	tablespoon lemon juice
1	tablespoon Worcestershire sauce
1	tablespoon Heinz 57® sauce
3-4	dashes Tabasco sauce
•	salt and pepper to taste
1/4	cup chopped parsley
3	cups cooked rice

Peel and devein shrimp and set aside in refrigerator. Small dice the onion, celery and pepper. In a large sauté pan, heat oil on medium high, and cook vegetables until soft. Stir in tomato sauce, sugar, lemon juice, Worcestershire, Heinz 57® and Tabasco. Simmer 15 minutes until thickened. Season with salt and pepper. Add shrimp and continue to simmer briefly 3-5 minutes until shrimp are just done. Do not overcook. Sprinkle with chopped parsley and serve over rice.

Pastor Lamar Moore of Lexington knows his way around a kitchen. His preparation of duck and quail at Timberlake's "Critter Dinners" is legendary among friends. One of his secrets for tenderizing duck – a quick 10 minutes in a pressure cooker. When he was working his way through seminary, Moore commuted to Morehead City to work weekends on busy shrimp boats. It winds up the Pastor cooks a mean Shrimp Creole, which he wanted to share.

Front Porch, 1975

Ben's Spicy Grilled Shrimp over grits with country ham

Ben Barker, co-owner and chef of the Magnolia Grill in Durham, prepared this dish for the late Julia Child and other participants in 1994 at a joint conference for the American Institute of Wine and Food and the International Association of Culinary Professionals that featured Southern foods. In 2000 Barker was named Best Chef in the Southeast by the James Beard Foundation. The recipe has several steps, but none are difficult. Consider this for a light entrée.

Average to Involved • Serves 4

- • Grits Cakes
- • Balsamic Vinaigrette
- 1 1/4 pounds large shrimp, about 24
- 8 6" wooden skewers
- 1 teaspoon cracked fennel seed
- • zest of 1 lemon, minced
- 1 teaspoon crushed red pepper flakes
- 5 cloves garlic, minced
- 1 teaspoon freshly ground black pepper
- 1/3 cup peanut or olive oil
- 1/4 pound thinly sliced country ham
- 1 tablespoon butter
- 1/2 pound mesclun, or mixed peppery greens

Make Balsamic Vinaigrette and Ben's Grits Cakes.

Peel and devein shrimp. Soak wooden skewers in water for 10 minutes. Divide shrimp into 4 equal portions. Allowing 2 skewers per portion, skewer shrimp through the top of each shrimp with one skewer, and through the tails of the shrimp with the other skewer. The shrimp will be equidistant on the skewers which will facilitate turning them on the grill. Place prepared shrimp in a Pyrex baking dish and set aside.

In a bowl whisk together fennel seed, lemon zest, red pepper flakes, garlic, black pepper and oil. Thoroughly coat skewered shrimp with marinade. Cover dish and refrigerate for 6-8 hours, but no less than 2.

Trim fat from the country ham and cut into thin julienne strips. In a sauté pan, melt butter and cook ham over medium heat until lightly browned and crisp. Remove from pan, drain, pat dry and reserve. Wash greens thoroughly and break into bite-sized pieces. Place greens and ham in a bowl and set aside.

Just before grilling shrimp, reheat grit cakes on a cookie sheet in a 400° oven. Toss country ham and greens with reserved vinaigrette. Grill or broil shrimp, turning once, and cook them until just opaque, about 4-5 minutes. Remove shrimp from the skewers.

To assemble dish, place grits cakes on 4 warm plates. Top them with dressed greens. Allowing 6-7 shrimp per plate, try to place the grilled shrimp so that tails point up decoratively.

Ben's Vinaigrette

- 1/4 cup balsamic vinegar
- 3 cloves garlic, minced
- 1/2 teaspoon crushed red pepper flakes
- 2 tablespoons fresh thyme leaves
- 1/2 cup olive oil
- • salt to taste

In a small bowl, whisk balsamic vinegar and herbs together. Pour olive oil in parts, blending well after each addition. Season with salt.

Ben's Grits Cakes

- 1 tablespoon butter
- 3 cups chicken stock
- 3/4 cup quick grits, preferably stoneground yellow, not instant
- 1/4 teaspoon salt, optional
- 1 egg, beaten
- 1 cup grated Parmesan or Sonoma Dry Jack cheese
- • salt and pepper to taste
- • Tabasco sauce to taste

Preheat oven to 350°. Grease a 9" x 13" baking pan with the tablespoon of butter. Bring chicken stock to a boil; add grits and salt, stirring. Reduce heat to medium low. Cook 5 minutes, stirring, until thickened.

Remove pan from heat. Add a large spoonful of the hot grits to the beaten egg and stir; spoon the egg mixture back into hot grits. Stir until blended, then add cheese. Stir over low heat for 1 minute until cheese is melted. Remove from heat. Season to taste with salt, pepper and Tabasco. Spread mixture in prepared pan. Bake for 25-30 minutes, or until firm. Cool and refrigerate.

Cut the chilled grit cakes into 4 large pieces. Cut each piece crosswise to make 2 triangles to arrange on 4 individual plates.

It's a Southern rite of passage, and hunters like Bob Timberlake remember the thrill of receiving their first shotgun – usually at Christmas. It's an important time. Such a gift means that you have been trained in the proper care and use of the weapon and are now trusted to use it responsibly. With your brother and your best friend – a liver-spotted pointer – you head for the meadow to flush out quail. Childhood is behind you. Now you are someone who can put food on the table.

Grilled Quail with Pecans and Currants

*Fall means quail season, and there's nothing better than grilling this succulent bird. **Taste Full** has provided two different side dishes so you can enjoy the game bird with savored variety.*

Easy • Serves 4

- 8 quail
- 2 cloves garlic, minced
- 1/2 cup olive oil
- 1/2 teaspoon thyme
- 1/2 teaspoon rosemary
- 1/2 teaspoon basil
- • salt and pepper to taste
- • Very Light Sauce

Butterfly quail by splitting each down the backbone and removing neck.

Combine garlic with oil and seasonings. Rub over the quail and marinate in the refrigerator for 2 hours. Make Very Light Sauce and keep warm. Grill quail on the breast side first for 3-4 minutes over high heat. Baste with oil marinade and turn, cooking another 3-4 minutes or until done. Do not overcook.

Couscous with Pecans and Currants:

Use larger size couscous for the perfect blend of sweet and nutty flavors. Available at well-stocked mainstream grocery stores.

- 1 cup uncooked couscous
- 1 1/2 tablespoons butter
- 1/4 cup chopped green onions
- 1/4 cup chopped pecans
- 1/4 cup currants

Cook couscous according to package directions.

In a small separate pan, melt butter and sauté green onions until soft. Add pecans and currants and cook over low heat about 5 minutes. Stir nut mixture into couscous and keep warm. Serve quail on top of couscous and spoon Very Light Sauce over the top.

Very Light Sauce

- 1/4 cup butter
- 1/4 cup minced shallots
- 1 1/2 cups chicken stock
- 1/2 cup white wine
- 2 teaspoons Dijon mustard
- 2 teaspoons lemon juice
- • dash Worcestershire sauce

In a small saucepan melt butter. Sauté shallots 2-3 minutes. Add remaining ingredients and bring to a boil. Reduce heat and simmer until sauce is reduced by half.

Spinach Potato Pancakes

- 2 large potatoes
- 1 leek
- 1/4 cup oil, divided
- 2 cups spinach leaves, packed
- 1/4 cup chopped basil leaves
- 2 eggs, lightly beaten
- 1/2 cup flour
- 1 teaspoon salt
- 1/2 teaspoon nutmeg

Peel and shred or grate potatoes. Slice leek thinly, then sauté in 1 tablespoon oil until soft. Remove large stems from spinach before coarsely chopping.

In a medium bowl, mix potatoes, leeks, spinach, basil, eggs, flour, salt and nutmeg. Shape into cakes 4" in diameter.

In a large skillet, heat 1 tablespoon oil on medium high. Cook cakes about 4 minutes per side. Add more oil as needed as you cook cakes in batches. Serve with 1 quail on each cake, and spoon Very Light Sauce over the top.

Makes eight 4" cakes.

PUMPKIN BREAD PUDDING WITH BUTTERED BOURBON SAUCE

Moist, rich and wonderful!

AVERAGE • SERVES 6-8

- 1/2 large loaf dry French or Italian bread (not a baguette)
- 4 tablespoons butter, softened
- 1 cup currants or golden raisins
- 4 eggs
- 1/2 cup brown sugar
- 1 15-ounce can puréed pumpkin
- 1 cup heavy cream
- 1/2 cup milk
- 1 teaspoon cinnamon
- 1/4 teaspoon nutmeg
- 1/4 teaspoon allspice
- 1 teaspoon vanilla extract
- • Buttered Bourbon Sauce

Slice bread 1/2" thick and spread 1 side of each slice with butter. Cut each in half and layer into a greased high-sided 2-quart casserole. Sprinkle currants or raisins on each layer as you fill casserole to the top with bread.

In a medium bowl, beat eggs with brown sugar and pumpkin. Mix in cream, milk, cinnamon, nutmeg, allspice and extract. Pour over bread and press gently with your fingers until bread slices settle as they absorb the cream mixture. Let sit a few minutes and press again; repeat several times for about 15 minutes. Preheat oven to 350°.

Bake for 1 hour 10 minutes or until a knife inserted in the center comes out clean. Let sit 5 minutes before serving warm. Spoon Buttered Bourbon Sauce over each serving.

Buttered Bourbon Sauce

- 2/3 cup dark corn syrup
- 1/2 cup bourbon
- 4 tablespoons unsalted butter

In a heavy saucepan, heat corn syrup and bourbon on medium-high until syrup dissolves. Simmer 2 minutes. Chop butter into small pieces and swirl into sauce; cook until it thickens. Serve warm. Or, if serving cold, chill and whip before serving. Makes 1 1/4 cups.

Autumn traditions require a family trip to a pumpkin farm where the cook seeks pulp for holiday pies and soufflés, while the children look for the perfect jack–o–lantern material. Since both want good, ripe pumpkins that are free from blemishes and heavy for their size, it's possible to compromise. Empty Mr. Jack and make this old-fashioned Pumpkin Bread Pudding with Buttered Bourbon Sauce from his flesh and everybody wins.

Rustic Apple Tart

A hint of orange and dried cranberries enhance this apple tart. The rustic look fits the casual mood of autumn.

Average • Serves 10

1 3/4	cups flour
1/2	teaspoon salt
10	tablespoons butter, divided
1	egg
3	tablespoons sugar
4	tablespoons ice water
5	Granny Smith apples
1	tablespoon Grand Marnier, optional
3/4	cup sugar
1	tablespoon flour
1	teaspoon cinnamon
1 1/2	teaspoons orange zest
1/2	cup dried cranberries
1/4	cup orange marmalade

To make crust: In medium bowl combine flour and salt. Using a pastry blender or fork, cut in 9 tablespoons butter until mixture resembles coarse crumbs. In separate small bowl, beat egg with sugar and ice water. Add to flour mixture and mix to combine. Bring into a ball; wrap in plastic wrap and chill 30 minutes.

On lightly floured surface, roll pastry into about a 14" circle. Fold in half and carefully transfer to 11" tart pan with removable sides (see note), leaving overlap to hang loosely. Transfer tart pan to a pizza pan or other baking pan and chill while preparing filling.

Preheat oven to 400°. Peel apples and cut into quarters. Remove core, then cut each quarter into 3 pieces lengthwise to make thick slices. Put slices into large bowl and toss with Grand Marnier. In separate small bowl, combine sugar, flour, cinnamon, orange zest and dried cranberries. Add to apples and toss to coat with sugar mixture. Arrange slices in 1 layer in tart pan lined with crust, starting with outer edge and packing in tightly. Continue lining in concentric circles to the center. Distribute dried cranberries over apples and scrape out any remaining sugar mix. Dot with remaining 1 tablespoon butter. Fold overlapping crust over the apples to cover about 2-3" for a rustic look. Bake for 10 minutes. Reduce heat to 350° and bake about 40 minutes more until crust is browned and apples are just tender. Remove to rack. While tart is still hot, warm orange marmalade in small saucepan. Spoon or brush over the apples that are not covered with crust. Let cool. To serve, remove sides of tart pan and display tart on cake stand or plate. Cut in wedges to serve. Serve warm or at room temperature.

Note: If you do not have an 11" tart pan, this tart could be baked free form on a pizza pan. Just bring edges of crust up around the apples, overlapping 2-3". Bake as above.

Bittersweet Chocolate Tart

This delectable tart comes with words of advice from the Fearrington House Restaurant: "Offer slender slices. It's very rich and very elegant!"

Easy • Makes one 9" tart

- • Pastry Shell
- 3/4 cup heavy cream
- 1/3 cup milk
- 4 ounces bittersweet chocolate, grated or finely chopped
- 1 egg, lightly beaten

Preheat oven to 375°. Make pastry shell and pre-bake.

In a medium saucepan, combine the cream and milk and bring to a simmer over moderate heat.

Place finely chopped chocolate in bowl and pour hot milk/cream over and stir to completely melt chocolate. Set aside to cool to lukewarm. Whisk in egg until thoroughly blended. Pour mixture into prebaked pastry shell. Bake in middle of oven until filling is almost firm, 12-15 minutes. Cool. Serve warm or at room temperature with whipped cream.

Pastry Shell

- 1 cup all-purpose flour
- 1 tablespoon sugar
- 1/4 teaspoon salt
- 6 tablespoons unsalted butter, cold, cut in pieces
- 1 egg yolk
- 2 tablespoons ice water

Combine flour, sugar and salt in food processor. Add butter and process until texture of coarse crumbs. Add egg yolk and ice water through the feed tube and process until the dough forms a ball. Cover with plastic wrap and refrigerate for 1 hour.

Preheat the oven to 425°. Roll dough out to 11" circle. Transfer to a 9" tart pan and press into the bottom and sides. Fold the overhang back towards the inside and crimp the edge. Prick the bottom with a fork and line with aluminum foil. Fill with pie weights or dried beans and bake until slightly golden, about 12-14 minutes. Remove from oven, lift off weights and foil and cool completely.

Pisgah's French Silk Pie

*A chocolate-lover's dream! This recipe was shared with **Taste Full** by the Pisgah Inn near Asheville, North Carolina, one of three restaurant inns commissioned by the U. S. Forest Service to operate on the Blue Ridge Parkway.*

Easy • Serves 8

- • Walnut Crust
- 4 1/2 ounces unsweetened baking chocolate
- 6 tablespoons butter
- 3/4 cup brown sugar
- 3 eggs, see note page 25
- 2 tablespoons raspberry brandy or amaretto
- 1 teaspoon vanilla extract
- 1/8 teaspoon salt

Make Walnut Crust.

In a double boiler melt chocolate, butter and sugar. Stir until smooth. Add each egg separately to the melted chocolate, whisking thoroughly between each addition. Stir in raspberry brandy, vanilla and salt. Pour filling into cooled crust and refrigerate for 4 hours before serving. Garnish with whipped cream, slivered almonds or fresh strawberries or raspberries.

Walnut Crust

- 1 1/2 cups walnuts
- 1/4 cup brown sugar, firmly packed
- 1/3 cup butter, softened

In a food processor, grind walnuts with brown sugar to prevent nuts from becoming too oily. Stop when nuts are finely chopped. Add butter and blend well. Butter a 9" pie plate and press crust mixture onto the bottom and sides of plate. Bake at 350° for 10 minutes and then let cool.

Orville & Wilbur's Favorite Rum Fig Cake

Fig cakes are a favorite dessert along the Outer Banks. This moist, spice cake shared by Nancy Aycock and Nancy Pugh, longtime residents on the prized barrier islands, features fig preserves and a rum syrup.

Easy • Serves 8-10

- 3 eggs
- 1 1/2 cups sugar
- 2/3 cup vegetable oil
- 2 cups flour
- 1 teaspoon baking soda
- 1 teaspoon salt
- 1 teaspoon cinnamon
- 1/2 teaspoon nutmeg
- 1/4 teaspoon ground cloves
- 1/2 cup buttermilk
- 1 teaspoon vanilla extract
- 1 cup fig preserves
- • Rum Syrup

Preheat oven to 350°.

In a mixing bowl, beat eggs with sugar until thickened. Blend in oil. In a separate bowl, sift together flour, baking soda, salt and spices. Add flour mixture to eggs alternately with buttermilk. Stir in vanilla and fig preserves. Pour into a greased and floured bundt pan. Bake for 40 minutes or until done. Remove cake from oven and pour 1/2 of the Rum Syrup over cake while cake is still in the pan. Cool in pan for 30 minutes then invert onto cake plate. Drizzle remainder of Rum Syrup over cake.

Rum Syrup

- 1/4 cup sugar
- 1/2 cup water
- 3 tablespoons dark rum

In a small saucepan, boil sugar in water until sugar is dissolved. Add rum.

When Orville and Wilbur Wright were ready to test their new flying machine, they left their bicycle shop in Dayton, Ohio, for Kill Devil Hills on the Outer Banks of North Carolina. Winds in these barrier islands gave proper lift to the wings of their craft, and the sand, whose dunes provided a platform for launching, allowed a soft landing. They found the folks in the land of Blackbeard the Pirate to be curious and friendly and the food, delicious. This moist, old-fashioned cake is made with Caribbean rum and fig preserves, produced from fruit of the Calimyrna trees that are part of nearly every eastern North Carolina garden.

NOSTALGIA COOKIES WITH PEANUT BUTTER, CEREAL & RAISINS

These cereal bars or cookies are reminiscent of the old Special K Bars that were popular in the 50s and early 60s. They provide a healthy, fun snack for children — one they can help make and give to their friends. Since cereal is the main ingredient, they are healthier than most treats, though they do contain a sugar wallop.

EASY • MAKES 12 LARGE COOKIES OR 24 SMALLER ONES

3/4 cup sugar

1 cup corn syrup

1 3/4 cups peanut butter

8 cups cereal (Special K, Corn Flakes, etc.)

2 cups raisins, optional, OR

1 1/2 cups coconut, optional

In saucepan, combine sugar and corn syrup. Bring to a boil over medium heat. Remove from heat and immediately add peanut butter, stirring until well-combined. Place cereal into large bowl; stir in raisins or coconut if using. Pour peanut butter mixture over and stir well to combine, making sure all of cereal is moistened. Press into 9" x 13" cake pan or, for fun shapes, lightly spray cookie molds and pack cereal mixture into them. Chill; then remove by flexing the plastic molds, or use a knife in 1 corner to get them started. Alternately, lay several large cookie cutters onto wax paper-lined pan. Pack cereal mixture into cutters. Chill, then remove cutters. Continue until all is used. (If you only have a few molds, just cover cereal mix until the first set has chilled. It should not take more than about 30 minutes.)

Cookie Jar, 1972

A Snappy Pumpkin Chiffon Pie

Everyone loves the spicy fall flavors of pumpkin pie, but when combined with a gingersnap and pecan crust, infatuation sets in! This chiffon version has a lighter quality than the traditional pie. The filling does contain raw eggs, so keep the pie refrigerated.

AVERAGE • SERVES 6-7

Gingersnap Crust:

1	cup gingersnap cookie crumbs (about 20 wafers)
1/2	cup finely chopped pecans
1/2	cup or 1 stick butter, melted

Filling:

1	envelope unflavored gelatin
1/4	cup cold water
3	eggs, separated, see note
1 1/4	cups puréed canned or fresh pumpkin
3/4	cup sugar, divided
1/2	cup milk
1/2	teaspoon salt
1/2	teaspoon ground ginger
1/2	teaspoon ground cinnamon
1/4	teaspoon ground nutmeg

Garnish:

1/2	cup whipped cream
1/4	cup chopped pecans

Combine gingersnap crumbs, pecans and butter in a bowl. Press into 9" pie pan.

Sprinkle gelatin over cold water in small bowl. Set aside for 3 minutes to soften. In the meantime, combine egg yolks, pumpkin, 1/2 cup of the sugar, milk, salt, ginger, cinnamon and nutmeg in top of double boiler. Cook over boiling water until smooth, stirring constantly for about 5 minutes until thick and mixture has reached at least 160°.

Stir in gelatin until dissolved, about 2 more minutes. Pour mixture into medium-sized bowl. Place in a large bowl with ice water. Stir until mixture starts to set, about 20 minutes.

Next, pour into a warm bowl. Stir a bit more to stop gelatin from clumping. Stir a bit more until filling reaches room temperature.

Whip egg whites to soft peaks. Gradually add 1/4 cup sugar, then beat to stiff peaks. Carefully fold egg whites into pumpkin mixture, just enough to blend. Pour immediately into pie crust. Refrigerate until set, at least 2 hours. Garnish with whipped cream and pecans.

Another recipe option: Leave off the crust and serve as a mousse by placing into individual compotes.

NOTE: Using raw eggs in recipes has become somewhat of a risk for salmonella. When cooking the egg yolk/milk mixture, be sure it gets to at least 160°. Also, pasteurized eggs are now becoming more available in the market and are a good substitute when a recipe calls for raw eggs.

Alexia's Sweet Potato Cake

Adapted from a carrot cake recipe and iced with orange flavor, this rich dessert adds the perfect finish to any meal.

Easy • Serves 10-12

- 1 1/2 cups plain flour
- 1 1/2 cups sugar
- 1 1/2 teaspoons baking powder
- 1 1/2 teaspoons baking soda
- 1 1/2 teaspoons cinnamon
- 3 eggs
- 3/4 cup vegetable oil
- 1 teaspoon vanilla extract
- 1 medium uncooked sweet potato, shredded to yield 2 cups
- 1 cup chopped pecans
- • Orange Cream Icing

Preheat oven to 325°. Grease two 8" cake pans and line with wax paper.

In a large bowl, combine flour, sugar, baking powder, baking soda and cinnamon. In a separate bowl, mix together eggs, oil and vanilla. Stir wet ingredients into dry ingredients and blend well. Add shredded sweet potato and pecans and mix well. Divide batter between prepared cake pans. Bake for 35 minutes until a toothpick inserted in the center comes out clean. Let cool 10 minutes on racks. Invert layers onto racks or plates and cool 10 minutes more. Remove wax paper liners and cool completely before icing between layers, top and sides with Orange Cream Icing.

Orange Cream Icing

This icing is extremely rich so spread thinly for the ultimate balance in flavors.

- 6 tablespoons butter
- 6 ounces cream cheese
- 1/4 cup orange juice
- 1 teaspoon orange zest
- 2 1/2 cups confectioners' sugar

In a medium bowl, mix together butter, cream cheese, orange juice and zest with an electric mixer. Gradually mix in sugar and blend until smooth.

Anne's Pecan Pie

***Taste Full** reader Anne Andrews once shared a particularly yummy pecan pie recipe from her husband's grandmother in Robeson County. It's not weighed down with corn syrup the way so many pecan pies are. Anne's pie makes a command performance each Christmas in the Andrews' household.*

Easy • Serves 8

- 4 tablespoons butter or margarine
- 1 1/2 cups light brown sugar
- 1 tablespoon flour
- 2 eggs
- 2 tablespoons milk
- 1 tablespoon vanilla extract
- 1 8" or 9" unbaked pie shell
- • pecan halves to cover pie

Preheat oven to 350°. Melt butter in saucepan. Stir sugar and flour together before adding to melted butter. Whisk eggs into mixture, 1 at a time. Add milk and vanilla. Pour into unbaked pie shell. Place pecans on top beginning at outside edge. Bake about 45 minutes. If pecans begin to brown too much, cover with foil.

Pumpkin Chip Muffins

Once featured in a children's Halloween menu, this easy muffin from Susan Dillard tastes like dessert – no icing or glaze necessary. Watch them disappear!

Easy • Makes 2 dozen regular or 4 dozen mini muffins

2	**cups flour**
2	**cups light brown sugar**
2	**teaspoons cinnamon**
1/2	**teaspoon salt**
2	**teaspoons baking soda**
1	**cup vegetable oil**
1	**15-ounce can pumpkin purée**
4	**eggs**
2	**cups chocolate chips**

Preheat oven to 350°. In a large bowl, combine flour, sugar, cinnamon, salt and baking soda. In another bowl, mix together oil, pumpkin and eggs. Make a well in dry ingredients and stir in pumpkin mixture. Fold in chocolate chips. Spoon into muffin tins lined with paper cups. Fill to top. Bake 15-20 minutes for mini muffins, and 20-25 minutes for the regular muffin size. Cool on racks.

The Great Pumpkin, 1999

Winter

Blue Ridge Shiitake Mushrooms

Chef Tom Young of Expressions Restaurant in Hendersonville, North Carolina, stuffs mushrooms with spinach and goat cheese. Easy to prepare and delicious.

Easy • Serves 4

- **1/2** **pound spinach leaves (cleaned, stems removed)**
- **6** **tablespoons melted butter, divided**
- **1** **teaspoon minced garlic**
- **1/8** **teaspoon nutmeg**
- **1/8** **teaspoon cayenne pepper**
- **1/2** **cup goat cheese**
- **16** **medium shiitake mushrooms, stems removed**
- • **salt and pepper to taste**

Preheat oven to 350°. Blanch spinach leaves in boiling water for 1 minute. Drain into strainer and press all of the water out of the leaves. In a sauté pan, place 3 tablespoons of butter and sauté the garlic until lightly brown. Add spinach, nutmeg, cayenne pepper and sauté for 3 minutes. Remove from heat. Fold in goat cheese and adjust seasoning.

Place the mushrooms on baking sheet, season with salt and pepper and fill mushrooms with spinach mixture. Dust mushrooms with cayenne pepper and drizzle with remaining butter.

Bake at 350° for 8-10 minutes. Serve immediately.

Mini Gorgonzola Tarts

The original idea for these delectable little tarts comes from the Five Diamond Fearrington House Restaurant in rural Chatham County near Chapel Hill, North Carolina. ***Taste Full*** *adapted them for the home cook by reducing their size and using frozen puff pastry. They can be baked at the last minute and served hot from the oven, or reheated, uncovered, for about 5 minutes in a 400° oven.*

Easy • Makes 3 dozen

- **1** **sheet of puff pastry (9" x 9")**
- **1** **tablespoon butter**
- **1/2** **cup finely chopped onion**
- **6** **ounces Gorgonzola cheese (about 1 cup)**
- **8** **ounces cream cheese**
- **1/2** **teaspoon cayenne pepper**
- **2** **eggs**

Preheat oven to 375°.

Thaw puff pastry according to package directions. Cut into thirty-six 1" squares with sharp knife. Lightly grease 3 mini muffin pans and set a square into each cup. Set aside.

Melt butter in a small skillet over medium-low heat, and sauté onion until soft, about 3-4 minutes; cool. With mixer, beat together the Gorgonzola, cream cheese and cayenne pepper. Add the sautéed onion and eggs. Beat until smooth and fluffy.

Spoon a scant tablespoon of filling into each pastry-lined muffin cup. Bake in 375° oven for 18-24 minutes until puffed and golden brown.

Previous page *Evening Flight*, 1999

Governor's Mansion Crab Dip

Served hot with crackers or toast points, this favorite of former North Carolina First Lady Dottie Martin is perfect for a festive buffet.

Average • Serves 12-14

1 pound fresh crabmeat
8 ounces cream cheese
1 clove garlic, minced
1/4 cup chopped celery
1/4 cup chopped onion
1 tablespoon butter
2 tablespoons pale, dry sherry
1/2 tablespoon Worcestershire sauce
3 dashes Tabasco sauce
3 green onions, chopped
• salt to taste
• white pepper to taste
• crackers or toast points

Pick through crabmeat and remove any bits of shell. Put crab and cream cheese in the top of double boiler, cover and heat on low. In a separate pan, sauté garlic, celery and onion in butter until transparent. Add sherry and flame. Reduce liquid by half. Add to crab in double boiler; stir until smooth. Add Worcestershire and Tabasco sauces. Add chopped green onions 10 minutes before serving. Add salt and pepper to taste and heat thoroughly.

Savory Cheesecake with Smoked Salmon & Dill

An easy, make-ahead hors d'oeuvre, this rich dish will be a party favorite. Decorate with a sprig of fresh dill and serve with crackers.

Easy • Serves 18-20

24 ounces cream cheese, room temperature
4 eggs
1/3 cup heavy cream
1/2 cup chopped red onion
1 tablespoon butter
1 tablespoon chopped fresh dill (or to taste)
1/3 pound smoked salmon, diced
1/2 cup grated Gruyére cheese
3 tablespoons Parmesan cheese
• salt and pepper to taste
1 8" cheesecake pan

Preheat oven to 300°. Place cream cheese, eggs and cream in electric mixer. Beat until blended thoroughly and smooth. Sauté onion in butter for 3 minutes. Add to cream cheese mixture. Fold in dill, salmon, Gruyére and Parmesan. Season with salt and pepper. Pour into buttered 8" pan. Place in water bath. Bake approximately 1 hour and 40 minutes. Cool at least 2 hours before unmolding.

Spanish Olive Spread

This interesting mixture blends a pungent medley of flavors reminiscent of Spain. It is good as a spread on crackers or as a dip for colorful peppers. Serve it with Sangria, beer or dry sherry.

Easy • Makes 1 1/2 cups

- 1 tablespoon olive oil
- 1/4 cup chopped onion
- 1 clove garlic, minced
- 1 7-ounce jar green pimento-stuffed olives, well-drained
- 1/4 pound blue cheese, crumbled
- 1 tablespoon capers, rinsed and dried
- 2 tablespoons slivered almonds
- 1 tablespoon anchovy paste
- 1/2 teaspoon paprika

Heat olive oil in small skillet over medium-low heat. Sauté onion and garlic until softened, about 3-4 minutes. In food processor bowl, combine olives, blue cheese, sautéed onion and garlic, capers, almonds, anchovy paste and paprika. Process until fairly smooth, but still textured, scraping down several times as needed. Chill until ready to use.

Hot Pumpkin-Cheese Dip

Shared by Pat Voorhees of Wilmington, North Carolina. She's always asked to bring this dish to parties.

Average • Makes 4-5 cups

- 1 round loaf French or sourdough bread, unsliced
- 3 cups shredded sharp cheddar cheese
- 1 8-ounce package cream cheese, softened
- 1 cup sour cream
- 3/4 cup solid packed pumpkin
- 1/2 cup chopped green onion
- 1/2 cup chopped parsley
- 2 packages sliced smoked beef or your choice of meat, chopped
- 1 tablespoon Worcestershire sauce
- • dash of hot pepper sauce

Preheat oven to 325°. Using a sharp knife, slice off top of bread. Hollow out bread with knife to create a bowl with 1" sides and bottom. Cube reserved bread. In food processor or large bowl, blend cheddar cheese, cream cheese and sour cream. Add pumpkin, green onion, parsley, beef, Worcestershire sauce and hot pepper sauce; blend well. Fill hollowed out loaf with mixture; pour remaining mixture into small greased casserole dish. Wrap loaf securely in foil; cover casserole with foil. Bake loaf for 2 hours; bake casserole during last 40 minutes of baking. Unwrap bread; stir dip and sprinkle with more parsley. Serve hot with cubed bread or crackers or chips. Use dip in casserole to replenish bread bowl.

Oysters On The Half Shell with Spinach Walnut Pesto

Elizabeth's father developed this outstanding oyster recipe. The pesto does not rely on fresh basil so it can be made year-round. You'll want to use it on more than oysters!

Easy • Serves 8-10

5 dozen oysters

Spinach Walnut Pesto:

1 pound fresh spinach leaves, washed
1 cup parsley leaves
2/3 cup grated Parmesan cheese
1/2 cup walnut pieces
4 anchovy fillets
2 cloves garlic
1 tablespoon dried basil
1 teaspoon salt
1/4 teaspoon fennel seed
1 cup olive oil

Wash oysters and prepare for shucking.

Remove stems from spinach. Drop into boiling water for 3-4 minutes to blanch. Drain and squeeze dry. Combine spinach in food processor with all ingredients except oil. Blend until smooth. Slowly add olive oil until incorporated into the mixture.

Shuck oysters and top with pesto. Bake in 375° oven until lightly brown.

Smoked Oysters Rockefeller Pastries

Much of the work for this elegant hors d'oeuvre may be done before the guests arrive. Pass the pastries warm from the oven.

Easy • Makes 24 hors d'oeuvres

24 pieces bread (white or rye)
1 tablespoon olive oil
1 5-ounce bag baby spinach, well washed and coarsely chopped
2 cloves garlic, minced
2 tablespoons mayonnaise
2 teaspoons grated lemon zest
• dash of Tabasco sauce
• dash of salt
1 3.6-ounce package small cocktail smoked oysters, drained

Preheat oven to 400°. Make bread shells according to recipe on page 15 using rye or white bread.

In medium sauté pan or saucepan, heat olive oil over medium-low heat. Add spinach and garlic and stir to coat with oil. Cover and cook until spinach is wilted, stirring occasionally, about 3 minutes. Put in a sieve to drain.

In small bowl, combine spinach with mayonnaise, lemon zest, Tabasco and salt. Put about a teaspoon of spinach mixture in each shell; top with a smoked oyster. These may be done ahead and refrigerated until serving time. Bake just long enough to warm spinach and oysters, about 4-5 minutes.

Eastern Shore Oyster Stew

The Surry bacon in this recipe shared by Sam McGann of The Blue Point Bar & Grill in Duck, North Carolina, is a salt-cured, hickory-smoked bacon from the Edwards Virginia Ham Shop in Surry, Virginia. Any bacon will work if Surry bacon is not available.

Easy • Makes 6 cups, Serves 4

1	carrot
1	stalk fennel
1	stalk celery
1	cucumber
1/2	pound Surry bacon
24	oysters, freshly shucked with juice (or 1/2 pint oysters with liquid)
1 1/2	cups heavy cream
1 1/2	cups half & half
1	tablespoon Worcestershire sauce
1/2	teaspoon salt
•	dash or two of Tabasco sauce
2	tablespoons unsalted butter
2	tablespoons freshly chopped dill
2	tablespoons freshly chopped chives

Peel and small dice the carrot. Small dice the fennel and celery. Peel, quarter and seed the cucumber; cut into thin julienne strips. Drop all the vegetables into a pot of boiling water and blanch for 3 minutes. Drain and set aside.

Cook the Surry bacon until crisp; dry and break into small pieces.

In a medium stainless steel saucepan, bring the oysters, bacon, vegetables, cream and half & half to a simmer over medium heat. Cook for 3-4 minutes. When the oysters are just cooked through, the edges will begin to curl. Reduce heat to low and season with Worcestershire, salt and Tabasco. Cook 1 minute more. Divide oyster stew among 4 bowls. Float a teaspoon of unsalted butter in each bowl (optional) and garnish with a sprinkle of chopped dill and chives.

> If he must be cooked, which is basically a pity, an oyster stew is probably the best.
>
> I do not have a favorite oyster. Any oyster, fresh and crisp from cold waters, is pure bliss for me.
>
> – M.F.K. Fisher

Tomato Florentine Soup

This flavorful soup, a specialty of the intimate Lakeside Restaurant in Highlands, North Carolina, has been adapted for the home cook.

AVERAGE • SERVES 6-8, MAKES 2 QUARTS

1 1/2 tablespoons olive oil
1/3 cup finely chopped onion
2 teaspoons minced garlic
3 tablespoons white wine
1 bay leaf
1 teaspoon dried basil
1 teaspoon Italian seasoning
1/2 teaspoon salt
1/2 teaspoon black pepper
1 1/2 tablespoons flour
1 1/2 cups chicken stock
1 28-ounce can tomatoes, chopped with juice
3 cups milk
1 10-ounce package frozen chopped spinach, thawed
1 tablespoon chopped fresh basil

In a large soup pot, heat oil over medium heat and sauté onion and garlic 3 minutes. Add wine, bay leaf, basil and seasonings and simmer 5 minutes until liquid is reduced to almost dry. Stir in flour and slowly add stock, whisking to make soup smooth and thick. Add chopped tomatoes and milk. Bring to a boil, lower heat and simmer 30 minutes. Stir in spinach and basil and simmer 15 minutes more.

New Year's Collard Soup

On New Year's Day in the South, there's lots of collard eating in the hopes of new wealth in the upcoming annum. This soup is a delicious beginning.

EASY • SERVES 8

2 tablespoons olive oil
12-14 cups raw collard greens, washed and cut in 1" pieces
2 cloves minced garlic, optional
1/2 cup water
4 tablespoons butter
1/2 cup finely chopped onion
4 cups mashed potatoes
4 cups chicken stock
• salt to taste

Heat olive oil in a soup pot. Stir in greens, adding more until pot holds all the greens. Add garlic and water. Cover. Steam 10 minutes until just tender. Remove cover and cook off any excess water. Remove greens from pot and set aside to cool. In the same pot, melt butter. Sauté onion until soft. Stir in mashed potatoes. Gradually stir in stock. Bring to a simmer. Meanwhile, finely chop cooked collards. (Do not use a food processor.) Stir greens into soup. Simmer for 15 minutes on low. Salt to taste.

J.K.'s Black Bean Soup

A wonderful everyday soup, but certainly not ordinary. Shared by J.K. Norfleet, who claims the secret is in the bay leaves.

Easy • Serves 8-10

1 pound dry black beans
1/4 cup olive oil
1 1/2 cups chopped onions
1/4 cup finely chopped green onions
2 cloves garlic, minced
2 stalks celery, chopped
2 red bell peppers, chopped
1 1/2 jalapeño peppers, seeded and minced
4 bay leaves
3 tablespoons chicken stock
1 ham hock
1 tablespoon oregano
1 teaspoon cayenne
1 tablespoon chili powder
2 teaspoons cumin
3/4 teaspoon crushed red pepper or ground red chilies
2 teaspoons salt
1 teaspoon pepper
1 tablespoon lemon juice
1/4 cup chopped parsley

In a large pot, soak the beans overnight and drain.

The vegetables should be chopped to 1/4"-1/2" dice, with no big chunks. In a soup pot, heat olive oil over medium heat and sauté both onions, garlic, celery, red peppers and jalapeños. When onions and celery are soft add beans, bay leaves and enough water to cover by 1 1/2". Bring to boil; add chicken stock and ham hock. Simmer uncovered for 30 minutes.

Add oregano, cayenne, chili powder, cumin, red pepper, salt and pepper. Cook 45 minutes or until beans are soft. Remove ham hock and bay leaves. Add lemon juice and parsley. Cook 10-15 minutes more. Makes 2 1/2 quarts.

Chopping wood, a neighborhood game of touch football, making snowmen, hauling the sled back to the top of the hill – winter brings such hard work! Thaw out and refuel with a bowl of hot soup.

Lobster Corn Chowder

This chowder is a meal in itself served with salad and bread.

Average • Serves 4-6

3	tablespoons butter
1	cup small diced celery
1	cup chopped green onions
1/2	cup small diced red bell pepper
2	tablespoons flour
1/4	cup white wine
2	cups lobster stock (made when fresh lobster is cooked)
1	cup half & half
3	cups cooked corn (frozen white or yellow corn)
1/2	teaspoon salt
1/4	teaspoon white pepper
2	cups chopped lobster meat
2	tablespoons sherry
•	chives for garnish

In a medium soup pot, melt butter over medium-high heat. Sauté celery, green onions and red pepper until soft, about 8 minutes. Stir in flour and cook 2-3 minutes more. Add wine, stock and half & half and return to a simmer. Chowder should thicken a little. Stir in cooked corn, salt and pepper and heat through. Just before serving, stir in lobster meat and sherry. Serve hot and ladle into bowls. Garnish with fresh snipped chives.

Mixed Cherry, Kiwi and Oranges

Sweet cherries, tangy oranges, grapes and heavenly kiwis make for a colorful, tasty salad during winter. A creamy lime dressing is the perfect accent.

Easy • Serves 8

- • Creamy Lime Dressing
- 1 pound cherries
- 2 large navel oranges
- 3 kiwis
- 1 pound red seedless grapes

Make the Creamy Lime Dressing. Wash cherries and remove pits. Peel and section oranges. Chop in 1" pieces. Peel kiwis. Slice into 1/2" rounds and cut each slice in half. Wash grapes and remove stems. Place fruit into a large serving bowl. Cover and refrigerate until ready to serve. Toss with dressing just before serving.

Creamy Lime Dressing

- 1/2 cup sour cream
- 2 tablespoons honey
- 2 tablespoons fresh lime juice
- 1/2 teaspoon lime zest
- 1/2 teaspoon salt
- 1 tablespoon chopped fresh basil

Mix sour cream with honey, lime juice, zest, salt and basil. Blend well. Refrigerate for 1 hour before serving. Makes 3/4 cup.

Winter Bean Penne Pasta Salad

A wintry pasta salad to serve alongside a simple supper.

Average • Serves 8

- • Pesto Dressing
- 1/2 pound fresh baby green beans
- 1 pound spinach penne pasta
- 1/2 pound mushrooms, sliced
- 1 16-ounce can cannellini beans, drained and rinsed
- 1/4 cup toasted pine nuts, see note

Prepare Dressing. Blanch green beans in boiling salted water 3-5 minutes, and then refresh with cold water. Cook pasta according to package directions, drain and cool. In a large bowl combine pasta, beans, mushrooms, cannellini and pine nuts. Stir in dressing as needed. Cover and refrigerate several hours to allow flavors to develop. Makes 2 quarts.

Note: To toast pine nuts, put into medium skillet over medium-low heat. Toss and stir until golden brown. Cool.

Pesto Dressing

- 5 tablespoons basil pesto, homemade or purchased
- 1/3 cup red wine vinegar
- 3 tablespoons orange juice
- 1 cup olive oil
- • salt and pepper to taste

Whisk ingredients together in a small bowl.

Radicchio Fruit Salad

Radicchio is a red-leafed Italian chicory with tender firm leaves and a slightly bitter flavor. This colorful salad blends tart and tangy flavors with sweet and smooth.

Easy • Serves 8

- • **Mint Vinaigrette**
- 1 **medium head radicchio**
- 4 **cups grapefruit sections, drained**
- 2 **ripe avocados**

Make the Mint Vinaigrette ahead and refrigerate. Cut radicchio into thin, julienne stips and arrange as a bed on each plate. Place 3-4 grapefruit sections in a fan at the top of the plate. Peel and thinly slice the avocados lengthwise and fan 3 slices at the bottom of the plate. Drizzle the dressing lightly over each salad and serve.

Note: You can buy 16-ounce jars of pre-sliced grapefruit in the refrigerated section of grocery stores; 16-ounces yields 2 cups.

Mint Vinaigrette

- 1/2 cup olive oil
- 1/2 cup raspberry vinegar
- 2 teaspoons Worcestershire sauce
- 1/4 cup fresh chopped mint
- 2 tablespoons fresh chopped parsley

In a small bowl, combine olive oil, vinegar and seasonings. Refrigerate for 20 minutes before serving. Stir before dressing each salad.

Apple & Pear Slaw

This palate cooling salad is a perfect accompaniment. Leave the skin on the apples to impart color to the salad. Raisins may be substituted for dried cranberries.

Easy • Serves 8

- • **Minted Lime Dressing**
- 4 **Bosc pears, peeled, cored and diced**
- 2 **apples, Granny Smith or Macintosh, cored and diced**
- 1 **tablespoon lemon juice**
- 3 **cups green cabbage, shredded**
- 1/2 **cup dried cranberries**

Prepare Minted Lime Dressing. Place pears and apples in a mixing bowl. Add lemon juice to prevent browning. Stir in cabbage and cranberries. Add Minted Lime Dressing. Cover and refrigerate at least 1 hour.

Minted Lime Dressing

- 1 cup plain yogurt
- 1 teaspoon fresh lime zest
- 1 teaspoon fresh lime juice
- 1 tablespoon honey
- 1/4 cup olive oil
- 1/4 teaspoon freshly ground pepper
- 2 teaspoons chopped fresh mint

Combine yogurt, lime zest, lime juice and honey in small bowl. Whisk in olive oil until smooth and thick. Stir in pepper and mint.

Simple Blue Salad

Fresh and colorful, you can whip this up in minutes. Its versatility as a salad to pair with other dishes is endless.

Easy • Serves 4

- 8 **cups lettuce greens**
- 1 **red pepper, julienned**
- 1 **cucumber, peeled, diced**
- 1/2 **cup thinly sliced red onion**
- 4 **ounces crumbled blue cheese**

Assemble ingredients in a medium bowl. Toss with vinaigrette.

Classic Dijon Vinaigrette

- 1/3 cup olive oil
- 3 tablespoons vegetable oil
- 1/4 cup red wine vinegar
- 1 teaspoon Dijon mustard
- 1/2 teaspoon salt
- 1/2 teaspoon black pepper

Whisk together in a bowl or shake vigorously in a glass jar.

Bob's Broccoli Salad

A versatile salad that works alongside a sandwich, baked chicken, or a simple soup and salad meal. Named for Bob Timberlake because broccoli is his second favorite food.

Easy • Serves 6-8

1/2	**cup golden raisins**
4	**cups broccoli florets (1 large bunch)**
12	**slices bacon, cooked and chopped**
1/2	**cup peanuts**
1/4	**cup chopped red onion**
1/2	**cup mayonnaise**
1/4	**cup sugar**
5	**tablespoons red wine vinegar**

Soak raisins in warm water for 30 minutes; drain. In a medium bowl, combine broccoli, bacon, raisins, peanuts and red onion. In small bowl, mix mayonnaise, sugar and vinegar. Spoon over broccoli and mix thoroughly. Chill.

Fig and Stilton Salad

Sweet and tangy port vinaigrette dresses an interesting combo of dried figs and Stilton cheese to make this winning dish shared by Randy Plachy of Blowing Rock.

Easy • Serves 4

1/2	**cup port**
2 1/2	**tablespoons red wine**
1 1/2	**tablespoons balsamic vinegar**
1	**tablespoon wine vinegar**
1/2	**teaspoon black pepper**
1	**tablespoon sugar**
2	**teaspoons Worcestershire sauce**
2	**teaspoons molasses**
1/4	**teaspoon onion powder**
2 1/2	**tablespoons vegetable oil**
1	**teaspoon hazelnut oil**
8	**dried mission figs, quartered**
4	**green onions, chopped**
4	**ounces Stilton cheese, sliced**
6-8	**cups mixed greens**

In a small saucepan, combine port with wine, vinegars, pepper, sugar, Worcestershire, molasses, onion powder and oils. Simmer until alcohol has cooked off. Remove from heat; cool off by whisking.

In a sauté pan, heat 1/2 cup vinaigrette and sauté figs and green onions. Combine sliced Stilton and mixed greens in a large bowl; toss with just enough dressing to coat, adding more vinaigrette if needed. Divide salad among 4 plates; spoon sautéed figs and green onions over the top.

HEARTY WINTER GARDEN SALAD

With the inclusion of red kidney beans, red onions, carrots and pear, this is a well-rounded green salad.

EASY • SERVES 4-6

- • Red Wine Vinaigrette
- 1 16-ounce can red kidney beans, rinsed and drained
- 1 head green leaf lettuce, washed, cored and torn
- 1/2 red onion, sliced paper thin
- 2 carrots, peeled and julienned
- 1 pear, diced

Prepare the Red Wine Vinaigrette.

In a medium mixing bowl, toss 1/4 cup vinaigrette with kidney beans. Set aside for 15 minutes while other salad ingredients are prepared. Combine lettuce, red onion, carrot, diced pear and kidney beans in a large salad bowl. Toss with remaining vinaigrette and serve.

Red Wine Vinaigrette

- 1 clove garlic, crushed
- 1/3 cup plus 2 tablespoons red wine vinegar
- 1/2 teaspoon dried oregano
- 1 heaping tablespoon fresh basil, chopped
- 1/2 teaspoon salt
- 1/4 teaspoon freshly ground black pepper
- 2/3 cup olive oil

In a small mixing bowl, combine garlic, vinegar, oregano, basil, salt and pepper. Whisk in olive oil. Make dressing at least 1 hour ahead and refrigerate so flavors blend.

RICE SALAD WITH LEMON TAHINI DRESSING

A hint of North Africa seeps into this delightful cold salad with its use of tahini and cumin, a great side dish for ribs.

AVERAGE • SERVES 8

- 4 1/2-5 cups cooked rice (1 1/2 cups uncooked converted rice)
- 1 cup sliced almonds
- 1/2 pound green beans
- 1/2 pound yellow wax beans (or use all green beans)
- 2 4-ounce cans diced green chilies
- • Lemon Tahini Dressing

Cook rice and cool.

Toast almonds in preheated 350° oven until golden brown, about 8 minutes, stirring occasionally. Set aside to cool.

Cut green and yellow beans into 1" pieces. Cook in large pot of boiling, salted water, uncovered, until crisp-tender, about 5 minutes. Drain and refresh under cold water to stop cooking. Dry on paper towels.

In large bowl combine rice, green and yellow beans, and green chilies.

Make Lemon Tahini Dressing.

Toss dressing with rice mixture. Chill several hours or overnight. Shortly before serving, stir in toasted almonds.

Lemon Tahini Dressing

- 2/3 cup lemon juice
- 2/3 cup tahini
- 2 cloves garlic, minced
- 1 teaspoon cumin
- 3/4 cup parsley, lightly packed
- 1 teaspoon salt
- 1/2 teaspoon pepper
- 2/3 cup extra virgin olive oil

Put lemon juice, tahini, garlic, cumin, parsley, salt and pepper into bowl of food processor (or blender). Process until well-combined, scraping down sides as needed. With motor running, gradually add olive oil through feed tube, until well-combined.

Wild Thing Pasta

The combination of flavors in this winter pasta is incredibly delicious. The addition of winter greens make it a healthy choice, too.

Easy • Serves 6

1/4	cup olive oil
4	garlic cloves, minced
3	cups sliced mushrooms (combination of shiitake, cremini, chanterelle or portobello)
12	ounces penne pasta
10	cups chopped mixed greens (mustard, kale, turnip)
•	salt and pepper to taste
1/4	pound Gorgonzola cheese, crumbled

Fill a large soup pot with water and bring to a boil. While water heats, sauté garlic in olive oil for 1 minute in a large sauté pan. Add mushrooms and cook until wilted, about 4-5 minutes.

Cook pasta in boiling water until *al dente*. Meanwhile, add greens to sauté pan and cook for 5 minutes, until just cooked and tender. Drain pasta. Add to sauté pan and mix together with greens. Season with salt and pepper. Sprinkle Gorgonzola over pasta and mix gently. Serve immediately.

Moravian Chicken Pie

This simply wonderful pie is from Old Salem, a restored 18th-century Moravian village in Winston-Salem, North Carolina. Cooking the chicken and making stock are the secrets to the essence of the sauce. Allow at least 3 hours for this step. Make sure you use a deep 10" pie pan – this pie is full of chicken. Make this!

Easy • Serves 6

Filling:

1	large whole chicken, with liver removed
•	salt and pepper to taste
2	bay leaves
•	Dough
1/4	pound butter
1/2	cup flour
1	quart chicken stock (made from ingredients)
1/4	cup white wine
1	pint half & half
1	dash Tabasco sauce
1	dash Worcestershire sauce
•	egg yolk

Dough

1	cup butter (2 sticks)
3	cups flour
1/2	cup ice water

Cut butter into flour, and add ice water to form a ball. This may be done in the food processor. Separate into two 10-ounce balls, and refrigerate at least 20 minutes, or overnight. If chilled overnight, remove 20 minutes before rolling out.

Roll 1 dough ball into a sheet large enough to fit a deep 10" pie pan. Lightly grease the bottom of the pie pan, and place the bottom sheet of dough in it. Refrigerate until ready to use. Keep other ball of dough chilled until ready to roll out for the top.

Cook chicken in a large pot with just enough water to cover. Cook until the meat is tender and falling off the bone. Let cool, then pick meat off bones, dice and set aside in a bowl. Reserve the cooking water.

Place remaining chicken bones and parts back in the cooking water with a generous amount of salt, pepper and bay leaves. Simmer 2 hours, then strain reserving 1 quart chicken stock.

Make the dough while the chicken is cooling.

For filling: Melt butter in saucepan. Add flour, whisking until smooth. Add reserved chicken stock and wine, and cook until thickened, stirring occasionally. Lower heat and add half & half, Tabasco and Worcestershire, stirring until smooth.

Add 1/2 of cream sauce to picked chicken meat. Pour into bottom piecrust. Cover with rolled-out top pie dough sheet, crimp the edges and make small slits to vent steam from cooking.

Preheat oven to 350°.

To make an egg wash: Mix 1 egg yolk with a small amount of water. Brush egg wash over crust for a glossy shine. Bake until golden, about 45 minutes. Spoon the remaining cream sauce warm over each slice of chicken pie at serving time.

Dottie's Everyday Roast Beef

This is Dottie Martin's recipe that she shared with ***Taste Full*** *while her husband, Jim, was governor of North Carolina.*

Easy • A large roast serves 12

- • **eye of round roast**
- 1 1/2 **cups soy sauce**
- 1/2 **cup honey**
- 1 **tablespoon curry powder**
- 1 **teaspoon salt**
- 1/2 **teaspoon cinnamon**
- 1 **tablespoon candied ginger (or ground ginger)**
- 3 **cloves garlic, minced**

Place meat in a plastic bag. In small bowl, whisk all ingredients together, then pour sauce over the roast. Marinate for 24 hours in refrigerator, turning the roast 2-3 times during the 24-hour period.

Remove roast from bag, and place in a roasting pan. Pour sauce over the roast. Bake, uncovered for 30 minutes at 350° (do not open oven door). After 30 minutes, turn heat back to 150° and leave roast in oven for 3 hours.

Roast will be medium rare (and delicious!). This is enough marinade for any size roast. The leftovers make delicious sandwiches.

Ragoût Of Pork And Sausage With Apples

Pork, tangy apples and onions steep winter warmth into this hearty casserole.

Average • Serves 8

- 2 **pounds loose pork sausage, cooked and drained**
- 1/4-1/2 **cup olive oil, divided**
- 3 **pounds pork loin, cut in bite-size cubes**
- 2 **cups celery, cut into 1" pieces**
- 3 **Granny Smith apples, peeled and diced**
- 1 **cup coarsely chopped white onion**
- 2 **tablespoons flour**
- 1 **teaspoon dried rosemary**
- 1 **teaspoon dried, rubbed sage**
- 1 **teaspoon dried leaf thyme**
- 2 **cups beef stock**
- 1/2 **cup chopped fresh parsley**

In a large skillet over medium-high heat, cook the sausage until brown and crisp. Remove to a heavy casserole dish. Heat 2 tablespoons olive oil. In the same skillet, brown the pork pieces. Remove pork and place in the casserole. Next sauté the celery, apple and onion in the same skillet until soft, adding more olive oil if needed; place in the casserole. Still using the skillet, now add the flour and dry seasonings (except for the parsley), adding more olive oil if needed to make a *roux* or paste. Whisk in the beef stock and bring to a boil on the stove top. Let mixture boil for 3-4 minutes only. Pour over casserole ingredients. Cover casserole and cook in a 350° oven for 1 1/2-2 hours. Serve over pasta or rice. Garnish each dish with parsley.

Eggs Timberlake

Named for a man who's a household name in the art world but among friends is known for his passion for good food – where to find and share it.

Easy • Serves 6

2 pounds North Carolina pork barbecue, preferably Lexington style
6 eggs
• salt and pepper to taste
• Zesty Tomato Sauce

Preheat oven to 400°.

Divide barbecue among 6 individual ramekins (or use an 8" x 8" pan). Put ramekins onto cookie sheet for easier handling. Cover with foil and bake in oven until hot, about 15 minutes. Remove from oven and remove foil. With the back of a spoon, make a well in the center of the barbecue in each ramekin. Break 1 egg into each. Sprinkle egg with salt and pepper. Return to oven and bake, uncovered, 8-10 minutes until eggs are cooked. Serve immediately, putting each ramekin on a serving plate. Top with Zesty Tomato Sauce.

Zesty Tomato Sauce:

4 strips bacon, cut up
1 cup diced green pepper
1/2 cup chopped green onions
1/2 teaspoon red pepper flakes
1/2 teaspoon dry mustard
1 14.5-ounce can diced tomatoes

In medium skillet, fry bacon over medium heat until fat is released, 3-4 minutes. Add green pepper and green onions and sauté 5 minutes, until tender. Sprinkle with red pepper flakes and dry mustard; stir briefly. Add tomatoes and bring to a boil. Reduce heat to low, cover and cook 5 minutes.

Note: This sauce can be made a day or 2 ahead and reheated just before serving.

Wine & Fruit Compote

A delicious way to prepare fresh fruit ahead, particularly delicate pears and apples without any worry of the fruit turning brown. Serve hot or at room temperature.

4 tablespoons butter
1 tablespoon cornstarch
2 tablespoons brown sugar
1/2 teaspoon cinnamon
1/2 cup orange juice
1/2 cup dry red wine
1 tablespoon orange zest
2 Granny Smith apples
2 red pears
1 cup red grapes, cut in half if large
1 orange, peeled and sectioned

Preheat oven to 350°.

In medium saucepan over low heat, melt butter. Mix together cornstarch, brown sugar and cinnamon. Add to butter and cook, stirring, 1 minute. Add orange juice and red wine and bring to a boil. Stir in orange zest. Core and slice apples and pears (no need to peel unless you prefer). Put into 11" x 8" or 9" x 9" baking pan. Top with grapes and orange sections. Pour sauce over the top. Bake in 350° oven for 40 minutes until fruit is tender.

An inscription carved into a table in Bob Timberlake's studio: Be not forgetful to entertain strangers, for thereby some have entertained angels unawares. – Hebrews 13:2

Roasted Quail with Goat Cheese

This recipe by Chef Tom Young of Expressions Restaurant in Hendersonville, North Carolina, features quail wrapped in hickory-smoked bacon and may be served as an appetizer or an entrée. Young suggests side dishes of polenta or wild rice cakes when serving this dish as an entrée.

Average • Serves 4

8	**quail (semi-boneless)**
•	**salt and cracked black pepper**
1	**cup goat cheese**
1/4	**cup sun-dried tomatoes, diced**
1/2	**teaspoon thyme leaves**
1	**tablespoon chopped parsley**
16	**slices bacon, hickory-smoked**
3/4	**cup olive oil**

Preheat oven to 350°. Cut quail in half and lay on baking sheet, skin side down. Season with salt and pepper. In mixing bowl, combine goat cheese, sun-dried tomatoes, thyme and parsley and mix together.

Dividing cheese mixture evenly among the birds, place a dollop of cheese near the breast section and wrap each half of quail with 1 slice of bacon (it will wrap around twice.) Place back on baking sheet. Drizzle quail with olive oil and cracked pepper and bake at 350° for 8-10 minutes or until done.

To serve, place on serving platter, drizzle with olive oil and fresh chopped parsley.

Jerry's Venison

This recipe for venison from Chef Jerry Rouse of Jerry's Food, Wine & Spirits in Wilmington, North Carolina, features either tenderloins or medallions of venison. Quickly sear on both sides over a charcoal fire and serve with fresh vegetables and robust wines.

Easy • Serves 6

6	**8-ounce venison steaks or 2 venison tenderloins**
2	**tablespoons minced garlic**
1/2	**bottle good Cabernet Sauvignon**
1/2	**cup Italian dressing**
1/2	**cup minced shallots**
1/2	**stalk upper leaves of celery, small diced**
1	**large red onion, sliced**
1	**cup olive oil**
1/2	**cup chopped fresh parsley**

Place venison in a large Pyrex dish. Prepare marinade by combining the remaining ingredients. Pour over venison. Marinate 4-6 hours in refrigerator.

Place on hot charcoal grill. Cook quickly on both sides to desired doneness. For tenderloins, grill about 6-8 minutes per side. Serve immediately.

Country Ham Risotto

A risotto made with two Southern favorites that will ensure your good fortune into the new year – country ham pork for health and turnip greens for lots of ready cash!

Average • Serves 6

1/2	pound country ham
1/2	pound turnip greens
1	tablespoon vegetable oil
2	tablespoons butter
3/4	cup chopped onion
1	cup Arborio rice
3	cups hot chicken stock
1	cup hot cooked corn

Cut ham into small pieces. Thoroughly wash greens by soaking twice in 2 changes of clean water. Drain dry and remove large stems. Cut greens into thin strips. In a large skillet, heat oil and sauté ham over medium-high heat until it begins to brown. Stir in greens and toss until they wilt. Set aside.

In a large heavy saucepan, melt butter over medium heat and sauté onions for 3 minutes. Stir in rice to coat well. Add hot stock 1/2 cup at a time and continue to stir until all the liquid is absorbed before the next addition. When all the stock is incorporated, about 20-25 minutes, the risotto will be creamy yet slightly firm. Remove from heat. Quickly reheat ham, greens and corn in the skillet, and stir into risotto. Serve immediately over the bed of Turnip Greens.

Turnip Greens

This is an essential recipe for your New Year's fortune. Earmark this recipe for lots more meals throughout the year.

3	pounds turnip greens
2	tablespoons olive oil
2	tablespoons minced garlic
2	teaspoons balsamic vinegar
•	salt and pepper to taste

Carefully wash greens by soaking them in at least 2 changes of clean water. Remove large stems and discard; coarsely chop leaves. In a large skillet, soup pot or high-sided sauté pan, heat olive oil and sauté garlic over medium-high for 2 minutes. Add greens and stir to cook evenly about 5 minutes or until greens have wilted and taste tender. Toss in balsamic vinegar, salt and pepper. Divide among 6 plates and use as a bed for risotto, black-eyed pea cakes and roasted vegetables.

Southern Game Hens with Pecan Cornbread Stuffing

Petite birds filled with pecan cornbread stuffing studded with colorful dried fruit. A quick and easy entrée for a smaller feast, even the Light Sherry Gravy, akin to an au jus, doesn't weigh the palate down. The hens are split in half for easier eating. The recipe calls for cooked cornbread but you may substitute cornbread stuffing.

Average• Serves 8

4 Cornish game hens
1 cup dried cranberries
1/2 cup chopped dried apricots
1/2 cup golden raisins
1/2 cup boiling water
1 cup dry sherry, divided
4 tablespoons butter
1 cup finely diced celery
2 tablespoons minced shallots
4 cups crumbled cornbread (or substitute 8 ounces cornbread stuffing)
1/2 cup chopped pecans
1 1/2 tablespoons minced fresh sage leaves
1 teaspoon ground thyme
1 teaspoon salt
1/2 teaspoon black pepper
2 cups chicken broth

Wash Cornish hens and pat dry. Split in half with kitchen shears by cutting down the center of the breast and then down the center of the back. Cut out backbone and remove excess skin. Set aside and make stuffing.

In a small bowl, soak dried fruit in boiling water and 1/2 cup sherry for 15 minutes. Drain fruit, reserving liquid. In a large skillet, melt butter and sauté celery and shallots until soft. Stir in cornbread, pecans, fruit, sage and thyme. Add enough reserved liquid to moisten; season with salt and pepper.

Preheat oven to 400°. Gently lift the skin of each hen half, loosening the pocket over the breast and thigh. Fill generously with stuffing. Brush birds with melted butter and sprinkle with salt and pepper. Bake at 400° for 15 minutes. Reduce heat to 350°, baste and bake 30 minutes more. The skin should be brown and crispy, and the juices will run clear when pierced with a fork. Remove hens to a large platter and keep warm.

To make Light Sherry Gravy: Deglaze the pan over the burner with remaining 1/2 cup sherry. Scrape drippings and sherry into a saucepan and add chicken broth. Bring to boil. Simmer 10 minutes and strain sauce into a gravy bowl and ladle over each serving.

The Ritual, 1986

In the rural South of Bob Timberlake's youth, a large stack of firewood was essential – for the fireplaces that heated the house, for the cast iron kitchen stove and for curing tobacco before barns were heated with kerosene. After the wood was split and stacked, it was time to go duck hunting.

Roasted Winter Vegetables with Colcannon

A savory vegetarian "stew" that has plenty of "oomph." Colcannon is traditionally an Irish dish of cabbage and potatoes; ***Taste Full*** *substituted kale for cabbage, and mashed the potatoes. So the vegetables won't cook to nothing in liquid, they are roasted and, once the dish is plated, moistened with a little fresh vegetable stock.*

Average • Serves 4

- 2 cups vegetable stock, see page 173
- • Colcannon
- 1 zucchini
- 1 yelow squash
- 1 red bell pepper
- 1 acorn squash
- 12 baby carrots, cut in half on the bias
- 6 tablespoons olive oil, divided
- 2 tablespoons chopped fresh rosemary, divided
- • salt and pepper to taste
- 2 portobello mushrooms, cut into julienne strips
- 2 leeks, white part only

Prepare vegetable stock (or use vegetarian bouillon cubes) and set aside. Ready ingredients for Colcannon and time according to roasted vegetable preparation.

Preheat oven to 425°. Cut zucchini, yellow squash and red peppers in half lengthwise and then into 1" pieces. Peel and dice acorn squash to match. Mix vegetables including carrots in a large bowl with 5 tablespoons of the olive oil and 1 1/2 tablespoons of the rosemary. Sprinkle with salt and pepper. Place in a roasting pan and bake for 10 minutes, tossing occasionally. Remove stems from mushrooms and cut into julienne strips. Cut the leeks to match. Toss with remaining olive oil and rosemary and add to the vegetables in oven. Roast about 20 minutes more, stirring occasionally until vegetables are lightly browned.

Make Colcannon.

To plate: In a shallow soup plate arrange Colcannon in center, piled high. Scatter roasted vegetables around potatoes, moisten all with hot vegetable stock, up to 1/2 cup. Garnish potatoes with rosemary sprigs.

Colcannon

- 5 large Idaho potatoes, peeled and quartered
- 1 large onion, cut in small dice
- 2 cups kale, rinsed and coarsely chopped
- 5 tablespoons butter, divided
- 1/2 cup milk
- 1/2 teaspoon salt
- 1/2 teaspoon pepper

Place potatoes and onions in large pot of cold salted water. Bring to a boil and cook until potatoes are tender. In large pan over medium heat, sauté kale in 1 tablespoon of butter for about 5 minutes until just wilted.

In small saucepan, combine milk and 4 tablespoons butter. Simmer for 3 minutes, turn off heat and set aside. Drain potatoes and mash with a hand masher. Add kale. Strain in enough of the milk mixture until potatoes are moist and fluffy. Adjust seasonings.

A vegetarian dish that non-vegetarians can love, Roasted Vegetables with Colcannon is so filling that you'll never miss the meat.

Rummed Pork Roast with Dried Cherries and Ginger

Outstanding! Cherry, pistachio stuffing and ginger marmalade glaze turn an everyday pork roast into something exquisite. Definitely try this one.

Average • Serves 10

1 cup dried cherries
1/2 cup dark rum
1 tablespoon candied ginger, chopped
1/2 teaspoon fennel seed, crushed
4 cups soft bread crumbs
6 tablespoons butter, divided
1/2 cup coarsely chopped pistachios
1 teaspoon salt
1 teaspoon pepper
1/4 cup chicken stock or apple juice (or a bit more as needed)
1 5-pound boneless pork loin roast
2 tablespoons olive oil
2/3 cup ginger preserves
1 tablespoon dark rum

Place the cherries, rum, ginger and fennel seed in a small glass bowl. Cover and microwave on high for 1 minute. Allow to stand covered for 1 hour.

Preheat oven to 400°.

Mix the breadcrumbs, 4 tablespoons of melted butter, pistachios, fruit mixture, salt, pepper and chicken stock or apple juice, adding more liquid if needed to make a moist stuffing. Set aside.

Cut the pork loin to form a long sheet: starting on the long side, cut meat about 1/2" above the level of the cutting board, continuously cutting and rolling the loin until a single even sheet is formed. (If the loin has been cut into 2 pieces when boned, just overlap slightly and continue cutting.)

Sprinkle with salt and pepper if desired.

Spread the stuffing on the pork and roll up the loin (similar to a jelly roll), tying it securely with butchers' string.

Heat remaining 2 tablespoons butter and the olive oil in a large heavy skillet. Sear and brown the stuffed loin on all sides. Put the loin into the oven, then reduce the temperature to 325° and roast, allowing a cooking time of 25 minutes per pound, or, until a meat thermometer registers 150°-155°. (A 5-pound loin will take around 2 hours or a bit longer.)

Combine ginger preserves and rum; brush over roast during the last 35 minutes of cooking time.

Allow roast to rest for 20 minutes before slicing. This preserves the juices. Remove string and slice.

Golden brown and succulent – what better way to chase winter's chill than with this Rummed Pork Roast? Hiding in the stuffing are dried cherries, a bite of last summer's harvest in the dead of winter.

BONELESS LAMB LOIN WITH BOURBON MOLASSES SAUCE

This lamb dish shared by the Five Diamond Fearrington House in rural Chatham County near Chapel Hill, North Carolina, is spectacular. Ask the butcher to cut boneless lamb loins. Each will be approximately the width of 2 lamb chops. Serve with Wild Basmati Rice Timbales on page 183 and the Cascade of Color Green Beans on page 176. The bourbon sauce could be made ahead and reheated before serving.

EASY • SERVES 4

4	**6-ounce boneless lamb loins**
•	**salt and ground pepper**
1/2	**cup bourbon**
1/2	**cup molasses**
3	**cups beef stock**
1	**bay leaf**
1	**rosemary sprig**
2	**shallots, chopped**
2	**cloves garlic, crushed**
2	**tablespoons butter, room temperature**

Preheat oven to 400°. Trim as much fat as possible from lamb loins. Season with salt and pepper.

In large, hot sauté pan, sear on all sides and both ends until caramelized. Transfer to rack on a baking pan and move to oven. Bake about 8-10 minutes for medium rare.

In small saucepan, combine bourbon and molasses and bring to a boil. Add beef stock, bay leaf, rosemary, shallots and garlic. Simmer until reduced to 1-1 1/2 cups. Strain into a bowl and swirl in butter.

Slice lamb loins against the grain into 4-5 slices per portion and top with sauce.

ROSEMARY LAMB WITH VEGETABLES

A quick and simple one-pan dish. Serve with caesar salad or winter greens.

EASY • SERVES 4

1 1/2	**teaspoons salt**
1/2	**teaspoon crushed rosemary leaves**
1/8	**teaspoon pepper**
4	**lamb shoulder steaks (about 6 ounces each)**
3	**tablespoons butter, divided**
1	**leek, sliced**
1	**cup finely chopped carrots**
1/4	**cup chopped onion**
2	**tablespoons flour**
1	**cup chicken broth**
1/2	**cup dry white wine**
•	**snipped fresh parsley**

Mix salt, rosemary and pepper; press onto steak surfaces. Heat 1 tablespoon butter in large skillet until hot. Brown steaks in butter; remove.

Add remaining butter to skillet; reduce heat and sauté leeks, carrots and onion until onion is golden, stirring constantly. Add flour. Cook and stir until bubbly. Stir in broth and wine. Heat to boiling, stirring constantly; reduce heat.

Return steaks to skillet. Simmer covered about 45 minutes. Serve steaks topped with vegetable mixture; sprinkle with parsley.

Boneless Lamb Loin with Bourbon Molasses Sauce

Lash Larue, Roy Rogers, Gene Autry – these silver screen cowboys from the 1940s and 50s mediated clashes on the western range between cattle ranchers who got there first and wanted to continue letting their cattle roam free, and the sheepherders who fenced their flocks and pastures. Huge herds of cattle and small flocks of sheep meant cattle was king. Hollywood embellished the conflict, but it's more than just a Hollywood tale that beef, being more plentiful, graced more tables. Traditionally lamb has been the other red meat in the United States. It's a flavorful, robust main course, and most worthy of a special occasion meal.

Stuffed Beef Tenderloin

Spinach, mushroom, and blue cheese stuffing is rolled up jellyroll fashion in the most tender cut of all – the tenderloin. Surround the beef slices with a wreath of broccoli-stuffed Italian tomatoes for a festive presentation. This stuffed tenderloin is good either hot or cold. To serve on a cold buffet, prepare as below. Cool, then chill and slice. When cold, the slices can be cut thinner to serve about 12.

AVERAGE • SERVES 8

- 2 1/2 pounds beef tenderloin, 8" long
- 1/2 cup chopped walnuts
- 1 10-ounce package fresh spinach, washed
- 4 tablespoons butter, divided
- 1/4 cup chopped shallots
- 1/2 pound mushrooms, chopped
- 1 clove garlic, minced
- 2 tablespoons Madeira
- 1 6-ounce Saga Blue Cheese (1 1/2 cups crumbled)
- 1/2 teaspoon thyme
- • salt and ground pepper
- 4-5 bay leaves
- • Saga Cream Sauce

To prepare tenderloin, cut into an 8" x 11" x 3/4" rectangle: cut the long edge of meat 1/3 of thickness down from top, across to about 1/2" from opposite edge; open out like a book. Starting from where the other cut ended, cut back in opposite direction. Open into a flat rectangle. Pound lightly to even the thickness of the meat. Set aside.

Toast walnuts on cookie sheet in 325° oven for 10 minutes, stirring occasionally. Set aside to cool.

Place spinach in large pot; do not add water. Sprinkle with salt. Cover and cook over medium heat until wilted, about 5 minutes. Drain and refresh under cold water. Squeeze water from spinach and dry on paper towels. Chop roughly to yield about 1 cup. Set aside.

Heat 2 tablespoons of butter in skillet over medium-high heat. Add shallots and mushrooms. Sauté 4 minutes. Add reserved spinach and garlic. Sauté a few seconds more. Add Madeira. Boil until reduced and fairly dry. Turn heat to low. Stir in crumbled blue cheese, reserved walnuts, thyme, salt and pepper. Cook, stirring, just until cheese melts. Cool.

Preheat oven to 425°. Sprinkle tenderloin with salt and pepper. Spread filling over meat leaving 1/2" margin on edges. Roll up like a jellyroll. Tie with butcher's string at 1 1/2" intervals. Tuck bay leaves in string. Rub with remaining 2 tablespoons butter. Place in shallow roasting pan. Roast until meat thermometer reaches about 140° for medium-done meat, about 40 minutes. Let sit 10-15 minutes before slicing. Remove string and discard bay leaves. Slice into 1" thick pieces. Serve with Saga Cream Sauce.

Saga Cream Sauce

- 1 cup whipping cream
- 2 tablespoons Madeira, divided
- 1/4 teaspoon thyme
- 1 2-ounce Saga blue cheese (about 1/2 cup crumbled)
- • salt and pepper

In medium saucepan combine cream, 1 tablespoon Madeira and thyme. Bring to a boil and reduce by half. Skim fat from roasting pan and add remaining tablespoon of Madeira to the pan. Deglaze by heating over medium-high heat scraping any browned bits from pan; add to cream sauce. Reduce heat to low. Add blue cheese; cook stirring just until melted. Season with salt and pepper. Spoon over slices of hot stuffed tenderloin.

To serve cold, leave out meat juices and chill. Thin with another tablespoon or so of Madeira until desired thickness. Serve with cold sliced tenderloin. Makes about 1/2 cup sauce.

Roasted Baby Pheasant with Caramelized Apples

Flanked by quickly caramelized onions and apples and finished off with a light sherry gravy, this pheasant entrée headlines a truly memorable dinner.

Allow 1/2 pheasant per serving with a few extra for the ever hungry. The most difficult part of the recipe is preparing the pheasant for the pan, which may be done hours ahead. Removing the wishbone prior to cooking will facilitate halving and eating the pheasant.

Average • Serves 8

- **8** — **3/4-1 pound farm-raised baby pheasant or six 1-1 1/4 pound farm-raised pheasant**
- **4** — **cups water**
- **1/2** — **onion, coarsely chopped**
- **1** — **medium carrot, coarsely chopped**
- **1** — **large celery stalk, coarsely chopped**
- **2** — **sprigs parsley**
- **•** — **salt and pepper to taste**
- **•** — **olive oil**
- **•** — **sage leaves (8 per pheasant) plus 1 large sprig for each**
- **1** — **large lemon, cut into 8 wedges**
- **•** — **butcher's string**
- **1/3** — **cup sherry**
- **4** — **Granny Smith apples**
- **3** — **tablespoons butter**
- **1** — **large onion, thinly sliced**
- **2** — **tablespoons balsamic vinegar**
- **1** — **tablespoon honey**
- **1** — **tablespoon chopped fresh sage**
- **•** — **Pheasant Gravy**

Remove giblets from pheasant. Wash both birds and pat dry. Place giblets in a large pot with water. Add onion, carrot, celery and parsley. Bring to a boil. Reduce heat and simmer 1 hour for broth. Strain and reserve broth for gravy.

Cut off wing tips of pheasants. Gently loosen skin from breast, upper legs and thighs, being careful not to tear. Season under the skin and inside the cavity with salt and pepper. Rub under the skin with olive oil and tuck whole fresh sage leaves under skin, pulling skin back to cover. Tuck a wedge of lemon and a large sage sprig inside each cavity. As these baby pheasant are too small to truss, tie each with string to secure legs and wings close to the body. Rub outside of bird with olive oil and sprinkle with salt and pepper. The pheasant can be made ahead to this point and stored in the refrigerator.

About an hour and a half before mealtime, brown pheasants under preheated broiler, turning to brown all sides, about 10 minutes. Do not crowd them, but broil in 2 batches for more even browning. Arrange in a roasting pan and roast in a preheated 325° oven for 15 minutes. Pour sherry over pheasant using 1 tablespoon per bird. Continue roasting until meat thermometer inserted just inside the leg joint registers 165°, about 10-15 minutes more. Do not overcook as pheasant dries out quickly.

Meanwhile, peel and core apples; cut in half, then slice each half into 1/2" slices. Melt butter in a large skillet over medium-high heat; add sliced onion and sauté 2 minutes. Add drained apples and chopped sage, cooking until apples are brown on both sides. Add vinegar and honey and simmer 1 minute more. Remove from pan and keep warm. Do not rinse skillet; save to make the gravy.

Remove string and split pheasant in half down the breastbone. Serve with Caramelized Apples and onions. Garnish with fresh sage. Serve gravy on the side.

Pheasant Gravy

- 1 — cup sherry
- 3 — tablespoons butter
- 2 1/2 — tablespoons flour
- 2 1/2 — cups reserved giblet broth
- 1 — teaspoon salt, or to taste
- 1/2 — teaspoon white pepper

Place roasting pan from cooked pheasant directly on a medium-high burner. Deglaze the pan by adding sherry and stirring to incorporate any browned bits from the pan. Set aside.

Using the apple/onion skillet, melt butter over medium-high heat. Stir in flour and cook until flour is quite brown, about 3 minutes. (This is called a brown *roux*.) Whisk in the 2 1/2 cups of the giblet broth, salt and pepper. Whisk until smooth; simmer 5 minutes to blend flavors.

Chestnut Mousse

This seasonal dessert is especially light and flavorful. It's a new and unusual way to finish Thanksgiving's bountiful feast.

Easy • Serves 8

1	**cup milk**
1	**pound chestnut purée (available in specialty food stores)**
1/2	**cup confectioners' sugar**
1	**tablespoon brandy**
2	**teaspoons vanilla extract**
1 1/2	**cups heavy cream, whipped**

In a double boiler, heat the milk with the chestnut purée and blend well with a mixer. Mix in confectioners' sugar, brandy and vanilla. Continue to blend until very smooth. Set aside to cool. In a separate bowl, beat the heavy cream until stiff. Fold in the cooled chestnut mixture until the brown and white colors are well mixed. Spoon into custard cups or ramekins and garnish with a dollop of whipped cream and/or chocolate shavings.

Scottish Cranachan

A dessert developed from the memory of a divine concoction of cream and toasted oatmeal on the Isle of Skye, Scotland. Drambuie, a Scotch-based liqueur sweetened with honey, adds the punch to this simple yet very appealing dessert. Oatmeal is such a staple of Scotland that it comes in three different grinds. The Gerber brand of baby oatmeal substitues well for the "fine" Scottish grind.

Easy • Serves 4-6

4	**ounces Gerber brand baby oatmeal**
3	**ounces Drambuie**
2	**tablespoons honey**
2	**cups whipping cream**
8	**ounces cream cheese, softened, cut into bits**
2-2 1/2	**cups fresh raspberries, depending on flute size**
•	**mint leaves for garnish**

Toast the oatmeal in a nonstick skillet for 2-3 minutes. Wet the toasted oatmeal with Drambuie and honey. In a medium bowl, whip cream until it doubles in volume; whip in softened cream cheese. Mix in the oatmeal/Drambuie mixture. To serve: spoon mix into champagne flutes, alternating with fresh raspberries and ending with cream mixture. Garnish with 1 raspberry and a mint leaf.

Christmas Crown Cake

Resembling a jeweled crown, this rich chocolate cake is sure to bring "oohs" and "aahs" from your holiday guests. It can be made ahead and frozen whole or sliced into layers, separated by sheets of waxed paper. Thaw and frost a day before serving.

Average • Serves 16

- 1 3/4 cups vegetable shortening
- 2 1/2 cups sugar
- 3 eggs, separated
- 2 whole eggs
- 2 teaspoons vanilla extract
- 3 cups cake flour
- 1 cup cocoa
- 1 1/2 teaspoons baking powder
- 1 teaspoon soda
- 1 teaspoon salt
- 3/4 cup strong coffee
- 3/4 cup milk
- • glacéed cherries
- 16 pecan halves

Grease a 10" heavy cast aluminum bundt pan. Preheat oven to 350°.

Cream shortening and sugar until light and fluffy. Beat in 3 egg yolks. Beat in 2 whole eggs and vanilla. In separate bowl, sift together cake flour, cocoa, baking powder, soda and salt. Combine coffee and milk. Add flour mixture to batter alternately with the liquid ingredients, beginning and ending with flour.

With clean mixer and bowl, beat reserved egg whites until stiff peaks form. Stir about 1/3 into cake batter. Fold in remaining egg whites. Pour into prepared pan. Bake for 55 minutes or until cake tester or toothpick comes out clean. Cool 5 minutes in pan. Turn out on wire rack to cool.

Prepare Cointreau Syrup, Orange Buttercream, Orange Filling and Candied Orange Peel on page 176. When completely cool, cut cake into 4 layers. Mark the cake for reassembling the layers with a vertical strip of frosting on 1 side. Set each layer on a cake circle or several layers of foil for easier handling. Place bottom layer on cake plate. Drizzle with 1/4 Cointreau Syrup. Spread with 1/3 of Orange Pecan Filling. Repeat with next 2 layers. Carefully drizzle bottom of top layer with syrup; set on top of cake. Ice with Orange Buttercream. Decorate with long strips of candied orange peel so that 2 pieces form a triangle with the bottom edge of the cake. Place a glacéed cherry at the top of each triangle. Arrange 16 pecan halves along top of cake. Chill thoroughly.

Cointreau Syrup

- 1/3 cup sugar
- 1/3 cup water
- 1/3 cup Cointreau

Bring sugar and water to a boil, stirring to dissolve sugar. Reduce heat. Simmer 5 minutes. Remove from heat. Add Cointreau. Cool.

Orange Buttercream

- 1 1/3 cups sugar, divided
- 3/4 cup orange juice
- 3 tablespoons corn syrup
- 3 egg whites
- 1 1/4 cups butter, softened
- 3 tablespoons Cointreau

In small saucepan, boil 1 cup sugar, orange juice and corn syrup until it reaches soft ball stage or 238° on candy thermometer. Beat egg whites until soft peaks form. Gradually beat in 1/3 cup sugar, until stiff and glossy. Add hot sugar syrup to egg white mixture in a stream, beating constantly, until very firm. Cool.

Beat butter until fluffy. Gradually add egg white mixture, beating constantly. Add Cointreau, beating until very smooth.

Orange Filling

- 1 cup Orange Buttercream
- 1 1/4 cups chopped pecans
- 1 cup orange marmalade

Combine all ingredients.

From the simplest homes comes the most eloquent food.

– Unknown

Walter's Chocolate Bread Pudding

This recipe from Walter Royal of the legendary Angus Barn in Raleigh, North Carolina, is what comfort food is all about. Serve with whipped cream.

Easy • Serves 6-8

1	**French baguette**
1 1/2	**cups semisweet chocolate chips, divided**
5	**eggs**
1 1/2	**cups sugar**
1 1/2	**cups milk**
1 1/2	**cups heavy cream**
3	**tablespoons melted butter**
1 1/2	**tablespoons vanilla extract**
1	**teaspoon cinnamon**
3/4	**cup raisins**

Cut bread into 1/4" thick slices, set aside. In top of double boiler, melt 1 cup of the chocolate chips, set aside. In a large bowl, whisk together eggs and sugar. Whisk in milk, cream, melted butter, vanilla and cinnamon. Grease the bottom and sides of an 8" x 8" baking pan and put a layer of the bread slices in the bottom. Drizzle with half of the melted chocolate and sprinkle with 1/3 of the raisins. Add another layer of bread slices; drizzle with remaining melted chocolate and sprinkle with 1/2 of remaining raisins. Add final layer of bread and sprinkle with remaining raisins. Pour milk mixture over the final layer and press bread with fingers. Let rest several minutes and press again. Repeat 2 more times to insure bread is saturated with milk. Place in a larger baking pan or roasting pan. Pour hot (almost boiling) water into pan going about 1/2-2/3 way up sides of pudding pan. Bake at 350° for 1 hour and 15 minutes or until knife comes out clean. Add remaining 1/2 cup chocolate chips to top of hot pudding. Let sit 5 minutes, then spread chocolate. (Or, melt chocolate and drizzle over top.) Let rest another 5 minutes before serving.

Mama's Soggy Coconut Cake

*Her grandmother's make-ahead dessert was shared with **Taste Full** by Jo Ann P. Foreman of Elizabeth City.*

Average • Serves 8-10

4	**eggs**
2	**cups sugar**
2	**cups flour**
1/2	**teaspoon salt**
3/4	**cup boiling water**
2	**teaspoons baking powder**
•	**Coconut Filling**

Heat oven to 350°. Line three 8"-cake pans with wax paper circles. Beat eggs well, then add sugar and beat. Measure flour, then sift with salt. Add to eggs and sugar. Pour boiling water over this mixture, then stir in baking powder. Divide evenly between the 3 cake pans. Cook about 30 minutes until layers are brown. Cool, then remove from pans.

Spread coconut filling between cake layers and on top. The sides are not iced. Refrigerate overnight before serving.

Coconut Filling

2	6-ounce packages frozen coconut
1/2	cup sugar
1 1/2	cups skim milk
1	teaspoon vanilla extract

Mix ingredients together.

Applejack Cake

A recipe fine-tuned over the years by a special subscriber, the late Laura Armstrong, who was both cook and friend to Elizabeth's paternal grandparents, and later her great aunt. Since Katy and Charlie Norfleet's grandchildren weren't big fans of the traditional fruitcake, Laura developed this cake as an alternative for the Christmas holiday.

Easy • Serves 14-16

- 2 cups sugar
- 1 1/2 cups corn oil
- 3 eggs
- 3 cups all-purpose flour
- 1 teaspoon baking soda
- 1 teaspoon salt
- 1/2 teaspoon cinnamon
- 1/2 teaspoon nutmeg
- 2 teaspoons vanilla extract
- 2 cups peeled apples, chopped
- 1 cup chopped pecans
- 1/2 cup golden raisins
- • Applejack Glaze

Cream sugar and corn oil together. Beat in eggs 1 at a time.

Sift flour with soda, salt, cinnamon and nutmeg into a separate bowl. Slowly beat into creamed mixture. Add vanilla. Fold in apples, pecans and raisins by hand.

Preheat oven to 300°. Pour batter into greased 8-cup Kugelhopf mold or large bundt pan. Bake 2 hours. Pour Glaze over cake in pan right out of the oven. Cool in pan, then remove to a cake tin. This cake is best made a few days before serving; the flavors just improve as they meld together. A little more Applejack never hurts either!

Applejack Glaze

- 1/2 cup applejack brandy
- 1/2 cup apple juice
- 1/4 cup brown sugar
- 2 tablespoons butter

In a small saucepan, mix brandy, apple juice, brown sugar and butter. Bring to a boil to dissolve sugar. Pour over cake.

Old-Fashioned Red Velvet Cake

This recipe was shared by Wanda Matthews Cardullo of New Bern. It was her mother, Valle Stallings Hollstein's recipe. Moist, old-fashioned – make it for your next family gathering.

Average • Serves 8-10

- 2 1/2 cups all-purpose flour
- 2 cups sugar
- 1 cup buttermilk
- 2 eggs
- 1 tablespoon cider vinegar
- 1 teaspoon baking soda
- 1 teaspoon vanilla
- 1 1/2 cups cooking oil
- 1 ounce red food coloring
- • Pecan Frosting

Preheat oven to 350°. Combine all ingredients and mix well by hand. Grease and flour three 8" pans. Bake for 25-30 minutes. Cool slightly and turn out onto a rack to completely cool. Carefully split the layers in half to yield 6 layers. Spread frosting between layers and over top, leaving sides alone to show off their red color. Garnish with pecan halves and cherries.

Pecan Frosting

- 1 stick margarine or butter
- 8 ounces cream cheese, softened
- 1 pound powdered sugar
- 1 cup chopped pecans

Cream butter and cream cheese. Beat in sugar. Carefully blend in pecans.

Banana Layer Cake with Cream Cheese Icing

For banana lovers, pecan nuts only enhance its richness.

Average • Serves 12

- 6 bananas, divided
- 1/2 cup butter, softened
- 1 1/4 cups sugar
- 2 eggs
- 1 teaspoon vanilla extract
- 2 1/4 cups all-purpose flour
- 2 1/4 teaspoons baking powder
- 1/2 teaspoon salt
- 1/2 teaspoon baking soda
- 1/4 pound pecan halves, divided
- • Cream Cheese Icing

Grease and flour two 10"-cake pans. Preheat oven to 350°.

In a large bowl, cream 5 bananas with butter, sugar and eggs. Beat for 3 minutes. Add vanilla and mix well. Add flour, baking powder, salt and baking soda; beat until well blended.

Finely chop enough pecans to measure 1/2 cup. Save a few pecan halves for garnish. By hand, mash the remaining banana and add with nuts into batter; mix until blended but still lumpy.

Divide batter among prepared cake pans. Bake for 25 minutes or until a toothpick inserted in the center of the cake comes out clean. Remove cakes from oven; cool on racks in pans for 10 minutes. Turn onto racks and cool completely. While the cakes are cooling, prepare the icing.

To assemble cake: Carefully slice each cooled cake layer in half with a long serrated knife to yield 4 layers. Dab a bit of icing on a cake plate to hold the cake in place. Place 1 cake layer on plate. Ice with 1/4 of the icing. Repeat the process with the other 3 layers. Do not ice the sides. Decorate top of cake with pecan halves. Store in the refrigerator.

Cream Cheese Icing

- 1 8-ounce package cream cheese, softened
- 1/4 cup butter, softened
- 1 tablespoon banana extract
- 1 teaspoon vanilla extract
- 1 teaspoon salt
- 1 1/2-2 cups confectioners' sugar
- • dash of nutmeg

In a medium bowl, cream the cheese with butter, banana extract, vanilla extract and salt. Beat until light and smooth. Slowly sift in the confectioners' sugar, beating until smooth. The amount of sugar you add depends on how thick you want the icing. Add the nutmeg, blending well.

Here are two recipes using a favorite fruit – bananas. The old-fashioned layer cake with Cream Cheese Icing is a nut cake made moist and sweet by mashed bananas in the cake mix. You would only need a scoop of vanilla ice cream to turn the chocolate cake into a banana split, but why do it when you have the outstanding Roasted Banana Sauce? Make them both with ripe bananas – the ones with little freckles.

REVIVAL CHOCOLATE CAKE WITH ROASTED BANANA SAUCE

Melt in your mouth goodness. This creamy, moist chocolate cake gives new meaning to a banana split! Shared by The Revival Grill in Greensboro, North Carolina, when ***Taste Full*** *featured sinful restaurant desserts.*

AVERAGE • SERVES 8

- $^3/_4$ cup unsalted butter, room temperature
- $1^1/_3$ cups sugar, divided
- 3 egg yolks
- $1^1/_3$ cups milk, divided
- $^1/_3$ cup heavy cream
- 1 teaspoon vanilla extract
- 6 ounces (1 cup) semisweet chocolate chips
- 2 whole eggs
- $1^1/_2$ cups cake flour
- 1 teaspoon baking powder
- $1^1/_2$ teaspoons salt
- • Roasted Banana Sauce

Preheat oven to 350°. Butter sides and bottom of a 10" springform pan. Line bottom with parchment paper, butter again and dust with flour. In a large bowl, cream butter and 1 cup sugar with an electric mixer on low speed for 2-3 minutes, or until butter loses its yellow color. Set aside.

In top of a double boiler, whisk together remaining $^1/_3$ cup sugar, egg yolks, $^1/_3$ cup of the milk, heavy cream and vanilla. Over simmering water, stir constantly with a wooden spoon until custard coats the back of the spoon. Do not allow to boil or yolks will curdle. Remove from heat; stir in chocolate chips until melted. Cool.

Beat whole eggs 1 at a time into butter mixture; add the cooled chocolate custard mixture. Sift together the flour, baking powder and salt. Add to batter alternately with remaining 1 cup milk, beating until smooth.

Pour batter into prepared pan. Place pan in a water bath. (That means set the pan with batter into a larger cake pan and surround with hot, almost boiling, water about $^1/_2$ way up the sides of the pan with the batter.) Bake at 350° for 60-70 minutes. Remove from water bath. Cool on a rack for 10 minutes. Remove sides from pan. Cool another hour. Slice and top with Roasted Banana Sauce.

Roasted Banana Sauce

- 4 ripe bananas
- 1 cup heavy cream
- $^1/_3$ cup confectioners' sugar
- 2 tablespoons dark rum
- 1 teaspoon vanilla extract

Place bananas with peels in a 350° oven for 20 minutes. Remove and let cool. Beat cream with confectioners' sugar to soft peaks. Add rum and vanilla and beat to stiff peaks. Shortly before serving, peel bananas and mash pulp with a fork; fold into whipped cream mixture.

Nell's Decadent Oatmeal Cookies

This recipe is from a menu ***Taste Full*** *developed for an Oscar party the year Jodie Foster was up for Best Actress for her dramatic role in* ***Nell****, filmed in and around Lake Lure in North Carolina. Foster's character loved oatmeal, and our staff was convinced that had Nell eaten these oatmeal cookies, she would have found the words to say, "I want this recipe!"*

EASY • MAKES 3 DOZEN

1	**cup butter**
1	**cup packed brown sugar**
1/2	**cup sugar**
2	**large eggs**
1	**teaspoon vanilla extract**
1/3	**cup milk**
1 1/2	**cups all-purpose flour**
1	**teaspoon baking soda**
1/2	**teaspoon salt**
3	**cups rolled oats (not quick)**
1/2	**cup chocolate chips**
1/2	**cup Hershey's Skor bar bits**
1/2	**cup chopped Macadamia nuts**

Preheat oven to 350°. Grease cookie sheet. In a mixer, cream butter and sugars. Add eggs 1 at a time. Mix in vanilla and milk. Sift flour, baking soda and salt into a small bowl. Slowly add into batter. By hand, stir in remaining ingredients. Drop by rounded tablespoonfuls onto cookie sheet. Bake for 10-12 minutes. Cool on pan then transfer to a wire rack.

French Lace Cookies

These paper-thin cookies are so named because of the lace-like way they spread during baking.

AVERAGE • MAKES 5 DOZEN

1/3	**cup dark corn syrup**
1/2	**cup butter**
2/3	**cup brown sugar**
1	**tablespoon grated orange zest**
2	**tablespoons frozen orange juice pulp**
1	**cup all-purpose flour, sifted**
1	**cup finely chopped pecans**

Preheat oven to 375°.

In medium-size heavy saucepan, bring corn syrup, butter, sugar, orange zest and pulp to a boil. Stir in flour and nuts. Remove from heat. Drop batter by the teaspoonful on a lightly greased baking sheet about 3" apart. Bake at 375° for 5-6 minutes. Remove from oven. Let stand for 5 minutes before removing with a spatula. If cookies become difficult to remove from pan, return to oven for 1 minute and try again.

Cherries, 1972

OLD TIME CHERRY CRUMB PIE

An easy two-step dessert shared by Louise Moore, a special friend of Bob Timberlake and the better half of Pastor Lamar Moore who shared his Shrimp Creole on page 115. Any fruit may be substituted in the same proportions.

EASY • SERVES 6-8

2	**quarts cherries or 2 16-ounce packages frozen cherries**
2	**cups sugar, divided**
3	**tablespoons cornstarch**
1 1/4	**cups all-purpose flour**
1	**stick butter**

Preheat oven to 400°. Pit and chop fresh cherries or thaw frozen cherries. Mix fruit, 1 cup sugar (When substituting fruits, add 1/2-1 cup depending on the natural sweetness of the fruit.) and cornstarch in 9" x 13" baking dish. In another bowl, mix remaining 1 cup sugar, flour and butter until crumbly. Spread over fruit. Bake about 1 hour or until brown. Serve warm with vanilla ice cream.

Stocks and Sauces

Homemade Tomato Sauce

This all-purpose tomato sauce is good for pasta, polenta, chicken, pork, veal parmigiana, eggplant parmigiana and more. It will keep up to a week in the refrigerator and for several months in the freezer for a quick emergency meal.

Easy • Makes 10 cups

- 3 tablespoons olive oil
- 2 cups chopped onions (about 2 medium)
- 5 cloves garlic, minced
- 4 14.5-ounce cans diced tomatoes
- 2 15-ounce cans tomato sauce
- 1 cup chopped Italian parsley
- 2 tablespoons balsamic vinegar
- 2 tablespoons dried basil leaves, crushed
- 1 tablespoon dried oregano leaves, crushed
- 1/2 teaspoon sugar
- 1/2 teaspoon pepper
- • salt to taste

Heat olive oil in large saucepan or soup pot over low heat. Add onion and garlic and sauté slowly until translucent, about 10 minutes. Add remaining ingredients except salt. Bring to a boil; reduce heat and simmer 45 minutes until thickened. Taste; add salt if necessary. The amount of salt will vary according to the saltiness of the tomatoes.

Basic Basil Pesto

Easy • Makes 1 cup

- 2 cups of fresh snipped basil leaves
- 1 teaspoon salt
- 1/2 teaspoon pepper
- 2 cloves garlic
- 2 tablespoons pine nuts or walnuts
- 1 cup olive oil
- 1/2 cup Romano or Parmesan cheese, grated

Combine all ingredients except cheese in a blender container. Cover and blend until smooth; stir in Romano or Parmesan cheese.

Refrigerate covered. Stir into soup or over hot pasta.

Vegetable Stock

Easy • Makes 2 quarts

- 1 tablespoon olive oil
- 3/4 cup chopped onion
- 1/4 cup chopped celery
- 1 leek, sliced
- 1 clove garlic, chopped
- 1/2 cup sliced mushrooms
- 2 quarts water
- • bouquet of thyme, bay, parsley, peppercorns

Sweat onion, celery, leek and garlic in olive oil about 6-8 minutes. Add remaining ingredients. Bring to boil and simmer 30-45 minutes. Strain and cool.

Chicken Stock

Easy • Makes 3 quarts

- 2-3 pounds chicken bones
- 1 cup chopped onion
- 1/2 cup chopped celery
- 1/2 cup chopped carrot
- 3 quarts water
- • bouquet of thyme, bay, parsley, peppercorns

Combine ingredients in a soup pot. Bring to boil and simmer 2 hours. Strain and skim fat from top.

Fish Stock with Vegetables

Average • Makes 1 1/2 quarts

- 1-2 pounds fish bones and heads
- 6 cups water
- 1 cup white wine
- 4 black peppercorns
- 2 sprigs parsley
- 1 teaspoon thyme
- 1/2 onion, sliced
- 1 small carrot, sliced
- 1 rib celery, sliced
- 1 clove garlic, crushed

Rinse fish bones and heads in cold water. Bring trimmings to a boil in a large pot with all the other ingredients. Turn down the heat and simmer for 30 minutes. Strain stock through a fine sieve.

Note: In a pinch, ***Taste Full*** most often uses Knorr Vegetarian Vegetable Bouillon Cubes.

Horseradish Sauce

page 13

Great with beef tenderloin or baked potatoes.

Aïoli

page 17

A good dose of garlic. Spread on bread or serve with vegetables.

Mediterranean Tartar

page 28

Make your own for all your fish dishes.

Barbecue Sauce

page 109

It's always nice to have a good homemade recipe on hand.

Very Light Sauce

page 119

Excellent for any kind of poultry.

Citrus Buerre Blanc

page 34

Featured on pecan-crusted chicken, this is also delicious on fish!

Cherry-Port Sauce

page 36

Try this with pork or lamb.

Meat Marinade

page 75

Delicious on pork or beef.

From the Cupboard

Beet Pickles

A recipe by Grace Willoughby Futrell shared from a family reunion menu.

Average

- 1 peck (2 gallons) small tender beets (Larger beets should be sliced before putting in jars with syrup)
- 1 quart water
- 1 quart vinegar
- 5 pounds sugar

Leave 1" stem on beets. Scrub with brush. Place beets in a large pot. Add water to cover and cook 35-40

Ella's Cupboard, 1971

Southerners have strong ties to the land. Owning land means you can sustain your family – with game from your woods, fish from your streams, fruits and vegetables from your garden.

Canning season starts in June and continues until first frost. By September, kitchen shelves overflow with colorful rows of butterbeans, corn, green beans, okra, squash, tomatoes, grape jelly and a dozen different kinds of pickles. Hidden behind the ventilated doors of the cupboard above may be root vegetables that will stay edible for weeks if kept in a cool, dark place.

minutes or until tender. Drain. Pour cold water over beets and drain again. Combine water, vinegar and sugar in pot, and bring to a boil. Add tender peeled beets to syrup and bring to a boil. Let boil 5 minutes. Pack beets into sterilized jars and cover with hot syrup. Seal.

Apple Raisin Chutney

Sam McGann at Duck, North Carolina's Blue Point Bar & Grill serves this chutney as a substitute for cranberry sauce.

AVERAGE • MAKES 1 1/2 QUARTS

10 Granny Smith apples
1 medium yellow onion
1 tablespoon peanut oil
2 cups sugar
1 teaspoon salt
1 tablespoon cinnamon
1 cup cider vinegar
1 1/2 cups golden raisins (or dried currants or dried cranberries)
1 lemon
1 lime
1 orange
1/2 cup fresh mint, chopped

Peel, core and cut apples in a medium dice. Chop onion coarsely. In a large covered saucepan over low heat, sweat (see note) apples and onion with the oil, sugar, salt and cinnamon. The sugar will bring the moisture out of the apples. Stir gently, being careful not to crush the apples. Cook at a simmer for 20 minutes. Add vinegar and cook another 10 minutes. Remove pan from heat and stir in raisins. Allow the mixture to cool.

Juice lemon, lime and orange, stir juices into chutney. Add mint. Chill chutney completely. Refrigerate until ready to use (up to 4 weeks).

NOTE: Sweat means to cook in a little fat over very low heat in a covered pot, so that the food exudes some of its juice without browning; used especially with vegetables.

Carolyn's Pear Chutney

This chutney calls for a firm flavorful pear such as the "old-fashioned" Kieffer pear which shows up in local farmer's markets in September; however, Bartlett pears make a fine substitute.

EASY • MAKES 6 CUPS

- 6-7 very firm pears
- • juice and zest of 1 large lemon
- 1 small onion, diced
- 1 small red bell pepper, diced
- 2 large cloves garlic, minced
- 1 cup light brown sugar, firmly packed
- 3/4 cup cider vinegar
- 1 cup golden raisins
- 1/2 teaspoon ground ginger
- 1/4 teaspoon allspice
- 1/2 teaspoon dried crushed red pepper
- 1 teaspoon salt
- 3/4 cup water

Peel pears; quarter and remove stringy center portion and seeds. Coarsely chop pears and combine in a heavy pot with remaining ingredients. Cook over moderately low heat until the sugars dissolve. Bring mixture to a boil, reduce to a simmer and cook about 1 hour, or until the mixture is thick and syrupy. Refrigerate in jars up to 1 week. To store, process in water bath according to canning directions.

Okra Pickles

Here in the South, these "pickles" are natural additions to summer picnics and barbecues.

AVERAGE • MAKES 6 PINTS

- 2 1/2 pounds small fresh okra pods
- 6 heads fresh dill weed
- 6 garlic cloves
- 3 tablespoons mustard seed
- 48 whole black peppercorns
- 12 serrano chile peppers
- 5 1/2 cups white vinegar
- 3 3/4 cups water
- 3 tablespoons kosher salt

Sterilize six 1-pint jars, lids and rings by boiling for 10 minutes. Remove and let air dry. Keep hot until ready to fill.

Wash okra thoroughly. Divide evenly among the sterilized jars. Repeat with dill, cloves, mustard seed, peppercorns and chiles. Combine vinegar, water and salt in medium saucepan. Bring to boil. Fill hot jars within 1/4" of top and seal immediately. Store for at least 6 weeks for best flavor.

Watermelon Rind Pickle

This recipe came from Trent Colbert's mother's second grade teacher, Ms. Marcie Jones. She used Lily's Lime or calcium hydroxide to pickle; store bought pickling lime is easier to find.

MAKES 3 QUARTS

- 5 pounds watermelon rind
- 1/2 cup pickling lime
- 1/2 cup salt
- 4 cups distilled white vinegar
- 10 cups sugar (5 pounds)
- 1 tablespoon whole cloves
- 1 tablespoon cinnamon
- 1 tablespoon mace

Trim pulp and green skin from rind and cut into 1" squares. Soak overnight in cold water with enough pickling lime to cover. Drain water and wash rind thoroughly. Place in a large pot with water to cover and salt. Bring to a boil and cook 20 minutes. Drain, rinse and wash again. Place back in pot with water to cover and boil 45 minutes. Drain, pat dry and let sit 30 minutes until dry.

In same large pot, make syrup with vinegar, sugar and spices. When syrup boils, add rind and simmer until tender, about 30-45 minutes. Put pickles in sterilized jars, fill to top with syrup and seal.

Yellow Squash Pickles

A delightful, sweet yet tart pickle. Choose tender yellow squash, about 10" long.

AVERAGE • MAKES 2 QUARTS

- 5 yellow squash, unpeeled
- 2 large onions
- 1/2 gallon water
- 1/2 cup salt
- 2 1/2 cups white vinegar

Yellow Squash Pickles

1 cup sugar
1/4 cup brown sugar
2 tablespoons whole mustard seed
1 tablespoon celery seed
1/2 teaspoon turmeric

Cut squash and onions into thin slices. Soak in a large pot of water and salt for 18 hours. Drain squash and onions in large colander in sink for 1 hour, but do not rinse.

In the same pot, combine vinegar, sugars and spices. Bring to boil and simmer 5 minutes. Add drained squash and onions and simmer another 30 minutes. Finally, bring the squash and onions to a boil, remove from heat and spoon into hot sterilized jars. Process in a water bath according to canning instructions if you plan to put them away. Refrigerate after opening.

Candied Orange Peel

This old-fashioned technique is the finishing touch to the Christmas Crown Cake on page 163.

AVERAGE • MAKES 2 CUPS

- **peel of 3 oranges (2 cups)**

2 cups sugar
1/2 cup water

- **sugar for rolling, optional**

Cut peel from oranges in large pieces. To remove bitter flavor, place in medium saucepan, covered with cold water. Bring to a boil. Drain well. Repeat this process 3 more times with fresh water, boiling peel 5-10 minutes the last time. Drain. Cut into long strips.

In saucepan over medium heat, stir sugar and water until sugar dissolves. Add peel. Simmer over low heat until translucent, but not caramelized, 1 1/2-2 hours. Drain in a sieve. While warm, roll each piece in sugar. Place on racks to dry for several hours or overnight. Store in an airtight tin.

VEGETABLE SIDE DISHES

Broccoli Stuffed Tomatoes

These colorful tomatoes featured on page 160 add a festive touch to any holiday meal. Italian or Roma tomatoes are the most flavorful during winter months.

AVERAGE • SERVES 8

8 Italian (Roma) tomatoes
1 head broccoli
2 tablespoons sour cream
1/2 teaspoon freshly grated nutmeg

- **salt and pepper to taste**
- **several drops of Tabasco sauce**

Cut each tomato in half; remove seeds and juice to make a shell. Sprinkle each shell with salt and turn upside down on paper towels to drain. Let shells sit about 15-20 minutes.

Cut broccoli into florets with stems short enough to fit into tomatoes. Slice stems to yield 2 cups. Steam stems until very tender, 10-15 minutes. Purée in food processor. Add sour cream and nutmeg. Season generously with salt, pepper and Tabasco. Steam florets just until crisp-tender, about 4-5 minutes.

Preheat oven to 400°. Place tomatoes in baking dish, just large enough to hold them. Spoon purée into each shell. Bake 8 minutes. Add broccoli floret to each shell. Return to oven. Bake until heated through and tomatoes are tender, about 5 more minutes.

Cascade of Color Green Beans

Julienned red and yellow bell pepper and green onions cut on the bias add festive splashes of color to plain old green beans.

EASY • SERVES 4

1/2 pound green beans (pole)
1/2 red bell pepper, cut in strips
1/2 yellow bell pepper, cut in strips
1-2 cloves garlic, minced
1 cup green onions, cut on 3/4" bias
1 tablespoon olive oil
1/4 cup vegetable broth

- **salt and pepper to taste**

Blanch green beans in large pot of boiling salted water (uncovered) until crisp, about 3-4 minutes. Drain and refresh under cold water to stop cooking. (May be done ahead to this point.)

In large skillet, sauté peppers, garlic and green onions in oil 3-4 minutes. Add reserved green beans and vegetable broth. Cover and cook just until vegetables are done, about 3-4 minutes. Season with salt and pepper.

Chayotes with Herb Butter

Chayotes are a gourd-like fruit about the shape and size of a large pear. Grown in Florida, California and Louisiana, prepare them as you would for summer squash. Readily available in the winter, they are an excellent source of potassium.

EASY • SERVES 8

- **Herb Butter**

8 chayotes
2 tablespoons butter
1 cup diced orange pepper
1 4-ounce Parmesan cheese wedge, freshly grated

- **salt and pepper to taste**

Make Herb Butter.

Peel chayotes and remove seeds. Slice lengthwise and steam as you would squash in a medium saucepan for 10 minutes until tender. Melt butter in a medium sauté pan and cook diced pepper until tender. Arrange chayotes in a Pyrex 9" x 11" baking pan. Sprinkle with sautéed peppers. Grate long strips of Parmesan and spread them out over the chayotes; save a small portion of cheese for garnish. Season with salt and pepper. Dot with Herb Butter. Cover and bake in a 350° oven for 15 minutes.

Herb Butter:

1/2 cup unsalted butter, softened
1 tablespoon minced garlic
1/4 teaspoon thyme
1/4 teaspoon crushed rosemary
1 tablespoon chopped parsley

In a small bowl, blend butter, garlic and herbs until smooth.

Creamed Spinach

A classic vegetable dish that complements prime rib. The nutmeg is the secret!

EASY • SERVES 10-12

- 4 **10-ounce packages frozen spinach**
- 2 **tablespoons olive oil**
- 2 **8-ounce packages of cream cheese, cut in pieces**
- 1/4 **cup fresh chopped chives**
- 1 **teaspoon salt**
- 1 **teaspoon pepper**
- 1/2 **teaspoon nutmeg**

Wash and remove the stems from the fresh spinach. In large pot, sauté the leaves in 2 tablespoons hot oil until they wilt. Place spinach in colander and press out all the liquid. If using frozen spinach, simply thaw and strain out all the liquid. Combine the spinach, cream cheese, chives, salt, pepper and nutmeg in a saucepan. Heat through and serve. Easily cut in half for a small crowd.

Spinach-Laced Brussels Sprouts

Clean, simple, full of green. Pre-steam Brussels sprouts and clean spinach ahead for quick and easy cooking at serving time.

EASY • SERVES 8

- 1 1/2 **pounds fresh Brussels sprouts**
- 1 **pound spinach leaves**
- 1 1/2 **tablespoons minced garlic**
- 3 **tablespoons olive oil**
- • **salt and pepper to taste**

Choose Brussels sprouts that are relatively similar in size and trim woody ends; cut a small X into the base of the core. Bring 1" water to boil in a steamer and add sprouts. Cook smaller sprouts 5-8 minutes, larger ones 8-10. Test with a fork until just tender. Remove from heat and cool to touch. Slice vertically into 2 or 3 parts depending on their size. Set aside. Wash spinach thoroughly, drain and dry. Remove large stems and chop coarsely. In a large sauté pan, cook garlic in hot oil for 1 minute. Add Brussels sprouts and spinach and stir until spinach wilts and Brussels sprouts are heated through. Season with salt and pepper, then serve immediately.

Dilled Cucumbers with Tomatoes

A refreshing side dish salad. At Old Stone Inn in Waynesville, North Carolina, Cindy Zinser often adds sliced fresh mozzarella to this salad and serves it with garlic toast to make a nice light lunch.

EASY • SERVES 6

- 1/3 **cup olive oil**
- 3 **tablespoons cider vinegar**
- 1 **tablespoon fresh dill weed, chopped or 1/2 teaspoon dried dill weed**
- 1/2 **teaspoon salt**
- 1/2 **teaspoon sugar**
- 1 **dash pepper**
- 1 **English cucumber, thinly sliced**
- 3 **large tomatoes, sliced**

Combine oil, vinegar, dill, salt, sugar and pepper in a medium glass bowl; whisk until well-blended. Add cucumber slices and toss until all are coated. Cover and chill at least 3 hours. Arrange sliced tomatoes on individual plates. Spoon cucumber mixture over tomatoes and serve.

Garlicky Green Beans

These green beans will be liked by even the most finicky vegetable eater.

EASY • SERVES 4

- 8 **cups water**
- 1 **teaspoon salt, plus more to taste**
- 1 **pound fresh green beans, ends removed only**
- 1/4 **cup olive oil**
- 4-5 **cloves garlic, minced**
- • **pepper to taste**

In a medium saucepan, bring water and salt to a boil. Add beans and blanch for 4 minutes. Pour into a colander; refresh with cold water. To the same pan, add oil and garlic, sautéing for 1 minute over medium heat. Add beans, salt and pepper; sauté for 3-4 minutes until tender but still very green and slightly crunchy. Serve immediately.

Honeyed Carrots with Marsala

Serve with poultry or fish.

EASY • SERVES 4-5

- 2-3 **tablespoons butter or margarine**
- 2 1/2 **cups carrots, thinly sliced**
- 1 **tablespoon honey**
- • **salt and pepper to taste**
- 1/2 **cup dry Marsala wine**

Melt butter in a medium saucepan. Add sliced carrots and sauté for 2-3 minutes. Stir in honey, salt and pepper. Add Marsala, cover saucepan and simmer over low heat 10-15 minutes until carrots are tender. Serve immediately.

Maple Squash and Apple Casserole

Native Americans taught the early settlers how to grow squash. This simple, colorful combination of butternut squash and unpeeled green apples makes a beautiful presentation in a large, round earthenware dish. For best flavor use real maple syrup, not a pancake syrup substitute.

EASY • SERVES 8

- 1 **medium butternut squash (about 2 pounds)**
- 2 **Granny Smith apples, unpeeled**
- • **salt and pepper**
- 2 **tablespoons butter**
- 1/2 **cup real maple syrup**

Butter a large flat earthenware casserole. Preheat oven to 350°. Peel squash. Cut the narrow end into 1/4" slices. Split the larger end in two lengthwise. Remove seeds. Cut each half into 1/4" slices. Do not peel apples. Cut each in half and remove core. Cut into 1/4" slices. Alternate squash and apple slices around sides

of casserole. Repeat with another layer; put odd shaped pieces in middle. Sprinkle with salt and pepper. Dot with butter and drizzle maple syrup over top.

Bake, uncovered, until just tender, stirring occasionally, about 30 minutes.

Carol Lewark and her husband, Joe, run the nineteenth-century Swan Island Hunt Club in North Carolina's Currituck Sound area where Bob Timberlake is a frequent guest. The pleasure Carol gets from cooking for Bob and his group of hunting buddies is evident in her voice when she speaks of them. Two of Bob's favorite side dishes are Carol's Stewed Tomatoes and mashed rutabagas freshly picked from Joe's garden.

Rutabagas

Joe Lewark grows rutabagas in his garden. Bob is crazy over these and wants them reheated for dinner each night if there are any left.

AVERAGE • SERVES 4-6

- **2 large rutabagas, peeled and cut up**
- **1/2 teaspoon salt**
- **4 thin slices salt pork**
- **1 tablespoon butter**
- **1/3 cup sugar**
- **1/4 teaspoon black pepper**

Combine rutabagas and salt in pot. Cover with water, bring to a boil, and cook until tender. Fry salt pork slices until golden brown, drain on paper towel – save grease. Once rutabagas are done, drain well and mash. Add salt pork grease, butter, sugar, black pepper and mix well. Take salt pork slices and chop very fine. Add to rutabagas.

Carol's Stewed Tomatoes

Bob loves these!

AVERAGE • SERVES 6-8

- **1 28-ounce can tomatoes, whole (Carol prefers the Red Glow brand)**
- **1 cup sugar**
- **1 teaspoon cinnamon**
- **2 cups cubed day old bread**

Chop tomatoes. Add remaining ingredients and mix. Pour into greased baking dish. Bake at 350° for 45 minutes or until firm.

Stocking Stuffed Squash

A side dish developed for a holiday menu, choose this for its taste and eye appeal. Ingredients are easily prepared ahead and then assembled 30 minutes before mealtime.

AVERAGE • SERVES 8

- **8 small yellow squash (4"-5" long)**
- **1 pound fresh baby spinach, washed and stems removed**
- **2 medium tomatoes (do not substitute canned)**
- **3 tablespoons olive oil**
- **2 tablespoons minced garlic**
- **• salt and pepper to taste**
- **1 cup breadcrumbs**
- **2 tablespoons melted butter**
- **1 teaspoon basil**

Trim the ends of the squash and cook in boiling salted water for 3-4 minutes or until tender. Remove squash and drop into large bowl of ice water immediately to stop cooking process. Cut squash in half lengthwise and scoop out flesh and seeds to make small boats.

Chop baby spinach. Peel, seed and dice tomatoes. In large sauté pan, heat oil; sauté garlic for 2 minutes. Add spinach and cook until just wilted. Stir in diced tomatoes. Season with salt and pepper and set aside. In a small bowl combine breadcrumbs, butter and basil. Cover and leave at room temperature.

A half hour before serving, arrange squash boats in a baking pan. Sprinkle salt down the center of each. Fill with spinach/tomato mixture and top with breadcrumbs. Cover and bake at 325° for 20-25 minutes until heated through. Just before serving run the squash under the broiler to brown the breadcrumbs. Serve 2 per plate.

Oven Fried Okra

In the South, some consider fried okra a favorite comfort food. Other folks would never consider swallowing okra that's been simply steamed (that runny-nosed green bean!) but would gobble down fried okra. We love okra all ways at **Taste Full**, *but to ease the okra tension in your home, we developed a method to serve the very popular "fried" okra without the greasy mess of deep-frying.*

EASY • SERVES 4-6

- 2 pounds fresh okra (or frozen)
- 2 cups dry breadcrumbs
- 1/2 teaspoon paprika
- 1 teaspoon salt
- 1/2 teaspoon pepper
- 1/2 cup butter, melted

Preheat oven to 450°.

Trim stems from okra and cut into 1/2" pieces. Combine breadcrumbs, paprika, salt and pepper in a small bowl. Dip okra in melted butter and then roll in breadcrumbs to coat evenly. Place on a large ungreased baking sheet and cook for 5 minutes on 1 side.

Turn okra pieces over and bake another 5 minutes until brown and crisp. Serve immediately.

Okra with Chives

A basic recipe using a star of summer's fresh produce.

EASY • SERVES 8

- 2 pounds fresh okra
- 1 cup water
- 2 tablespoons butter
- 1/4 cup chopped fresh chives
- • salt and pepper to taste

Wash okra and trim off the tops. Bring water to boil in a large saucepan. Add okra, cover and steam about 8 minutes or until tender. Smaller okra will take less time. Drain okra and return to pan. To the same saucepan, add butter and chives and return to medium heat. Toss well. Season with salt and pepper.

Roasted Asparagus & Leeks

Roasted seasonal vegetables flavored with balsamic vinegar — what a treat.

EASY • SERVES 8-10

- 4 carrots
- 2 leeks
- 4 stalks celery
- 1 bunch asparagus
- 4 garlic cloves, thinly sliced
- 1 teaspoon salt
- 1/4 cup extra virgin olive oil
- 1 teaspoon sugar
- 1 tablespoon balsamic vinegar

Preheat oven to 400°. Prepare vegetables by cutting them into 2" batons. Toss with garlic, salt, oil and sugar. Spread evenly on a baking sheet and bake for 20-25 minutes. Vegetables will be *al dente* — tender but not too soft. Toss with balsamic vinegar. Serve warm or at room temperature.

Sugar Snap Peas with Cherry Tomatoes

A beautiful and very simple side dish.

EASY • SERVES 6-8

- 1 pound sugar snap peas (fresh or frozen)
- 2 tablespoons butter
- 2 teaspoons minced garlic
- 20 small cherry tomatoes
- 2 tablespoons fresh chopped thyme
- • salt and pepper to taste

Remove strings from sugar snap peas and blanch in boiling water for 1 minute. Drain and set aside.

In large sauté pan, melt butter over medium heat and sauté garlic for 3 minutes. Add sugar snap peas, cherry tomatoes and fresh thyme. Cover and cook another 2-3 minutes until vegetables are heated through. Stir at least twice during cooking. Season with salt and pepper.

Thick-Cut Fried Cornmeal Tomatoes

Consider this for a fish dinner, or even for brunch along with eggs and bacon.

EASY • SERVES 6

- 4 beefsteak tomatoes, cut into 3/8" slices
- • cornmeal
- • salt
- • pepper
- 2 tablespoons bacon drippings, if available, or good olive oil

Dredge tomato slices in cornmeal that has been lightly seasoned with salt and pepper. Coat skillet with drippings or oil and fry tomatoes until golden brown on both sides.

Tomatoes Rockefeller

When summer tomatoes are ripe and juicy, this recipe makes a delicious and attractive side dish for meat, poultry or seafood.

EASY • SERVES 6

- 2 1/2 cups chopped fresh spinach leaves
- 1 teaspoon minced garlic
- 1 tablespoon minced shallots
- 2 tablespoons minced celery
- 3 tablespoons melted butter
- 2/3 cup breadcrumbs
- 2 tablespoons chopped fresh parsley
- 2 tablespoons grated Parmesan cheese
- 1 egg, slightly beaten
- 2 dashes Worcestershire sauce
- 1/2 teaspoon salt
- 1/4 teaspoon cayenne pepper
- 6 thick tomato slices

Sauté the spinach leaves quickly in a little oil, until they are limp. Remove from pan to a bowl. Next, sauté garlic, shallots and celery in butter until soft. Combine in bowl with the spinach. Add the other ingredients except the tomatoes and mix together. This mixture may be made ahead in the day and it also freezes well. To prepare: Preheat oven to 350°. Mound the spinach mixture on top of the tomato slices and bake for 20 minutes.

Sautéed Trio of Greens

Heeding Grandma's advice to "Eat your greens!" is a welcome task when this seasoned mixture is on the plate, another winner shared by Walter Royal of the Angus Barn in Raleigh, North Carolina.

EASY • SERVES 4-6

- 1 bunch kale
- 1 bunch Swiss chard
- 1 bunch spinach
- 5 tablespoons butter
- 2 tablespoons minced garlic
- 1/4 teaspoon ground nutmeg
- 1/2 teaspoon salt
- 1/4 teaspoon freshly ground black pepper

Remove stems from kale, chard and spinach. Immerse greens in cool water and drain. Repeat this process until water is clear. Drain well and roughly chop.

In a large pot, heat butter over medium-high heat. Add garlic and brown lightly, about 1 minute. Add greens and cook covered, tossing every 30 seconds until lightly wilted, approximately 4 minutes. Season greens with nutmeg, salt and pepper.

Winter Greens with Caramelized Shallots

The caramelized shallots mellow the strong flavor of the greens. Choose a medley of mustard greens, collards, and chard.

AVERAGE • SERVES 6

- 3 pounds mixed greens, thoroughly washed, stems removed, coarsely chopped
- 4 tablespoons butter
- 6-8 medium shallots, cut lengthwise into thin slivers
- 5-6 medium garlic cloves, minced
- 1 tablespoon sugar
- 2 tablespoons olive oil
- 2 tablespoons balsamic vinegar

Place washed, chopped greens in large stockpot with 4 cups water. If using a variety of greens, cook tougher varieties (collards or turnips) approximately 20 minutes before adding the remaining more tender varieties (Swiss chard, spinach, young mustard).

Cook combined greens approximately 30 minutes longer. Drain in colander. The recipe may be done up to this point the day before.

A half hour before serving, melt butter in a saucepan large enough to accommodate the cooked greens. Place shallots, garlic and sugar in butter and cook over very low heat until golden and tender. When shallots are caramelized, stir in cooked greens, olive oil and vinegar. The amount of vinegar may be adjusted up or down depending on personal taste. Heat to serve.

NOTE: Chard stems may be chopped and cooked with the first greens; they add additional color and texture to the finished dish.

Asian Sweet and Sour Slaw

Tangy and colorful. Serve on top of or alongside Seared Tuna Sandwiches on page 112. This can easily be doubled and served as an accompanying salad.

EASY • SERVES 4

- 2 tablespoons fresh lime juice
- 2 tablespoons minced shallots
- 2 tablespoons soy sauce
- 1 tablespoon minced fresh ginger
- 1 teaspoon minced garlic
- 1 tablespoon honey
- 2 tablespoons sesame oil
- 1/4 cup peanut or vegetable oil
- 2 cups finely sliced red cabbage
- 1/2 cup shredded carrots
- 1/2 cup finely chopped red pepper
- 1/2 cup finely chopped yellow pepper
- 1/4 cup sliced green onions
- 2 tablespoons chopped fresh cilantro
- 2 tablespoons unsalted peanuts
- 1 teaspoon sesame seeds
- 1/2-1 teaspoon salt
- 1/2 teaspoon black pepper

In a small glass bowl or jar, combine lime juice, shallots, soy sauce, ginger, garlic, honey, sesame oil and peanut oil. Whisk or shake covered jar vigorously to blend. Set aside.

In a medium bowl, combine cabbage, carrots, peppers, green onions, cilantro, peanuts and sesame seeds. Toss to mix. Pour dressing over mixture and toss thoroughly. Add salt and pepper. Cover and refrigerate for at least 30 minutes and up to 5 days.

Fruited Coleslaw

The fruit of the moment makes this slaw different each time you offer it. ***Taste Full*** *tested the slaw with apples, mango and oranges. Make the salad the night before for best flavor.*

EASY • SERVES 3-4

- 1/2 pound cabbage, shredded fine
- 2 tablespoons sugar
- 1/2 teaspoon salt
- 1/4 cup white wine vinegar
- 1/4 cup canola oil
- 1 teaspoon celery seed
- 3/4 cup peeled, seeded and cubed fruit (peaches, nectarines, plums, mangoes, apples or oranges)

Place cabbage in bowl. Combine sugar, salt and vinegar in small saucepan and bring to a boil. Stir until sugar dissolves. Add oil and celery seed. Pour over cabbage. Cool completely before adding fruit.

J.K.'s Coleslaw

Just the right tang – or perfect cool down for spicy barbecue. Add to barbecue sandwiches or eat as a side dish.

EASY • SERVES 8

- 4 pounds cabbage, shredded
- 2/3 cup apple cider vinegar
- 2 tablespoons olive oil
- 1 teaspoon salt
- 2 tablespoons sugar
- 1 teaspoon white pepper
- 1 1/2 cups mayonnaise

Core the cabbage head, then shred. In a large bowl, toss cabbage with vinegar and oil. Season with salt, sugar and pepper and then mix in the mayonnaise. Adjust seasonings to your taste. Refrigerate until ready to serve.

Simmered Apples

Homespun delicious.

EASY • MAKES 3-4 CUPS

- 8 **Granny Smith apples**
- 1/4 **cup butter**
- 2 **teaspoons brown sugar**

Peel and thinly slice apples. Sauté apples in butter. Season with brown sugar. Let simmer 20 minutes or until soft.

Hot Cranberry Relish

From Mary Duke Grubbe of Palatine, Illinois. Her sister, Stagg, introduced it into her family and ever since this recipe has been a hotly requested item. Very kid friendly, serve warm as a complement to turkey, pork, Cornish hen or quail.

EASY • SERVES 6-8

- 3 **cups cranberries**
- 3 **cups chopped apples**
- 1 1/4 **cups sugar**
- 1 **cup butter, softened**
- 1/2 **cup brown sugar**
- 3/4 **cup instant oatmeal**
- 3/4 **cup nuts, preferably pecans**

Preheat oven to 350°. Combine cranberries, apples and sugar; pour into large (12-cup) greased casserole dish. Combine butter, brown sugar, oatmeal and nuts; spread on top of cranberry/apple mixture. Bake for 1 hour. Serve warm.

Cranberries Madeira

Madeira-infused cranberries are a perfect accompaniment to the Stuffed Beef Tenderloin.

EASY • SERVES 8

- 1 **12-ounce package cranberries**
- 3/4 **cup Madeira**
- 1/2 **cup sugar**
- 1/8 **teaspoon cinnamon**

Wash cranberries. In saucepan, bring Madeira, sugar and cinnamon to a boil, stirring until sugar dissolves. Add cranberries; reduce heat. Boil gently until cranberries are cooked, 5-8 minutes.

POTATOES, RICE AND MORE

Spinach Potato Pancakes

page 119

An excellent choice for an easy vegetarian lunch.

Au Gratin Potatoes

This creamy, cheesy potato dish is comfort food on a chilly January day.

AVERAGE • SERVES 6-8

- 4 **large baking potatoes**
- 1 **4-ounce package cream cheese**
- 2 **teaspoons minced garlic**
- • **salt and pepper to taste**
- 1/4 **cup milk**
- 4 **tablespoons butter**
- 2 **tablespoons heavy cream**
- 1/4 **pound Gruyère cheese, grated**

Preheat oven to 350°.

Peel and slice potatoes. In a well-oiled 9" x 13" casserole, alternate layers of sliced potatoes with pats of cream cheese, sprinkled with minced garlic, salt and pepper.

In a small saucepan, heat milk and butter. Simmer for 2 minutes. Remove from heat. Stir in heavy cream. Pour over potatoes. Top with grated Gruyère. Bake 45-50 minutes until top is brown.

Herb Roasted Potatoes

Fresh herbs are the secret to these potatoes. If thyme and rosemary are not available, substitute other fresh herbs such as sage, parsley or chives.

EASY • SERVES 4

- • **cooking spray**
- 7-8 **medium white potatoes, cubed with skin on**
- 2 **tablespoons fresh chopped thyme**
- 2 **tablespoons fresh rosemary**
- 1 **teaspoon salt**
- 1 **teaspoon pepper**
- 4 **tablespoons vegetable oil**

Preheat oven to 400°. Spray a baking dish with cooking spray.

In a medium-sized bowl, combine remaining ingredients. Transfer to prepared dish and cover with foil. Bake for 40 minutes. Remove foil and continue baking for 20 minutes. Remove and serve. Potatoes will stay warm, covered, for 10-15 minutes.

Homemade French Fries

You have never tasted real fries until you have tasted them homemade!

EASY • SERVES 3-4

- 2 **large baking potatoes**
- • **vegetable oil (soy or canola)**
- • **salt**

Wash potatoes and cut (unpeeled) into long strips about 3/4" in diameter. Hold in a large bowl of cold water until ready to use.

Heat about 1/2" of vegetable oil in heavy skillet (cast iron works best) over medium-high heat until hot. Thoroughly dry some of the potato strip on paper towels and add to oil. Do not crowd. Fry, turning occasionally until crisp and brown, about 5 minutes. Drain on paper towels, sprinkle with salt and keep warm in 275° oven while frying the rest of the potatoes. Serve immediately.

Two Potato Gratin

Two staples – red and sweet potatoes – come together in this easy side dish.

EASY • SERVES 8

- 2 1/2 **pounds red potatoes**
- 3 **large sweet potatoes**
- 4 **tablespoons butter**
- • **salt and pepper to taste**
- 2 **tablespoons fresh thyme leaves**
- 2 **cups half & half**
- 1/4 **cup Parmesan cheese**

Preheat oven to 375°. Thinly slice red potatoes leaving peel on. Peel and slice the sweet potatoes.

Alternately layer in a 9" x 13" baking dish, dotting each layer with butter. Sprinkle each layer with salt and pepper and thyme leaves. Pour half & half over. Cover and bake at 375° for 45 minutes. Uncover and sprinkle Parmesan over top evenly and continue to bake another 30 minutes until golden brown.

Cornwallis Yams

One of the best sweet potato recipes ever from the former Colonial Inn in Hillsborough, North Carolina.

EASY • SERVES 10

- 6 medium sweet potatoes
- 1/2 teaspoon ground cinnamon
- 1/2 teaspoon ground nutmeg
- 1/4 pound butter
- 3 eggs
- 1/2 cup crushed pineapple
- 1 cup sugar
- 1/2 cup grated coconut
- 1 1/2 cups milk
- • more grated coconut for garnish

Preheat oven to 350°.

Boil sweet potatoes until soft. Peel and mash. Season with cinnamon, nutmeg and butter. Beat the eggs and add to the potatoes. Combine with the remaining ingredients. Pour into a greased 11" x 7" casserole. Bake until light brown, about 1 hour. Top with a sprinkle of coconut.

Glazed Sweet Potato Wedges

Simple and good, this recipe features two southern staples – sweet potatoes and molasses.

EASY • SERVES 4-6

- 3 large sweet potatoes, cut into 8 long wedges
- 3 tablespoons extra virgin olive oil
- • salt and pepper to taste
- • scant 1/8 teaspoon cayenne
- 2 tablespoons molasses

Preheat oven to 375°.

In large bowl, toss sweet potato wedges with remaining ingredients and place on large baking sheet. Bake until easily pierced with fork, approximately 20-25 minutes.

Smashed Sweet Potatoes with Turnips

Jalapeño and ginger impart a refreshing zing to the classic North Carolina staples, a winning side dish from Walter Royal of Raleigh's Angus Barn.

EASY • SERVES 4-6

- 2 pounds sweet potatoes
- 4 3/4 teaspoons salt, divided
- 1 pound white turnips
- 1 jalapeño pepper, seeded and minced
- 1 tablespoon ginger root, peeled and minced
- 4 tablespoons butter, softened
- 1/4 teaspoon fresh ground black pepper
- 1/4 teaspoon ground nutmeg
- 1 teaspoon soy sauce
- 1 tablespoon honey

Peel sweet potatoes and cut into 2" chunks. Place in a large pot and cover with cool water and 2 teaspoons salt. Bring to a boil and cook over medium-high heat until soft, 20-25 minutes. Peel, cut and cook turnips in the same manner with 2 teaspoons salt using a second pot. Turnips will take 30-35 minutes to fully cook.

Drain potatoes and turnips, and place in a large bowl. Add jalapeño, ginger, butter, the remaining 3/4 teaspoon salt, pepper and nutmeg. Mix well using a potato masher. Stir in soy sauce and honey, adjust seasoning if necessary.

Sweet Potato Polenta

Great with lamb or pork.

EASY • SERVES 4

- 1 baked medium sweet potato
- 10 large cloves garlic, unpeeled
- 4 cups water
- 1 cup polenta
- • salt and pepper to taste

Preheat oven to 350°. Bake sweet potato until soft, about 1 hour. A liquid should appear between the skin and flesh when poked with a fork. Coat unpeeled garlic cloves with olive oil. Bake in the same oven for 20 minutes, until soft. Cool and press each clove to yield about 2 tablespoons roasted garlic pulp. Set garlic and sweet potato aside.

In a medium saucepan, boil water. Slowly stir in polenta. Reduce heat. Simmer 20 minutes, stirring occasionally. Peel sweet potato, then whip into polenta with reserved garlic, salt and pepper.

Baked Cheddar Cheese Grits

Serve these baked grits in place of potatoes or rice. We promise they'll be a hit.

EASY • SERVES 8

- 3 cups milk
- 1 cup grits
- 1 teaspoon salt
- • dash pepper
- 7 tablespoons butter
- 3/4 cup water
- 2 eggs, slightly beaten
- 1/2 teaspoon garlic salt
- 3/4 cup shredded cheddar cheese
- • dash Tabasco sauce
- • handful of shredded cheddar cheese
- • Parmesan cheese, grated

Preheat oven to 350°.

In medium saucepan, heat milk, grits, salt, pepper and butter until the mixture begins to thicken. Stir in water and eggs. Add garlic salt, cheddar cheese and Tabasco sauce. Pour into greased 8" x 8" casserole dish. Sprinkle with remaining cheddar cheese and top with grated Parmesan. Bake 35-40 minutes.

THOUGH THE NAME OF THIS SOUTHERN STAPLE IS ALWAYS IN REFERENCE TO "HOMINY GRITS," THE TERM "GRITS" ACTUALLY REFERS TO ANY COARSELY GROUND GRAIN SUCH AS CORN, OATS OR RICE.

Hobgood's Baked Beans

This side dish is the rib-tickling creation of Sam Hobgood of what was once Hobgood's Family BBQ in Hillsborough, North Carolina.

EASY • MAKES 2 1/2 QUARTS • SERVES 10

- 2 cups diced onions
- 2 tablespoons butter
- 1 pound ground beef
- 1 1/2 cups Kraft-style barbecue sauce
- 2/3 cup brown sugar
- 1 31-ounce can pork and beans

Sauté onions in butter; add beef and cook until well done; add remaining ingredients and bake, covered, in a greased, shallow, baking dish at 350° for 30-45 minutes; uncover and cook for 30 minutes more.

Wild Basmati Rice Timbales

A simple rice dish made more elegant by placing in a small, high-sided, drum-shaped mold called a timbale, available at cookware stores.

EASY • SERVES 8

- 2 tablespoons butter
- 4 ounces chopped mushrooms (about 1 1/2 cups)
- 1/2 cup wild rice, rinsed and drained
- 2 1/2 cups vegetable broth
- 1/4 teaspoon salt
- 1/2 cup Basmati rice
- 2-3 tablespoons snipped chives
- • mushroom slice, optional

Melt butter in medium, heavy saucepan. Add chopped mushrooms and sauté until they release their liquid and it evaporates, about 4 minutes. Add wild rice, vegetable broth and salt. Bring to boil; cover and simmer 20 minutes. Add Basmati rice and return to boil. Cover and cook about 20 minutes more, until liquid is absorbed. Remove from heat and stir in chives.

Pack into lightly greased 1/2-cup timbales or custard cups. Recipe may be made a day ahead to this point.

Preheat oven to 400°. Place filled timbales in baking pan. Add boiling water to come 1/2-2/3 up side of timbales. Bake 20 minutes until heated through. Carefully remove from oven. Run knife around edge of each timbale and turn out on individual serving plates. Garnish with mushroom slice if desired.

Herbed Rice Cakes

This will become your new "favorite" side dish.

EASY • SERVES 6 LARGE

- 2 cups cooked brown rice
- 1 teaspoon salt
- 1/2 teaspoon pepper
- 1 egg, lightly beaten
- 1/4 teaspoon curry powder
- 1/4 teaspoon garlic powder
- 1/2 cup minced onion
- 2 tablespoons chopped parsley
- 2 tablespoons chopped chives
- 2 tablespoons chopped fresh thyme
- 2 Roma tomatoes, finely chopped
- 1 1/2 cups cornbread crumbs
- 1 cup olive oil
- 4 tablespoons sour cream

Combine cooked rice, salt, pepper, egg, curry and garlic powders, onion, parsley, chives, thyme and tomatoes with cornbread crumbs. Pat into 12 small cakes. Refrigerate 30 minutes. Heat oil in frying pan over medium heat. Fry 4 cakes at a time until golden on each side. Remove to paper towels to drain. Place on tray in 200° oven until all cakes are fried. Garnish with sour cream.

Pecan Scallion Rice

A delicious side dish shared by Sam McGann of Blue Point Bar & Grill in Duck, North Carolina.

AVERAGE • SERVES 4

- 2 tablespoons clarified butter
- 4 tablespoons minced red onion
- 1 bay leaf
- 1 teaspoon Blue Point Seasoning Mix, recipe below
- 3/4 cup white rice
- 1 1/2 cups water or chicken stock
- 4 tablespoons chopped roasted pecans
- 4 tablespoons chopped green onion

Preheat oven to 350°. Heat clarified butter in medium saucepan. Add red onions, bay leaf and seasoning mix. Add rice and stir. Be sure to coat the rice well with the butter. Add water, bring to a boil and cover. Bake for 18 minutes. Remove from oven and uncover. Stir in pecans and green onions. Taste for seasoning.

Blue Point Seasoning Mix:

- 1 tablespoon ground black pepper
- 1 teaspoon white pepper
- 1 teaspoon cayenne pepper
- 1 tablespoon salt

Combine all ingredients and blend.

Wild Rice Oyster Dressing

The wild rice adds a somewhat nutty flavor to the menu, and combined with oysters makes an outstanding dressing.

AVERAGE • SERVES 8-10

- 2 tablespoons vegetable oil
- 2 cups finely chopped onion
- 1 cup finely chopped celery
- 1 cup finely chopped carrots
- 1 cup chopped mushrooms
- 24 ounces fresh oysters with liquid
- 1 16-ounce package stuffing mix
- 1 teaspoon sage
- 1 teaspoon thyme
- 4 cups cooked wild rice, see note
- 2-3 cups chicken broth
- 1 teaspoon pepper
- 1/2 teaspoon salt

Heat oil in a large skillet over medium heat. Cook onion, celery and carrots for 10 minutes. Add mushrooms and cook for 2 more minutes. Add oysters with liquid and simmer for 4 minutes. Remove from heat.

In a large bowl combine the stuffing mix with sage and thyme. Stir in wild rice, blending well. Add vegetable/oyster mixture to bowl. Stir in chicken broth 1 cup at a time until the stuffing is very moist. Add salt and pepper. If you are not stuffing the turkey cavity, grease a 9" x 13" Pyrex dish and fill with dressing. Bake, uncovered, at 325° for 30-40 minutes. The dressing will keep warm, covered, for up to 30 minutes.

NOTE: Use real wild rice, not a blended, seasoned mixture. The texture of wild rice will hold up much better for this length of cooking. Also, blended packages tend to contain an abundance of salt, which is not necessary for this recipe. Cook rice according to package directions.

Wild Rice

Pure wild rice is a flavorful side dish.

EASY • SERVES 8

- 1 cup wild rice
- 2 tablespoons butter
- 1 cup thinly sliced celery
- 1 cup thinly sliced carrots
- 1 clove garlic, minced
- 1 can vegetable broth plus water to make 2 1/2 cups
- 1 teaspoon salt
- 1/2 cup sliced green onion with tops

Thoroughly wash wild rice. Heat 2 tablespoons butter in medium saucepan. Cook celery, carrots and garlic in butter over medium-low heat until almost tender, about 10 minutes. Add rice, vegetable broth and water. Bring to a boil, cover and simmer 45 minutes, until rice is tender. (Different brands of wild rice vary in cooking time.) Add green onions and cook a few minutes more.

Confetti Orzo

This simple side dish will dress up any plate. Substitute it for rice.

EASY • SERVES 6

- 2 cups orzo
- 3 tablespoons olive oil
- 1/2 cup chopped green onions
- 1/4 cup shredded carrots
- 2 tablespoons chopped parsley
- 1 1/2 teaspoons salt
- • freshly ground pepper

Cook orzo in 3 quarts boiling water for 8 minutes. Meanwhile, heat olive oil and sauté green onions, carrots and parsley over medium-high heat 2-3 minutes until soft. Drain orzo and stir in vegetables. Season with salt and pepper and serve hot.

Variation: Substitute the carrots with dried cherries for a hint of sweet.

Black-Eyed Pea Cakes

Lots of good luck are packed into these pan-fried patties.

AVERAGE • SERVES 6

- 2 pounds cooked black-eyed peas (2 cans)
- 1 tablespoon minced garlic
- 1/2 cup finely chopped onion
- 1/2 cup finely chopped red pepper
- 1/2 cup finely chopped pecans
- 1/2 cup breadcrumbs
- 2 tablespoons chopped parsley
- 2 teaspoons brown sugar
- 2 eggs
- 1 teaspoon salt
- 1/4 teaspoon black pepper
- 1/4 teaspoon cayenne
- 1/4 teaspoon mace
- 1/8 teaspoon allspice
- 1/8 teaspoon thyme
- 1/8 teaspoon sage
- 2 tablespoons butter, divided

Rinse and drain black-eyed peas and puree half of them in food processor. Transfer to a bowl and stir in remaining whole black-eyed peas. Mix with garlic, onion, red pepper, pecans, breadcrumbs, parsley, sugar, eggs and spices. Shape into 12 cakes; cover and chill for at least 30 minutes. In a large skillet melt 1 tablespoon butter over medium-high heat and cook half the cakes about 5 minutes per side until browned. Keep warm in a 300° oven as you repeat the process with remaining cakes. Makes 12 cakes.

Brown Butter Corn

This side dish can replace rice or pasta in your meal planning when appropriate.

EASY • SERVES 4

- 1/2 stick butter
- 3 cups cut fresh corn
- • salt and pepper to taste
- 1 tablespoon chopped fresh cilantro

On medium heat, melt butter in a skillet and continue cooking butter until it browns. Add corn and sauté until tender. Season with salt and pepper. Add cilantro just before serving. If using dried cilantro, add with salt and pepper.

Corn Custard

A delightful light corn dish inspired by the late Beth Tartan, the late food editor of the Winston-Salem Journal.

EASY • SERVES 10-12

- 2 1/2 cups fresh or frozen corn kernels
- 4 large eggs, beaten
- 2 1/4 cups heavy cream
- 2 teaspoons salt
- 1 teaspoon pepper

In a large bowl, combine all ingredients, stirring to blend well. Pour into a buttered 11" x 7" casserole dish. Place inside a larger baking pan and fill with hot water until it is 1" deep around the outside of casserole dish. Bake at 325° for 1 1/4 hours or until a knife, when inserted, comes out clean.

LUNCH AND BRUNCH

Italian Beefsteak Tomato Sandwich

A meaty slice of tomato adorned with an herbed mascarpone cheese is best served on a tomato basil bread.

EASY • SERVES 4

- 4 ounces mascarpone cheese
- 2 teaspoons chopped fresh parsley
- 2 teaspoons chopped fresh basil
- 2 teaspoons chopped fresh chives
- • freshly ground pepper
- 2 beefsteak tomatoes
- 8 slices good bread

Combine cheese with herbs and pepper. Slice tomatoes 1/4" thick.

Generously spread mascarpone on each bread slice and layer with luscious tomato.

The Goat Lady's Tomato Sandwich

with Vidalia Relish

A fresh Vidalia Relish is a perfect topping for this sandwich starring a goat cheese spread and vine-ripened tomatoes. Make the sandwiches a few hours ahead, wrap tightly and refrigerate. You will find the juices from the sweet onion relish will deliciously soak into the bread.

AVERAGE • SERVES 4

- 1 **loaf crusty French baguette or sourdough bread**
- • **The Goat Lady's Spread**
- 1 **cup arugula, washed and gently patted dry**
- 4 **vine-ripened tomatoes, sliced**
- 1 **cup Vidalia Relish**

Cut baguette in half lengthwise. Spread a thin layer of The Goat Lady's Spread over 1 baguette half. Layer arugula, tomato slices and Vidalia Relish, then close the sandwich with remaining baguette. Slice into 4 equal pieces on the diagonal. Wrap tightly in plastic and refrigerate until ready to serve.

The Goat Lady's Spread:

- 3 **ounces goat cheese**
- 2 **tablespoons heavy cream or half & half**
- 1 **tablespoon thyme leaves**

Blend all ingredients in a mixing bowl. Refrigerate until ready to use.

Vidalia Relish:

- 4 **Vidalia onions**
- 1 **small red bell pepper**
- 1 **small green bell pepper**
- 3 **tablespoons olive oil**
- 2 **tablespoons fresh thyme leaves**
- 1/3 **cup cider vinegar**
- 3 **tablespoons water**
- 1/3 **cup sugar**
- 1/2 **teaspoon salt**
- 1/4 **teaspoon pepper**

Slice onions into whole 1/4" thick slices. Slice peppers and cut into a 1/4" dice. Heat oil in a dutch oven over medium-high heat. Sauté onions until they begin to caramelize, about 10 minutes, stirring occasionally. Add peppers and sauté 2 more minutes.

Combine thyme, vinegar, water, sugar, salt and pepper and add to onions. Reduce heat, cover and simmer for 30 minutes. Relish will hold up to 2 weeks in the refrigerator. Makes 4 cups.

Okra Tomato Spoonbread

Spoonbread is a Southern original – not quite bread and not quite a soufflé. This densely textured and slightly sweet version is inspired by favorite southern staples. Packed with okra, tomatoes and corn, serve as a main dish or side dish. Either way, make sure to eat it with a spoon as the name implies.

AVERAGE • SERVES 6

- 1 **cup okra, 1/4" slices**
- 1 **medium tomato, diced**
- 3 **green onions, diced**
- 1 **cup corn kernels**
- 1 **tablespoon minced thyme leaves**
- 1/3 **large jalapeño pepper, finely minced**
- 1 1/2 **cups milk**
- • **salt and pepper to taste**
- 1 **teaspoon sugar**
- 1 **cup yellow cornmeal**
- 3 **tablespoons butter**
- 1 **cup buttermilk**
- 3 **eggs, separated**
- 2 **teaspoons baking powder**
- 1/2 **teaspoon baking soda**

Preheat oven to 375°.

Combine okra, tomato, green onions, corn, thyme and jalapeño in small bowl and reserve. (If using frozen corn, defrost first.) In a medium saucepan, heat milk, salt, pepper and sugar. Bring to a boil, then slowly add cornmeal, stirring constantly until smooth and thick. Remove from heat, add butter, buttermilk and egg yolks to saucepan, stirring until thoroughly mixed. Add baking powder and baking soda, stirring until well mixed. Stir in reserved vegetables.

Meanwhile, in a medium bowl, beat egg whites until stiff. Fold into cornmeal mixture and transfer to a greased 10" casserole. Bake for 35-40 minutes. Spoonbread will be golden and slightly puffy. Serve at once.

Country Ham Quiche

Southern farm flavors mixed with milk, eggs and cheese make this a delightful meal for breakfast or dinner when served with salad and a vegetable.

EASY • SERVES 5

- 4 **eggs**
- 1 **cup whipping cream**
- 1/2 **cup milk**
- 1/2 **teaspoon salt**
- • **dash pepper**
- • **pinch of ground nutmeg**
- 1/3 **cup finely grated Gruyere cheese**
- 1/3 **cup finely grated Swiss cheese**
- 1 **unbaked 9" pie shell**
- 1 **cup chopped, cooked country ham**

Preheat oven to 350°.

Beat eggs, add whipping cream, milk, salt, pepper and nutmeg. Blend in cheeses.

Line bottom of pie shell with chopped ham. Pour remaining mixture over ham. Bake 1 hour to 1 hour 15 minutes, or until knife inserted in center comes out clean. Let stand 10-15 minutes before slicing.

Shrimp, Sausage and Pepper Frittata

Pretty and full of flavor, serve for brunch or Sunday supper.

EASY • SERVES 4

- 1-2 **tablespoons oil for cooking**
- 1/2 **cup chopped white onion**
- 1 **cup red, yellow and orange peppers, julienned**

- 1/4 pound shrimp, peeled, deveined and chopped
- 1 cup boiled potato, cubed in 1/2" pieces
- 1/4 pound Italian sausage, cooked and crumbled
- • salt and cayenne pepper to taste
- • Italian parsley, minced
- 4 eggs, lightly beaten
- 1 cup heavy cream

Preheat oven to 350°.

Heat oil in pan. Add chopped onion and peppers and sauté for 3 minutes over moderate heat. Add the shrimp and cook over moderate heat until pink. Add potatoes, sausage and seasonings. Remove from heat.

Whisk eggs and cream together in medium bowl. Add ingredients from the sauté pan. Pour into greased 9" round or square glass pan. Bake for 45 minutes or until fork inserted in center comes out clean. Cut into wedges or squares and serve warm.

Squash Feta Casserole

Lillian Kroustalis of Westbend Vineyards in Lewisville, North Carolina, had never written down the recipe for this dish – a traditional Greek zimaropita her mother used to make – until she shared it with ***Taste Full*** *in the summer of 1993. When the summer garden overflows with squash, this is the casserole to prepare. Best served right out of the oven, it works well with zucchini or yellow squash. It can work as a side dish but is substantial enough for a vegetarian entrée.*

AVERAGE • SERVES 8

- 2 1/2 cups corn meal
- 1 1/2 teaspoons baking powder
- 3 tablespoons sugar
- 4 cups grated summer squash
- 3 eggs
- 1 cup cottage cheese
- 1 1/2 cup crumbled feta cheese
- 1 cup milk
- 1/2 cup butter, cut in pieces

Preheat oven to 375°. Grease and flour a 9" x 14" x 2" baking pan. Mix together the cornmeal, baking powder and sugar. In a separate bowl, combine the squash, eggs, cottage cheese, feta and milk. Add cornmeal mixture to squash; blend ingredients well. Pour into prepared pan. Dot top of mixture with butter. Bake until browned on top, about 1 hour.

Apricot Cream Scones

BREADS

Homemade Crackers

page 12

Serve with cheese tray or your favorite soup or dip.

Angel Biscuits

These angel biscuits are divine!

EASY • YIELDS ABOUT 2 1/2 DOZEN

- 1 package dry yeast
- 1/4 cup warm water
- 2 cups buttermilk
- 5 cups self-rising flour
- 1/4 cup sugar
- 1 cup Crisco solid shortening

Dissolve yeast in warm water and set aside. Four buttermilk into a measuring cup and microwave 1 minute to take off the chill. Mix together flour, sugar and shortening in large bowl of mixer, using lowest speed, until mixture is well-blended. Mix buttermilk and the yeast together and add to flour mixture. Blend, then increase speed and beat on high about 10 seconds. Scrape into a large clean bowl, cover with plastic wrap and refrigerate overnight.

Preheat oven to 400°. When ready to bake, turn the biscuit mixture out of the bowl onto a well-floured board. Knead lightly, making several turns to smooth out dough. Roll to a thickness of 1/2" and cut into small 2" rounds with a floured biscuit cutter. Bake on a lightly greased cookie sheet for 10-12 minutes.

Spoon Rolls

This recipe was shared by Squire Watkins Inn in Dillsboro, North Carolina, in ***Taste Full****'s early years. These rolls taste like your best memory.*

EASY • MAKES 16 ROLLS

- 1 **package dry yeast**
- 2 **cups warm water (105°-115°)**
- 1/2 **cup butter, melted**
- 4 **cups self-rising flour**
- 1 **egg, slightly beaten**
- 1/4 **cup sugar**
- 2 **tablespoons butter, melted**

Dissolve yeast in warm water and let stand for 5 minutes. Combine yeast mixture, melted butter and flour in a large bowl, mixing well. Stir in egg and sugar (mixture will be a very soft batter). Cover and refrigerate batter overnight.

Next day, preheat oven to 350°. Spoon batter into greased muffin pans, filling 2/3 full. Bake 20 minutes at 350°. Remove from oven and brush tops with 2 tablespoons melted butter. Bake 5 more minutes.

Batter may be stored, covered in the refrigerator, for up to 4 days.

Apricot Cream Scones

A moist scone with a hint of apricot and lemon. A great hostess gift.

EASY • MAKES 12 SCONES

- 2 **cups all-purpose flour**
- 1/4 **cup plus 2 tablespoons sugar**
- 1 **tablespoon baking powder**
- 1/2 **teaspoon salt**
- 3/4 **cup chopped dried apricots (about 4 1/2 ounces)**
- 1 **tablespoon plus 1 teaspoon grated lemon peel**
- 1 1/4 **cups whipping cream**
- 3 **tablespoons unsalted butter, melted**

Preheat oven to 425°. Mix flour, 1/4 cup sugar, baking powder and salt in a large bowl. Stir in apricots and 1 tablespoon lemon peel. Add whipping cream and stir just until dough forms. Do not overmix. Turn dough out into a lightly floured surface; knead gently 1 minute. Form dough into a 10" diameter, 1/2" thick round. Cut dough into 12 wedges. Transfer wedges to a baking sheet, spacing evenly.

Combine 2 tablespoons sugar with 1 teaspoon lemon peel in a small bowl. Brush scones with melted butter, then sprinkle tops with sugar mixture. Bake until light golden brown, about 15 minutes. Cool slightly before serving.

Buttermilk Cranberry Muffins

These muffins are as light as air! A delight for breakfast or as a bread accompaniment to any warming, winter meal.

EASY • MAKES 24-26 MEDIUM-SIZED MUFFINS

- 1 1/2 **cups cranberries**
- 1/3 **cup orange juice**
- 1/2 **cup light brown sugar**
- 3 1/2 **cups all-purpose flour**
- 1 1/2 **cups sugar**
- 1 **teaspoon salt**
- 4 **teaspoons baking powder**
- 1 **teaspoon baking soda**
- 1 **teaspoon orange rind**
- 2 **eggs**
- 2 **cups buttermilk**
- 1/2 **cup vegetable oil**
- • **juice of 1/2 lemon**

Preheat oven to 375°.

In a small saucepan, combine cranberries, orange juice and brown sugar. Lightly boil for 5 minutes until most of the cranberry skins have popped. Set aside.

In a large mixing bowl, whisk together flour, sugar, salt, baking powder, baking soda and orange rind. In another bowl, combine eggs, buttermilk, oil and lemon juice until mixed together well. Add wet ingredients to dry and stir until batter is just blended. Do not stir too much or the muffins won't be as light.

Pour cranberry mixture into batter and gently distribute fruit evenly.

Spoon muffin batter into greased muffin pan. Fill each cup until almost full. Bake for 20-25 minutes until brown on top. Let cool in pans for a few minutes, then remove.

Focaccia

A good basic recipe for this versatile Italian flatbread.

EASY • SERVES 6-12

- 1 **package dry yeast**
- 1 **cup lukewarm water (105°–115°)**
- 1/3 **cup olive oil**
- 1 **tablespoon fresh chopped rosemary**
- 3 **cups unbleached flour**
- 1 **teaspoon salt**

In a small bowl, dissolve yeast in water; let stand 5 minutes. Heat olive oil with rosemary for 3 minutes on medium. Set aside to cool. In a large bowl, combine flour, salt, yeast and olive oil until dough forms a ball. Turn out onto a floured board and knead 10 minutes dusting with more flour as needed. The texture should be very smooth and elastic.

Oil bottom and sides of bread bowl with olive oil. Turn dough over in bowl to coat; cover and let rise in a warm place until doubled in size, 45-60 minutes.

Preheat oven to 375°.

Dust a large cookie sheet (11 1/2" x 17") with flour. Stretch dough out with your hands to form a rectangular shape and press out evenly with your fingertips to the pan's edges, leaving dough about 1/4" thick overall. Bake 20 minutes or until lightly browned. Remove from pan with a spatula; cut into 16 squares, then cut squares in half diagonally to create finger food wedges.

Herb and Ricotta Muffins

These are delicious dinner muffins. A recipe to enjoy and share.

AVERAGE • MAKES 12 MUFFINS

3 tablespoons butter
2/3 cup finely chopped red onion
1/4 teaspoon rosemary
1/4 teaspoon sage
2 cups all-purpose flour
1 tablespoon baking powder
1/2 teaspoon salt
1/2 teaspoon crushed red pepper
1 cup ricotta cheese
2 eggs
1/3 cup grated Parmesan cheese
1/2 cup milk

Preheat oven to 400°.

In a medium saucepan, melt butter and sauté onion, rosemary and sage over medium heat for 5 minutes until onions are soft. Remove from heat.

In a large bowl combine flour, baking powder, salt and red pepper. In a small bowl mix ricotta with eggs, Parmesan and milk; blend well.

Add both the milk/cheese mixture and the onions to the flour. Stir until just moistened; the batter will be lumpy.

Spoon into greased muffin tins filling cups to the top. Bake for 20 minutes. Cool in the pans for 5 minutes before removing. These may be made a day ahead and kept in the refrigerator. Reheat in a covered pan at 300° for 20 minutes.

Sawgrass Cornbread

This cornbread is a moist and flavorful variation of the Southern standard – just perfect for the Fourth of July.

EASY • SERVES 9-12

2 tablespoons butter
1/4 cup green pepper, chopped
1/4 cup red bell pepper, chopped
1/4 cup green onions, finely chopped
1 1/2 cups yellow cornmeal
1 teaspoon salt
3/4 teaspoon baking soda
2 eggs
1 cup sour cream
1 8 1/4-ounce can cream style corn
1/2 cup vegetable oil

In medium skillet, melt butter over medium heat; add green and red pepper and green onions. Sauté until soft, about 4-5 minutes. Set aside to cool. In small bowl combine cornmeal, salt and baking soda. Set aside. In mixing bowl, whisk together the eggs, sour cream, corn and vegetable oil. Stir in cornmeal mixture just until combined. Fold in sautéed vegetables.

Pour into greased 8" x 8" baking pan. Bake in preheated 350° oven for about 40 minutes, until a toothpick comes out clean.

Maple Sweet Potato Muffins

A muffin that's chock full of moist goodness.

EASY • MAKES 18 MUFFINS

1 cup whole wheat flour
1 cup all-purpose flour
1 tablespoon baking powder
1 1/4 teaspoon cinnamon, divided
1 1/4 teaspoon ginger, divided
1/2 teaspoon salt
1/2 teaspoon nutmeg
1/4 teaspoon cloves
2 eggs
1/2 cup milk
1/2 cup real maple syrup
1 cup applesauce
2 tablespoons vegetable oil
2 cups shredded, raw sweet potato (about 3/4 pound)
1 cup chopped pecans, divided
1 cup currants
1/2 cup coconut

Preheat oven to 375°. Spray muffin pans with cooking spray.

In medium bowl, combine whole wheat flour, all-purpose flour, baking powder, 1 teaspoon cinnamon, 1 teaspoon ginger, salt, nutmeg and cloves. Set aside.

In separate bowl, whisk together the eggs, milk, maple syrup, applesauce and oil. Stir in the shredded sweet potatoes. Add to flour mixture and stir just to combine. Fold in 3/4 cup pecans, currants and coconut. Divide among prepared muffin cups filling each about 2/3 full. In small bowl, combine remaining 1 cup pecans, 1/4 teaspoon cinnamon and 1/4 teaspoon ginger. Sprinkle over top of batter in pan. Bake for 30 minutes, until lightly browned and a toothpick inserted in center comes out clean. Cool in pan 5 minutes then remove from pan. Serve hot or reheated.

Rye Beer Bread

The bread dough can be shaped into small rounds or into larger ovals. Serve with a winter stew or as a base for a cheese spread.

AVERAGE • MAKES 3 SMALL LOAVES

1/2 cup warm water (105°–115°)
2 packages dry yeast
1 tablespoon sugar
1/4 cup honey
1 cup beer, at room temperature
2 teaspoons salt
4 tablespoons melted butter
1 1/2 cups rye flour
3 1/2 cups white flour, preferably high gluten or unbleached flour

Put warm water in large mixing bowl. Sprinkle in yeast and sugar; stir until dissolved.

Let sit until it bubbles up, about 5 minutes. Stir in honey, beer, salt and melted butter.

Add rye flour and 1 1/2 cups white flour. Combine and beat with electric mixer or by hand for 2 minutes. Begin adding remaining white flour a little at a time until it forms a soft dough. Turn out on floured surface and let rest 5 minutes.

Knead until smooth and elastic, about 10 minutes. Dough may be a bit sticky but do not work in too much extra flour (not more than 1/2 cup more) or the bread will be heavy.

Put into greased bowl, turning dough to coat. Cover and let rise in warm place until double in bulk, about 1 1/2 hours. Punch down. For 3 round loaves, divide dough into 3 equal portions. Shape into round loaves by rotating dough on work surface with your palms and pinching any cracks or creases. Rotate until very smooth. (For 2 larger oval loaves, divide dough into 2, shape and smooth.) Transfer to cookie sheet. Cover and let rise again until double, 30-45 minutes.

Preheat oven to 375°. Make 2 slashes on top of each loaf with sharp knife or razor blade. Rub gently with a bit of flour for a rustic look. Bake for 25-30 minutes or until loaf makes a hollow sound when bottom is tapped with your fingers. Put on rack to cool.

Baked Herbed Crouton Sticks

An easy baked method. Pair with soups and salads.

EASY • MAKES 24 STICKS

- **4 tablespoons butter**
- **1 tablespoon minced garlic**
- **24 3" x 1" bread strips (crusts removed and cut from firm-textured bread)**
- **1/2 teaspoon salt, optional**
- **2 teaspoons dried basil or other dried herb**

Preheat oven to 400°.

In microwave or small saucepan over low heat, melt butter with the garlic. Let sit for about 15 minutes for garlic flavor to permeate butter. Brush both sides of bread strips with the garlic butter and lay onto cookie sheets. Put into hot oven and bake about 8 minutes, until browned on the bottom. Turn and bake until well browned, about 5 minutes more.

Meanwhile, combine salt and basil in a heavy-duty plastic bag. Add hot bread strips to the bag about 1/2 at a time and toss to coat with herbs. Lay on racks to cool. Repeat with remaining hot bread strips. When cool, store in tight tin. They will keep for several days.

Tomato Rosemary Rolls

Delicious on their own or for pork or beef tenderloin sandwiches served on a buffet.

MAKES 16 ROLLS

- **1/3 cup sun-dried tomatoes, finely chopped**
- **1/3 cup onion, chopped**
- **2 tablespoons olive oil**
- **1/2 teaspoon black pepper**
- **1 teaspoon dried rosemary**
- **3-3 1/2 cups bread flour**
- **1 teaspoon sugar**
- **2 teaspoons salt**
- **1 package dry yeast (1/4 ounce)**
- **1 1/2 cups water (1/4 cup warm and 1 1/4 cups cold)**
- **• oil**

Sauté sun-dried tomatoes and onion in the olive oil; add pepper and rosemary. Set aside.

In a large bowl, combine flour, sugar and salt. Add the tomato/onion mixture. In a separate bowl, dissolve yeast in warm water and let sit 5 minutes. Add yeast to flour mixture; add cold water. Blend ingredients well.

Knead dough on a floured board 8-10 minutes, adding more flour as necessary to keep the dough from sticking. Place dough in a large, lightly oiled bowl and cover with plastic wrap. Let dough rise in a warm place for 1 1/2-2 hours until it has doubled in size. Punch down and let rise again for another 45 minutes to 1 hour.

Preheat oven to 400°. Divide the dough and shape into two 12" long pieces. Cut into 1 1/2" pieces and place on an ungreased baking sheet. Let rise again for 1 hour. Bake for 20 minutes. These rolls can be made up to 2 days ahead. Store in cool place, well sealed.

Walnut-Cherry Bread

This hearty bread from Fearrington House Restaurant is doubly pleasing with the crunch of walnuts and the sweet bites of dried cherries — a perfect companion to everything from a winter soup meal to a lamb dinner.

AVERAGE • MAKES 2 LOAVES

- **1 1/2 ounce package dry yeast**
- **1 1/4 cups warm water (80°–100°)**
- **1/3 cup dark brown sugar, firmly packed**
- **2 tablespoons shortening, melted**
- **3-4 cups unbleached bread flour, divided**
- **1 cup whole wheat flour**
- **1 1/2 teaspoons salt**
- **1 1/2 teaspoons freshly ground black pepper**
- **1 1/2 cups chopped walnuts**
- **1 cup dried cherries**

In a small bowl, dissolve yeast in water; stir in sugar. Let rest 5 minutes, then add melted shortening.

In separate bowl, combine 2 cups bread flour, whole wheat flour, salt, pepper, walnuts and cherries. Using dough attachment of heavy-duty mixer, mix dry ingredients. Add yeast and mix at medium speed for 5 minutes.

Reduce speed to low. While dough is mixing on low, add up to 2 cups bread flour, 1/2 cup at a time, until dough forms a ball and pulls away from sides of bowl. You may not need to use all flour. Remove dough from bowl and knead 5 minutes, or until smooth and elastic.

Place in large, oiled bowl and cover. Put in warm area and allow dough to rise until doubled in size (at least 1 hour).

Punch dough down and divide in half. Form 2 balls and cover with

suggestions for a

FESTIVE CHEESE BOARD

by Carolyn Booth

When entertaining calls for distinctive, tasty appetizers, bring on the cheese. Not just spreads and balls or little cubes on the ends of toothpicks, but rather wedges, rounds or slabs of world-class cheese, artfully arranged and presented as the classic cheese board.

The variety of cheese available today is endless, but are normally grouped by their characteristics:

- Fresh cheeses may be drained or undrained but they are usually moist and milky like farmer's cheese, cottage cheese, French *fromage blanc*, unaged *fromage de chèvre* and Italian Mascarpone.
- Soft-ripened or bloomy rind cheeses have a semisoft consistency and a thin white velvety crust, such as French Brie, Camembert and triple-crèmes such as Gratte-Paille and Pierre Robert, Italian Paglia-style and Toma.
- Washed-rind cheeses have been washed, immersed or rubbed during the ripening process with brine, wine, beer or brandy, to promote a mold that produces the characteristic flavor of cheeses such as French Epoisses, Livarot and Pont-l'Evêque, Italian Taleggio, Spanish Mahón and most Trappist or monastery-style cheese.
- Natural rind cheeses have thin self-formed rinds, are denser in texture and usually are aged longer. Examples include English Stilton, French Roquefort, Italian Gorgonzola and Spanish Cabrales.
- Uncooked, pressed cheeses are made from curd which has not been heated. Instead, the curd is pressed to drain the whey and achieve a firm texture. Examples include English Cheddar, French Morbier and Tomme de Savoie, Italian Montasio and Spanish Manchego.
- Cooked, pressed cheese is made from curd that has been heated before pressing. Examples include Dutch Gouda, English Cheshire, French Cantal and Gruyère, Italian Parmigiano-Reggiano, Swiss Appenseller and French and Swiss Emmental.

*For help in selecting your cheese board, **Taste Full** suggests locating a knowledgeable cheese seller and asking for recommendations. Below are tips for creating a tantalizing selection:*

- Think color, texture and contrast of flavor when selecting cheese.
- Select only three or four cheeses.
- Follow a theme, like all Spanish or French, or have a variety of types, like a firm, a blue and a soft cheese.
- Hard or very firm cheeses are best arranged and served in small slices, while a wedge or block of the softer cheese may be cut with a good utility knife.
- Allow one ounce of each cheese per person.
- Always serve cheese at room temperature.
- Skip the crackers! Status cheeses deserve rustic handmade loaves of crusty bread.
- Small handmade or purchased labels visually enhance the cheese selections.
- Decorate with fresh or dried fruits like figs and cranberries, or green and black olives and sprigs of herbs or other edible greenery.

a lightweight dish towel. Let rise again until double in bulk (45 minutes or more).

Preheat oven to 400°. Bake for 25 minutes or until internal temperature registers 180°. The crust may get very dark, so use a thermometer to be sure the bread is done. The loaf should sound hollow when tapped.

Lillian's Blueberry Bread

*One of the best bread recipes **Taste Full** ever tested comes from Lillian Kroustalis of Westbend Vineyards in Lewisville, North Carolina. The small, award-winning winery was the first private vineyard in North Carolina to plant the vinifera and French-American hybrid grape vines that produce fruit for Chardonnay, Merlot, Cabernet Sauvignon and more.*

EASY • MAKES 1 LOAF

1/2 cup butter, softened
1 cup sugar
2 eggs
1 2/3 cups flour
1 teaspoon baking powder
1/2 teaspoon salt
1/2 cup milk
1 cup fresh blueberries
1/2 teaspoon grated lemon zest
1/4 cup lemon juice
1/3 cup sugar

Preheat oven to 350°. Grease a 9" x 5" x 3" loaf pan; set aside.

By hand (or with mixer), whisk together softened butter and sugar; beat in eggs. In a separate bowl, sift flour with baking powder and salt. Add to butter mixture alternately with the milk. Mix until just combined. Fold in blueberries and lemon zest. Pour bread batter into prepared pan and bake in a 350° oven for 50 minutes.

While bread is baking, heat lemon juice and sugar in a small saucepan. Cook until mixture is the thickness of syrup. Pour glaze over baked bread while it is still in the pan. Allow bread and glaze to cool before removing from pan.

Suggested Menus

A Lucky New Year's

Spanish Olive Spread 134
Oysters on the Half Shell with Spinach Walnut Pesto 135

Country Ham Risotto with Turnip Greens 151
Black-Eyed Pea Cakes 184
Applejack Cake 166

Valentine's Day

Mini Gorgonzola Tarts 132

Oven-Barbecued Lamb Shanks 39
Winter Greens with Caramelized Shallots 180
Sweet Potato Polenta 182
Walter's Chocolate Bread Pudding 165

Easter

Asparagus Wrapped in Smoked Salmon 13

Crabmeat Vichyssoise 18
Boneless Lamb Loin with Bourbon Molasses Sauce 158
Pecan Scallion Rice 183
Cascade of Color Green Beans 176
White Chocolate Raspberry Cheesecake 49

Mother's Day

Pecan Chicken with Citrus Beurre Blanc 34
*Steamed Asparagus **
Wild Basmati Rice Timbales 183
Crème Celeste with Strawberries 42

Father's Day

Succotash Chowder 95
Seared Tuna Sandwiches with Honey Ginger Glaze 112
Asian Sweet and Sour Slaw 180
Nanette's Fresh Blackberry Cake 83

Memorial Day

True Blue Pimento Cheese with Homemade Crackers 12

Vidalia Onion Soup with Fresh Thyme 19
Skewered Shrimp with Green Chile Salsa 69
Warm Madras Greens' Salad 24
Sour Cream Blueberry Pie 42

Fourth Of July

Black Bean Gazpacho 60
Grilled Chicken Pitas 76
Homemade French Fries 181
Bob's Broccoli Salad 143
Red-White-And-Blue Ice Cream Cake 81

Family Birthday

Black Bean Hummus 90

Red Pepper Soup 61
Silver Queen Crabcakes 69
Fiesta Salad 64
*Fresh Okra **
Old-Fashioned Red Velvet Cake 166

Porch Supper

Black-Eyed Pea Salsa 56

Chilled Honeydew Watermelon Soup 59
Derby Down Fried Chicken 75
Mama's Soggy Coconut Cake 165

Kid's Night

Bratwurst Rounds in Mustard Sauce 89

Barbecued Turkey 109
Two Potato Gratin 181
Mountain Apple Salad 101
Pumpkin Chip Muffins 128

Bridge Club Luncheon

Sherried Pecans 88

Curried Asparagus Soup 21
Phyllo Chèvre Tart 92
Spring Salad with Strawberries 22
Revival Chocolate Cake with Roasted Banana Sauce 169

Dinner At The Coast

Pâté in "Pastry" Shells 15

Sunny Corn Soup 59
Paella Carolina 70
Simple Blue Salad 142
Orville and Wilbur's Rum Fig Cake 125

Tailgating Picnic

Black Eyed Pea and Chicken Gumbo 100
Sawgrass Cornbread 188
Fruited Cole Slaw 180
Black Bottom Cupcakes 44

Blue Ridge Bound

Blue Ridge Shiitake Mushrooms 132

Smothered Pork Chops with Gingered Applesauce 107
Wild Rice Salad with Lemon Honey Mustard Dressing 104
Pisgah's French Silk Pie 123

Thanksgiving

Pine Nut Cheese Puffs 14

Eastern Shore Oyster Stew 137
Grilled Quail with Spinach Potato Pancakes 119
Sugar Snap Peas with Cherry Tomatoes 179
Pumpkin Bread Pudding with Buttered Bourbon Sauce 120

Dessert Party

Chestnut Mousse 162
Spirited Ambrosia 47
Bittersweet Chocolate Tart 123
Chocolate Strawberry Pecan Torte 40
Alexia's Sweet Potato Cake 128
Rustic Apple Tart 112
Specialty Coffee Bar 193

Hors D'Oeuvres Party

Governor's Mansion Crab Dip 133
Savory Cheesecake with Smoked Salmon and Dill 133
Chutney and Brie Bites 15
Carolina Bluefish Caesar Salad 25
Classic Grilled Tenderloin 75
Tomato Rosemary Rolls 189
Roasted Asparagus & Leeks 179

Spirited Ambrosia 47
Nell's Decadent Oatmeal Cookies 170
French Lace Cookies 170
Edinburgh Shortbread 46

Christmas Feast

Quick & Elegant Crab Salad 14

Freddy Lee's Pumpkin Soup 98
Rummed Pork Roast with Dried Cherries and Ginger 157
Garlicky Green Beans 177
Corn Custard 184
Spoon Rolls 188
Christmas Crown Cake 163

** recipe not included*

a word on WINE PAIRING by J.K. Norfleet

EDITOR'S NOTE: My father, J.K. Norfleet, is the kind of wine connoisseur I like. He discusses wine as one might talk about the day's sports. A partner in two restaurants on the Outer Banks, he helps develop each location's wine list. His skill at creating a well-rounded, well-priced list has been acknowledged in the wine press nationally.

The popularity of wine has made it possible for new vineyards to spring up and compete with the old established wineries for a share of the market. North America, France, Europe, Italy, Australia, New Zealand, South Africa and other countries have aggressively produced wines for the world market creating a real opportunity for the consumer to buy good wines in all price ranges. Never in history have there been so many quality wines from which to choose. Although the best estates generally have become more expensive, with a little research, the wine buyer can find good wines from other sources at reasonable prices. To assist your wine and food pairings, I have suggested general types and styles and married them with the range of foods and preparations found in this great collection. We have not selected particular vintages.

In the marvelous world of wine there are all sorts of styles. Every style has a place on the table. Most people who dabble in wine today know to forget the old saying that white wines go with fish and chicken, and reds only go with red meats. This listing crosses those lines to give you a broad selection of varietals to pair your meal. The main thing to remember is not to overpower the wine with your food, nor overpower your food with your wine selection.

I encourage you to visit a well-stocked wine merchant and take advantage of the 10% to 15% case (12) discounts most offer. Ask the salesperson to assist you in selecting a variety of everyday wines in an affordable price range. Such experimentation not only will enhance your wine knowledge but your mealtime pleasure.

The Seasonal Palette presents a terrific opportunity for cooks of varying experience to shine before their families and guests. To help complete the total enjoyment of the meal, I have contributed a general listing that pairs available wine varietals with food.

FISH AND SHELLFISH

- Grilled, baked or broiled with simple sauces: Sauvignon/Fumé Blanc (light to medium bodied), Chardonnay, Pinot Blanc, Semillon.
- Fish with more distinct flavors such as salmon, shad and tuna go well with a Pinot Noir, Syrah, Beaujolais or Zinfandel in addition to the whites.
- Fish and shellfish prepared with a substantial sauce requires more substantial wines. A heavier bodied Chardonnay or a complex Sauvignon/Fumé Blanc will fill the bill.
- Raw oysters, clams and cold shrimp cry out for a Muscadet from France, crisp Chardonnay, Pinot Gris or Pinot Grigio or Sauvignon/Fumé Blanc.
- Lobster – broiled or steamed – marries well with a heavy-bodied Chardonnay with some oak flavors.

POULTRY

- Grilled chicken and Cornish game hens: This is where we can really broaden our list. Chardonnay, Sauvignon/Fumé Blanc, Pinot Blanc, Riesling, Gewürztraminer, Pinot Gris, Pinot Grigio for the whites. Red varietals would include Pinot Noir, Beaujolais, Zinfandel and Syrah.
- Roasted chicken and game hens go well with a light-to-medium-bodied Chardonnay. If you add a flavorful sauce, use the list of wines for grilled chicken.
- Roast turkey: This marries well with a heavy Chardonnay or light red such as a Pinot Noir.

GAME

- Quail: A real round, hearty Chardonnay and any of the reds such as a light Cabernet, Pinot Noir, Beaujolais, Zinfandel and Syrah.
- Duck: A stout Cabernet Sauvignon, a complex and full-bodied Burgundy or Pinot Noir.
- Venison: Consult the same listing as Grilled Beef.

PORK

- Grilled Pork: Consult the same list as featured with the grilled chicken list.
- Roast Pork: Because of its delicacy it's wonderful with a light Chardonnay, Pinot Blanc, Riesling or Gewürztraminer.

BEEF

- Grilled Beef – New York strips, rib eye or sirloin, filet and flank steak: When beef is grilled it has so much flavor, it's very easy to let it overpower the wine. Think young and robust when picking a wine. Young Cabernet Sauvignon, Merlot, Syrah, Zinfandel, Bordeaux, Shiraz and Rhone wine such as Châteauneuf-du-Pape. All of these will go well and they should not be expensive.
- Roasted beef cuts – particularly the standing prime rib roast, whole tenderloin, strip loin, sirloin tips, and eye of round – are more mildly flavored than the grilled meats. A mature Cabernet Sauvignon, Bordeaux, Pinot Noir or Burgundy, or an aged Zinfandel. Think smooth

and flavorful with low evidence of tannin.

• Veal chops and tenderloins: Treat these as grilled beef.

• Roast Veal: This goes really well with a full-bodied Chardonnay along with light soft reds such as Merlot and Pinot Noir.

Lamb

• Grilled lamb chops, racks or legs: These are the most flavorful meats for the table, and sometimes tricky to pair with wine. Follow the same guidelines as for grilled beef, but as a rule of thumb, a young, robust Cabernet Sauvignon is very well-suited for grilled lamb.

• Roast leg of lamb, loin or rack: These should be complemented with more flavorful wine than roasted beef. Turn to a complex Merlot (generally a more expensive one), a Cabernet Sauvignon that still is holding on to its tannins or a Zinfandel. No matter how you prepare lamb, you must have a wine that will stand up to the unique flavor inherent in these fabulous meats.

Meat Stews

• Beef, Lamb and Veal Stews: Marry with big robust wines as described above. I would stay with the reds and, depending on the ingredients you can determine the degree of complexity and heartiness of the wine. Do not let the stew overpower the wine.

Specialty Coffee & Liqueur Bar

Here are some suggestions for creating a coffee bar for your next party.

Set up a self-service coffee bar. Several companies make inexpensive thermal coffee carafes. Fill and label each carafe, and place them on the bar. Use a variety of mugs and save your china for another occasion. Include stirring spoons and some festive napkins. Arrange your coffee bar in a central place that is accessible from aides. Invite guests to serve themselves and encourage them to fix a second cup.

Coffees

At least one decaffeinated; allow 50 cups for 20 guests

Colombian Supremo
Mocha Java
French Roast
French Vanilla
Swiss Chocolate Almond

Liqueurs

Amaretto
Brandy/Cognac
Crème de Menthe
Galliano
Grand Marnier
Harvey's Bristol Cream
Kahlúa/Tia Maria
Irish Whiskey

Other Flavorings

Torani Italian Syrups
Sweetened Whipped Cream
Brown Sugar/Rock Sugar Crystals
Ground Cinnamon
Orange/Lemon Zest

Chocolate Spoons

A creative addition to your bar and easy to make.

For 10 dark chocolate spoons, melt 8 ounces of semisweet chocolate in microwave. Stir to melt completely. Line sheet pan with wax paper; spray with cooking spray. Dip plastic spoons into chocolate, rotating spoons to cover the bottom-side and top of each spoon. Place on sheet pan.

Cover sheet pan with foil and place in freezer until ready to serve. Arrange spoons on large, flat serving platter. Instruct guests to stir spoons into hot coffee to flavor and sweeten their cups. These spoons make a fun party favor; simply tie several spoons together with curly holiday ribbon.

INDEX

Acknowledgements

*The following people developed recipes at different times during **Taste Full** magazine's 10 years of publishing that were included in **The Seasonal Palette**:*

Carolyn Booth
Geraldine Congdon
Susan Dillard
Debrah Lovan
Courtney Motley
Dorette Snover
Tracy Yunker

The following people also contributed photography included in this book:

John Tesh
Melva Calder

Special thanks to:

Frank Stoner and
Pam Sink of The Bob Timberlake Gallery,
and Dan Timberlake of Bob Timberlake, Inc.

with additional thanks to:

Beth Moore

*The following restaurants, inns, and winery were featured in **Taste Full** and shared their recipes:*

The Angus Barn
Highway 70 at Aviation Parkway
Raleigh, North Carolina
(919)787-3505

Barley's Taproom
42 Biltmore Avenue
Asheville, North Carolina
(828)255-0504

Bernardin's Fine Dining
Center Stage Shopping Center
373 Jonestown Road
Winston-Salem, North Carolina
(336)768-9365

Blue Point Bar & Grill
1240 Duck Road
Suite 1, Water Front Shops
Duck, North Carolina
(252)261-8090

Expressions
114 North Main Street
Hendersonville, North Carolina
(828)693-8516

Fearrington House Restaurant & Fearrington Inn
2000 Fearrington Village Center
Pittsboro, North Carolina
(919)542-2121

Fort Lewis Lodge
HCR #3, Box 21A
Millboro, Virginia
(540)925-2314

The Frog & Owl
46 E. Main Street
Franklin, North Carolina
(828)349-4112

Jerry's Food, Wine & Spirits
7220 Wrightsville Avenue
Wilmington, North Carolina
(910)256-8847

Lakeside Restaurant
531 Smallwood Avenue
Highlands, North Carolina
(828)526-9419

Lulu's On Main
612 W. Main Street
Sylva, North Carolina
(828)586-8989

Magnolia Grill
1002 Ninth Street
Durham, North Carolina
(919)286-3609

Old Stone Inn
109 Dolan Road
Waynesville, North Carolina
(828)456-3333

Pisgah Inn
408.6 Blue Ridge Parkway
Waynesville, North Carolina
(828)235-8228

The Revival Grill
604 Milner Drive
Greensboro, North Carolina
(336)297-0950

West Bend Vineyards
5394 Williams Road
Lewisville, North Carolina
(336)945-5032

For additional props for photos:
Lydia's Gifts & More
8845 Six Forks Road
Raleigh, North Carolina
(919)846-0555